A People's History
of the New Boston

A
People's History
OF THE
New Boston

Jim Vrabel

University of Massachusetts Press

AMHERST AND BOSTON

ISBN 978-1-62534-076-4 (paper); 075-7 (hardcover)

Designed by Steve Dyer
Set in SabonNext
Printed and bound by Sheridan Books, Inc.

Library of Congress Cataloging-in-Publication Data
Vrabel, Jim.
A people's history of the new Boston/Jim Vrabel.
pages cm
Includes bibliographical references and index.
ISBN 978-1-62534-076-4 (pbk. : alk. paper)—ISBN 978-1-62534-075-7
(hardcover : alk. paper) 1. Boston (Mass.)—History—20th century.
2. Boston (Mass.)—Social conditions—20th century. 3. Social
change—Massachusetts—Boston—History—20th century.
4. Community life—Massachusetts—Boston—History—
20th century. 5. Urban renewal—Massachusetts—
Boston—History—20th century. I. Title.
F73.52.V73 2014
974.4'61043—dc23
2014008143

British Library Cataloguing-in-Publication Data
A catalogue record for this book is available from the British Library.

publication of this book
is supported by a grant from
FIGURE FOUNDATION

*To the neighborhood residents, activists,
and community organizers in Boston in the
1960s and 1970s, who made the city better,
and to ALAN LUPO,
who wrote about them so early,
so often, and so well.*

Contents

Contents

A People's History
of the New Boston

Introduction

Boston, today, is seen as one of America's best cities — one that works for its residents, generates jobs, welcomes visitors, remembers its past, and embraces its future. But this latest incarnation of what the Massachusetts Bay Colony's first governor, John Winthrop, called the "City on a Hill" is a fairly recent one. The "New Boston" only came into being in the second half of the twentieth century. The "Old Boston" that preceded it didn't work very well for anyone, and was described as a "hopeless backwater" and "tumbled-down has-been" of a city.[1]

Credit for building the New Boston usually goes to a small group of "city fathers"—all of them men, all of them white, and most of them well-off. That story usually focuses on the bricks-and-mortar improvements made to the city's downtown.

But that is only half of the story. As the late, great, and very local journalist Alan Lupo wrote, the building of the New Boston was really "a tale of two cities." "One city was that newer Boston, brimming with confidence, attracting money and the middle class, [the other] the old Boston, increasingly angry . . . at what it perceived to be an insensitive government . . . and distrustful now of all outsiders, preachers, planners, reformers, and do-gooders."[2]

A People's History of the New Boston attempts to tell the other half of the story. It gives credit to many more people—women as well as men; black, brown, and yellow as well as white; the poor and working class as well as the well-off. This story focuses on how those people made Boston a more humane and a morally better city, and it extends to Boston's neighborhoods.

This book also attempts to explain how they made Boston better—by engaging in an era of activism and protest the likes of which the city hadn't seen since the fight for abolition and, prior to that, the beginnings of the American Revolution. Like that revolution, this one was directed at an insensitive or inept government and selfish business interests. That first revolution, however, was directed at a king, a parliament, and companies an ocean away. This one took aim at government and business interests here at home. That first revolution gave birth to a new nation, conceived in liberty and equality. This one helped make a city much more *of, by,* and *for* its people.

Boston has a long history when it comes to activism and protest. It was founded in 1630 by Winthrop and others who were out to purify Protestantism. After Boston's early activists sparked the revolution that gave the United States its political independence in the eighteenth century, the city's preachers, philosophers, and writers helped the country achieve its spiritual and intellectual independence in the early nineteenth century. Boston was a hotbed of abolitionism and strongly supported the effort to preserve the union in the middle of that century. It was very much involved in the labor, temperance, and suffrage movements at the end of it. But in the twentieth century, just as the city's economic fortunes declined, so did its involvement in activism and protest.

In the 1950s, by the time the Great Depression and World War II were over, the people of Boston—like those in the rest of the country—seemed interested in nothing more than going back to work, raising their families, and getting on with their lives. Conformity, not confrontation, was the order of the day, and politics had less to do with protest than personalities.

"Politics was all very familial back then," recalled Neil Savage, who grew up in Roslindale, lives in West Roxbury, and is the author of *Extraordinary Tenure: Massachusetts and the Making of the Nation.* "Political offices were often seen as 'belonging' to certain families. If you knew the family, you worked on their campaigns. Voting was seen as a civic obligation, and winning candidates were obliged to do what they could for their supporters. The only people who didn't like the way things were run back then were the 'reformers' and 'do-gooders,' mostly liberals and women, who thought it was a corrupt system. But as far as demonstrations, well, they were for radicals. It just wasn't done."[3]

"Bostonians had developed a docile attitude toward government, especially city government," added Henry Lee, a Beacon Hill Brahmin who, much to his own surprise, became an activist himself in the 1970s. "You didn't know what was going on, and even if you did, you didn't feel like you had any say in it."[4]

"City Hall wasn't a place to fight back then," agreed Gerry Burke. He grew up in Jamaica Plain, and his family has long operated Doyle's, a tavern where politics is always the favorite topic of conversation. "City Hall was a place to get a job or to ask for a favor, not a place to fight. There were no 'issues' back then. There was no such thing as 'activism.'"[5] That began to change, though, in the 1960s—and even those who changed it point to different reasons why.

Moe Gillen of Charlestown attributed it to the large number of military veterans who had returned home to Boston after World War II and Korea. "They had been at D-Day and Inchon and were going to do what was right. A mere politician didn't scare them."[6]

Dan Richardson of Roxbury claimed, "All the issues of the times created us ... created the circumstances that allowed us to do what we did ... to foment protest around urban renewal and civil rights ... and plans to build new highways through the city."[7]

Tom Corrigan, back then a young priest working in Jamaica Plain, called John F. Kennedy's election as president "the catalyst for a lot of the activism in Boston. His election excited a lot of people."[8]

Fred Salvucci of Brighton maintained, "The Vietnam War was a big part of it all. People had been in the habit of thinking that government knew more than they did. But the Vietnam War changed all that. The war was this giant red sign that said government doesn't always know what it is doing ... and that sometimes we knew better than government what the right thing to do was."[9]

That last notion—that sometimes the people knew better—appears to have been the common denominator in all the protest that followed. Some of that protest and activism was directed against a government that tried to force people to accept flawed plans, policies, or programs; some at the failure by government to provide people with the services they needed and deserved. Some of it involved fights for social and economic justice or against U.S. foreign policy. Some was directed at landlords or developers or big companies who put profit over people. One of those protests was directed at a federal court that tried to tell people how to live their lives.

Some of the battles were simple cases of a good, grassroots *us* against a bad, monolithic *them*. Some were more complicated. They divided people into factions of "militants," or "moderates," or "conservatives," and pitted people of goodwill against one another. Some of the protests were successful, in whole or in part; some were not. Most of those involved conducted themselves nobly; some did not.

But all of the protest and activism sprang from a desire on the part of the people to gain more power over their lives and to make Boston better — and, in most cases, they succeeded.

This book is a *selective* history. It contains only some of the many remarkable stories of protest, and profiles only some of the many activists who took part in this tumultuous chapter of the city's recent history. Each story deserves its own book.

It is a *collective* and a *collaborative* history, one assembled as much as written, from interviews with those who took part in it, from stories by the journalists who covered it, and from the books written by historians since then.

It is sometimes a *detailed* history, in order to explain what sparked so much protest and to show how people were able to improve on those details.

It is a *partisan* history, and assesses the city's leaders, particularly its mayors, through the somewhat narrow lens of how willing they were to listen to the people of Boston and to share power with them.

The book is a *roughly chronological* history. It tells each story in the order it began, follows that story to its climax, then doubles back to tell the next one. There was so much protest over so many different things at the same time that maintaining a strict chronological narrative proved impossible.

Finally, this is a *collected* history. Some of these stories have been told before and some have not. Gathering them together here, I hope, will illustrate what the longtime community activist Mel King has called the "chain of change" that made the New Boston the city it has become.

CHAPTER 1

◂◦▸

The Old Boston
and the New Boston

"BOSTON IS A DEAD CITY, LIVING IN THE PAST. IF YOU WANT
to be successful in any business, get out of Boston."[1] As the 1940s gave way
to the 1950s, this was the kind of advice being given young entrepreneurs
in the Old Boston. Boston wasn't the only dead city in the United States at
the time. Many of them, especially older cities in the Northeast and Mid-
west, were struggling against powerful forces that they had to confront if
they wanted to survive. But a case could be made that Boston was "deader"
than most.

Part of the reason for Boston's demise was economic. As Alexander Ganz,
the research director of the Boston Redevelopment Authority, explained,
"The Depression that lasted from ten to twenty years elsewhere lasted
thirty years here."[2] Boston's original economy, the one that made the city
the primary U.S. port from colonial days until the 1830s, had been based on
shipping. That economy was eventually replaced by one based on manufac-
turing and trade, as the city imported raw materials for the textile, shoe, and
garment mills throughout New England, and then exported their finished
products. After World War I, those industries fell prey to competition from
the non-union South and from overseas, where labor was much cheaper.[3]
After World War II, the new economy that was emerging was based on
something called "high technology," but those new high-tech companies
were bypassing Boston for the suburbs, where land was cheaper and the
labor force better educated.

By 1950, Boston had lost a quarter of its tax base over the previous twenty-five years.[4] Its tax rate was the highest of any major city in the country, and its bond rating one of the lowest. Only a handful of new office buildings had been built since the Depression—the most recent the "Old John Hancock Building" in 1947. In 1956, the city's skyline was so unprepossessing that the dean of the business school at Boston College recalled flying into Logan Airport, looking out of the window of his plane, and wondering, "Where's Boston?"[5]

Part of the reason for the city's demise was demographic. In 1950, Boston's population peaked at 800,000 and over the next ten years it lost more than 100,000 residents, the biggest drop of any major city in the country.[6] Long before, most of the wealthy had left Boston, fleeing before the waves of arriving immigrants. Now it was the turn of the middle class, drawn to suburbs made suddenly affordable by federally backed mortgages and accessible by federally funded highways. Most of those remaining in Boston were poor and working class, which prompted Murray Levin, a Boston University professor, to write, "The traditional image of Boston as the city of old-world charm and elegant living is replaced by one of rooming houses, tenements, and slums."[7]

Part of the reason for the city's demise was political. "The Brahmins who built Boston had all but abandoned it to the politicians," an article in *Newsweek* would later state.[8] That abandonment had started all the way back in 1910, when John F. Fitzgerald, grandfather of John F. Kennedy, defeated the Yankee banker James Jackson Storrow to become mayor and put the Irish in charge of running the city. Ever since, mayoral candidates had cultivated ethnic and class conflicts in order to appeal to an electorate now made up primarily of not only the poor and the working class but also recent immigrants.

No one was a better cultivator of conflict than James Michael Curley, who succeeded Fitzgerald as mayor in 1914. A large man and grandiloquent orator, Curley was born and raised in Roxbury, the son of Irish immigrants. When his father died, the ten-year-old Curley was forced to go to work after graduating from the Dearborn Grammar School, and the career that he ended up choosing was politics.

Curley, who dominated the politics of the Old Boston for forty years, served four terms as mayor, four terms in Congress, one term as governor, and two terms in jail. To some, he was the "Mayor of the Poor," a public servant who built roads and bridges, beaches and bath houses, health clinics and a new city hospital that provided services and created jobs to make life a little better for his struggling constituents. But to others, he was the "Rascal King," a profiteer who took a commission for himself on every municipal contract he signed.

Curley's behavior in office was so egregious that, in 1918, the Massachusetts legislature passed a law prohibiting the mayor of Boston from serving consecutive terms, which forced him to leave the office frequently. He managed to return to it every decade, but eventually, Curley's ability to prosper politically and financially ended when the public investment he so expertly manipulated dried up after World War II. The city suffered as a result, however, because, thanks to Curley's class-baiting politics and the corruption that had so alienated Boston's business community, there was no private investment to take its place. "Curley had lived off the Yankee-Irish animosity, which he cultivated for his own political ends," recalled Henry Lee of Beacon Hill. "It should have died fifty years before that."[9] The fact that it didn't was a big reason for the Old Boston's demise.

The birth date of the New Boston is usually celebrated as Election Day, November 8, 1949. That's when the seventy-four-year-old James Michael Curley was denied reelection to a fifth four-year term as mayor. (The Massachusetts legislature had repealed the law prohibiting the mayor from serving consecutive terms in 1938, under the mistaken impression that Curley's time had passed.) The man who defeated Curley in the 1949 mayoral race was John Hynes, whose background was similar to Curley's but who was unlike him in every other way.

Hynes, too, was the son of Irish immigrants. He was born in the South End and grew up in Dorchester, and he, too, had had to leave school and go to work. In Hynes's case, he left the Mary Hemenway School at fourteen after his mother died. But Hynes was twenty years younger than Curley and so "shy and unassuming" that he was called Whispering Johnny.[10] Rather than run for office, Hynes had become a career civil servant. He did serve briefly as acting mayor of Boston—while Curley was serving time in federal prison on a postal fraud conviction—but probably wouldn't have run for the office if Curley hadn't boasted on his return from prison, "I have accomplished more in one day than has been done in the five months of my absence."[11]

As Curley's biographer, Jack Beatty, described it, "A corrupt mayor, a corrupt City Council, a corrupt press, a swollen city payroll, a dying city economy, and the highest taxes beneath the wandering moon: such was the Boston scene as the 1949 election began."[12] During the campaign, the contrast between the two men was striking. The combative Curley derided Hynes as a "little city clerk" and "the Republican candidate of the State Street wrecking crew." The mild-mannered Hynes promised to "Restore Dignity to Boston" and guaranteed a "clean, honest and efficient administration." [13] On Election Day, the people of Boston showed they were tired of corruption and combat and ready for manners and honesty. They elected Hynes with 138,000 votes to 126,000 for Curley, and in doing so set not only a new tone but also a new direction for the city.

In that same election, the people also voted for a new city charter. It replaced the sometimes corrupt and always parochial city council, to which twenty-two members had been elected by ward, with a nine-member body elected at-large in hopes its members would spend less time looking out for themselves and the narrow interests of their district and more time looking out for the city as a whole. But an unintended result of this was that greater voter turnout in wards around the edges of the city yielded more representation than their populations deserved, and the less politically active neighborhoods in the city's inner core got none at all.

The new charter also increased the power of the already-powerful office of mayor, which had been described after the last such change as a "municipal monarchy." The hope here was that by giving a mayor not named Curley more power he (a woman would even not appear on the mayoral ballot until 1967) might be able to bring the dead city back to life.

In making the charter change, the people of Boston were making a leap of faith—one that some would come to regret. Because if they ever wanted any of that power back—as they soon would—they would have to either fight whoever was mayor to get it or else elect someone who was willing to share it.

In John Hynes the people elected a mayor who wasn't so much interested in wielding power as in mending fences. The fences he sought most to mend were those that divided "the people who 'owned' Boston (the Brahmin business community) from the people who 'ran' it" (the Irish-Catholic politicians).[14] Thomas O'Connor's *Building a New Boston: Politics and Urban Renewal, 1950 to 1970* is the best account of how the new mayor tried to do that.

Hynes set out first to win the business community's confidence by streamlining city government and reducing the waste and corruption that had been part of it for so long. This won him the confidence of the people of Boston, too. In 1951, they responded by reelecting him in the early election called for by the new charter. Once again, Curley was his opponent. But this time Hynes beat him by an almost two-to-one margin, 154,000 votes to 76,000. It was during the 1951 campaign that Hynes's vision for the city began to emerge, and he began to use the "New Boston" slogan for which he and the city would thereafter become known.

In his second term, Hynes continued to court the business community to become a partner in that vision, and he took advantage of the recently established Boston College Citizens Seminars to do it.[15] On October 26, 1954, he delivered a speech titled "Boston, Whither Goest Thou." Although his rhetoric was less than soaring, Hynes declared that the "most efficacious, the most logical and the quickest way [out of the] morass in which we find ourselves" was "to broaden the present tax base of the city . . . by tearing down old structures and the building of new ones."[16]

In trying to build Boston back to health, Hynes spent the rest of his tenure cultivating not conflict but what the political scientist John Mollen-kopf later called the "pro-growth coalition" of government and business leaders, labor unions, and newspaper publishers.[17] His biggest single success came when he persuaded the Prudential Insurance Company to locate its regional headquarters in Boston and construct what would become at that time the tallest building in the United States outside of New York City. But Hynes's broadest impact came from hitching Boston's wagon to the star of a new federal program called "urban renewal."

In doing this, Hynes did more than set a new direction for the city. He shifted the balance of power away from the neighborhoods, where it had resided since the Irish politicians had wrested control of the city from the Brahmins fifty years earlier, and back to the downtown interests that Curley had called the "State Street wrecking crew." Hynes was reelected in 1955, defeating Massachusetts State Senate President John E. Powers of South Boston by 124,000 votes to 111,000. But the fairly narrow margin of his victory suggested that a significant number of people in the New Boston weren't entirely happy with that shift.

To Hell with Urban Renewal

Urban renewal, created by Congress under Title I of the Housing Act of 1949, would later be described as a kind of domestic "Marshall Plan" for declining cities such as Boston.[1] But urban renewal was initially less about rebuilding cities than promoting what was described back then as "slum clearance," since Title I pledged that the federal government would repay cities two-thirds of what it cost them to buy and clear "blighted areas" and loan private developers up to 90 percent of what it cost to build something new there.[2]

To qualify for this federal largesse, cities had to come up with redevelopment plans and create local planning authorities to carry them out. Other cities—even smaller ones like Pittsburgh and New Haven—were quicker to jump on the urban renewal bandwagon. It took Boston some time to realize the new program held so much promise. It took the people of Boston a little longer than that to realize it posed such a threat.

Langley Keyes's *The Rehabilitation Planning Game: A Study in the Diversity of Neighborhood* is the best account of Boston's early experience with urban renewal, which began in 1950 when the Boston Planning Board drew up a "General Plan for Boston." It called for rebuilding almost a quarter of the city—areas it described as "so clearly substandard . . . that sweeping clearance of buildings is the only way they can be restored."[3] This clearance was to start in the North, South, and West Ends, the neighborhoods closest to downtown, then proceed all the way to the outer neighborhoods of Roxbury, Jamaica Plain, Dorchester, Charlestown, and East Boston.[4] A Redevelopment Division was set up within the Boston Housing Authority (BHA) to implement the plan. The first urban renewal plan in Boston was for a neighborhood that not many people remember today.

The New York Streets *was that part of the South End closest to downtown. The area had been developed soon after the nearby Boston & Albany Railroad Station opened in 1881, and its streets were named for the cities and Native American tribes in upstate New York. Over time, the neighborhood's brick row houses and wood-frame tenements filled with immigrants from many countries, and, by the 1950s, it had come to be described as a "League of Nations" of working-class families.*

Mel King grew up on Seneca Street and would become the leading community activist of his time. "The thing about Mel," said Langley Keyes, "was he took the big, universal issues and embedded them into the small, neighborhood issues." King was one of eleven children whose parents had emigrated from the West Indies to Boston. He said that growing up, "The kids I played ball with were named Cohen, Finnegan, De Cicco, Kowalsky, and some were Chinese." He first learned about the New York Streets urban renewal plan while attending college in South Carolina, when his parents sent him clippings from the *Boston Herald-Traveler,* which strongly backed the plan. The paper called the area "Boston's skid row." "I was surprised," King later wrote, "because I had always called it home."[5]

The New York Streets plan called for clearing 24 acres and dislocating the 858 families that lived there in *hopes*—no commitments had yet been made—that businesses and industries would build on the cleared land.[6] The BHA Redevelopment Division justified tearing down all those homes and evicting all those families by claiming that, "the most cursory inspection of the New York Streets establishes it as a blighted and deteriorated neighborhood."[7]

But there were other reasons the neighborhood was chosen for Boston's first experiment with urban renewal. One was its location, close to downtown Boston and with "easy access to major roads, the railroad, the Fort Point Channel, and the proposed Southeast Expressway."[8] Another was its lack of political clout. The days of the local ward bosses who could protect their turf were over, and none of the members of the new, at-large city council called down-at-the-heels neighborhoods like the New York Streets home.

Another reason the New York Streets area was chosen, according to a report by the BHA Redevelopment Division, was that "any vestige of pride in the surroundings has long since been abandoned by the people there."⁹ Gloria Ganno lived on Florence Street back then and years later disputed that charge. "It wasn't that we didn't have any pride, it was that we weren't very well educated. When the city told us we had to go, we didn't know any better, so we went."¹⁰

In January 1952, eviction notices were sent to the residents of the New York Streets. Just to be sure they left, Ganno recalled, "the city shut off the power to the street lights, leaving the neighborhood in the dark and making it dangerous to walk home after work." In September 1957, when the last building in the area was torn down, Mayor Hynes proclaimed it the "beginning of the New Boston."¹¹

But if the New York Streets project was a beginning, it was a stalled one. For years, the cleared land sat vacant and failed to attract any of those hoped-for new businesses and industries. The first new building didn't open until July 12, 1959—and just happened to be the new headquarters of the *Boston Herald-Traveler,* which had led the campaign to wipe the neighborhood off the map. It was built on the spot where Mel King's house had stood on Seneca Street, but the new streets there were now named "Herald" and "Traveler," after the new "neighborhood's" pioneer occupant.

Because the residents of the New York Streets didn't know better and left quietly, their neighborhood is almost forgotten today. But that wouldn't be true of the residents or the next neighborhood chosen for urban renewal.

The WEST END *is on the tip of Boston's downtown peninsula, wedged in between Beacon Hill, today's Government Center, and North Station. Early in its history, the West End was home to such preindustrial activities as ropewalks and distilleries. For a brief period, it became a somewhat upscale residential area. But from the end of the nineteenth century on, the West End came to house successive waves of immigrants in its brick four- and five-story tenements.*

By the 1950s, it was a melting pot of poor and working-class families, mostly Italian American, but with large helpings of Syrian, Irish, Jewish, and African American families mixed in, all living in close quarters. "I don't want to make it sound like heaven," said Jim Campano, who grew up on Poplar Street, "but we all did get along. If I could figure out what it was, I'd bottle it and sell it."¹²

Once the West End was chosen for urban renewal, the BHA Redevelopment Division published a pamphlet for residents that explained— in an excruciatingly patronizing way—why. "Sooner or later the old parts of a city wear out and have to be replaced," it read. "These things are not the fault of the people of the West End; it is not the people who are substandard, but their neighborhood." Bruce Guarino, who grew up there, claimed those substandard conditions didn't just happen—they were caused. "The city told property owners there was no point in fixing up their buildings and it stopped collecting trash regularly. Then they took pictures to show the people in Washington how much it had deteriorated."[13]

But just as with the New York Streets, the West End wasn't chosen so much for its condition but for its location. "They were looking for a slum in a good location," Campano explained. The "they" in this case was not limited to the city. Kane Simonian, then the director of the BHA Redevelopment Division, later told a *Boston Globe* reporter, "People forget that the project was supported by Jordan's, Filene's, Gilchrist's, Raymond's, the Chamber of Commerce, MGH [Massachusetts General Hospital], the Retail Board, Real Estate Board, the *Herald,* the *Post,* the *Record-American* and your own goddamn newspaper, and do you know why? Because it would provide warm bodies to buy silk stockings and pantyhose from the stores."[14]

And just as with the New York Streets, the West End was also chosen because of its lack of political clout. In the early decades of the century, it had been the home of Martin Lomasney, the most powerful ward boss in the city. But Lomasney was long gone, and there was no place in the New Boston for politicians who practiced the old-school constituent-oriented politics they way he did.

On April 11, 1953, Mayor Hynes officially announced the West End plan. It called for clearing 48 acres, displacing all the neighborhood's approximately 2,700 households (approximately 7,000 residents), and demolishing more than 700 buildings to enable construction of approximately 2,000 apartments in a cluster of high-rise buildings.[15] More than half of the new apartments were to be priced low enough so that many of the families who were losing their homes could remain in the neighborhood.[16]

But two not-so-funny things happened before the plan was implemented. The first was that the development team chosen to build the new project just happened to include Jerome Rappaport, a young lawyer who had served as Hynes's personal secretary and "almost single-handedly" organized the New Boston Committee that helped reelect Hynes mayor in 1951.[17] The second was that the plan was subsequently revised so that all of the units in the new buildings became what were called back then "luxury apartments," putting them out of the price range of any soon-to-be-evicted West Enders.

But unlike residents of the New York Streets, the West Enders didn't go quietly. Frank Lavine, who called himself "just a kid at the time," remembered grabbing a pamphlet that described the plan and running it up to the South Russell Street home of Joseph Lee Jr., an eccentric Brahmin and school committee member who had started a program that taught West End kids the genteel sport of sailing on the Charles River. "When I got to his house," Lavine recalled, "I said, 'Joe. Joe. We're all gettin' kicked out.' I'll never forget the look on his face after he read the pamphlet and said to me, 'They wouldn't dare!' "[18]

The sociologist Herbert Gans wrote a book about the West End, called *The Urban Villagers: Group and Class in the Life of Italian-Americans*, which became not just a classic study of the working class but a primer on the impact of urban renewal. In it, Gans lamented the "inability of the West Enders to organize in their own behalf."[19] But looking back, it seems they did everything they could to try to save their neighborhood.

Lee and others formed a group called the Committee to Save the West End, rented a storefront office on Staniford Street, and paid homage to Boston's rebellious past by displaying a sign in the window that read, "West End Minutemen." They held meetings and demonstrations and packed hearings. On May 14, 1953, more than 500 "irate West End residents" packed a city council hearing described as "one of the stormiest scenes in recent City Hall history."[20] Residents turned out in similar numbers and with similar fury at meetings and hearings in subsequent years.

In the fall of 1957, the Boston Redevelopment Authority was created to take over responsibility for implementing urban renewal in Boston. On November 16, 1957, the BRA held its first public hearing on the plan at the West End Branch Library and hundreds of residents packed the meeting room. Hundreds more picketed outside, some carrying signs that read, "Don't Give the West End to Rappaport." Several people were ejected before the hearing even got started, and scores lined up to testify against the plan.

Joe Lee Jr. called the plan a "land grab" that was being perpetrated "because of the cultural and geographic advantages of the area." One of the neighborhood's two state representative asked, "What's going to happen to these people?" The other asked the BRA to give residents more time so they could come up with a plan of their own that would allow them to stay in their homes.[21]

A BRA board member admitted to being "impressed with the protest." But with Mayor Hynes, most of the city council, and the city's business community and newspapers all behind it, the plan was impossible to stop. After deciding that "the process had gone too far to be reversed," the BRA board approved it, and the city council, state, and federal government quickly followed suit.[22]

Using its power of eminent domain, the BRA took all of the property in the project area and, on April 25, 1958, sent eviction notices to all of the residents. West Enders came to call that day "The Taking," and it sparked another round of protests. More than 500 people turned out for a rally on Staniford Street. One speaker urged residents not to let inspectors into their homes. Another called on them to get arrested if necessary. A march on city hall was proposed. Although the march never took place, a delegation of West Enders did go to Washington to ask the Massachusetts congressional delegation to stop the project, and a dozen residents went to court to try to get an injunction to keep it from moving ahead.

Even neighborhood teenagers pitched in. One night, Jim Campano and his friends dropped cinder blocks from rooftops onto construction equipment. Another night, someone tossed a Molotov cocktail into the cab of a crane. "You should've seen when it went off," Campano remembered gleefully, "it lit up the street like Fenway Park at a night game."[23]

But nothing residents did could stop the plan from going forward. In June 1958, when the school year ended, most of the families in the West End moved out. Within a year-and-a-half, all of the residents were gone. The BRA claimed it tried to help them find new places to live. But that help seems to have consisted of little more than referring them to public housing (which most residents refused) or giving them a $25 per room "relocation allowance" (which they scornfully accepted). "They gave us a hundred bucks and told us to take a hike," Campano recalled.[24] In the diaspora that followed, West Enders scattered to other Boston neighborhoods or nearby cities and towns. By 1960, except for a handful of historic buildings that were spared, the neighborhood had been leveled. Photos taken at the time show a landscape that looked like the bombed-out sections of European cities during World War II.

Asked many years later why residents hadn't been able to save their neighborhood, Lavine echoed what Gloria Ganno, his counterpart from the New York Streets, had said. "Looking back, we really didn't have the education we needed. Most people were afraid. The schools let us down. I went to the Blackstone, and, back then, the schools trained you to be a good citizen—which basically meant to keep your mouth shut. It wasn't until years later that people like Saul Alinsky came around and taught people there was another way to be a good citizen and that was to stick up for your rights."[25] It would be another twenty-five years before Alinsky,

Demolition of the West End along Chambers Street in 1959. Photo courtesy of the
West End Museum.

a Chicago-based community organizer, published a book called *Rules for
Radicals,* which would serve as a long-overdue handbook for grassroots
community organizing.

On March 8, 1960, more than 100 political and business "leaders" (all
men, all white, and all, it appears from photographs, wearing fedoras), took
part in the groundbreaking ceremony for the new Charles River Park residential complex, which replaced the West End. Jerome Rappaport, one
of the developers, called it "the first child of the New Boston." Most news
accounts emphasized in boosterish prose what the city was expected to
gain: "bold blight-ridding rehabilitation," and "an entirely new idea in gra-
cious city living."[26] Only a few acknowledged what it had lost: "families
whose lives were interwoven in the community affairs of the tightly knit
and proud district."[27]

Soon, however, thanks to the all the noise the West Enders made before
they left and to Herbert Gans's book, the destruction of the West End became something else—a textbook example for cities across the country and
even around the world on how *not* to implement urban renewal. *Fortune*
magazine called it a "disaster" and "a bitter warning to all of the timeworn
Boston neighborhoods of what renewal might mean to them, too." Langley

Keyes called it a lesson to the people of Boston "that you better watch out because they're going to do something to you—*they* being the Port Authority, the T [Metropolitan Boston Transit Authority], the city or whomever." [28]

In 1959, John Hynes, the mayor who announced the goal of building the New Boston and who chose urban renewal to do it, announced he would not run for another chance at a job he admitted could be "pretty agonizing at times." In looking back on his tenure, Hynes was characteristically charitable and described the people of Boston as having been "forgiving, patient, and understanding for the most part." [29] It was a description that wouldn't hold true for much longer.

John Hynes had outlined a "bold vision of a modernized city," wrote the historian Thomas O'Connor, but it was his successor, John Collins, "who made things happen." [30] Collins grew up in Roxbury, graduated from Suffolk Law School, and served as an Army intelligence officer in World War II. Returning home to Boston, he moved to Jamaica Plain, started a family, and began his career in politics by getting elected first to the Massachusetts House of Representatives and then to the state senate.

In 1955, after losing a statewide race for attorney general, Collins was forced to start over by running for the Boston City Council, but during the campaign he was stricken with polio. Although he would never walk without assistance again, Collins stayed in the race and won a spot on the council. After serving as Suffolk County Register of Probate, he was persuaded to run for mayor.

In the 1959 mayoral race, Collins's opponent was Massachusetts Senate president John E. Powers, who had lost to Hynes four years earlier but was heavily favored to win this time. During the campaign, Collins sounded like the cautious, prudent clerk that candidate Hynes had been before being elected mayor. Collins called for things like "a policy of rigid economy and entrenchment." Powers, on the other hand, sounded like the visionary Mayor Hynes had become. Powers called for the city's political and business community to "work together with a common purpose" and proposed a "blueprint for action to solve the city's fiscal and economic problems." [31]

But what Collins lacked in message, he more than made up for with his mastery of the new medium of television, which was widely used for the first time in a Boston mayoral campaign. "Powers came across as short and stubby on TV, like your typical pol," recalled Collins's campaign manager, Henry Scagnoli, "but Collins came across as young and handsome." In his

TV ads, Collins appeared seated, with just one arm of his wheelchair visible "so he couldn't be accused of trying to hide his disability," according to Scagnoli. Then he looked into the camera and said, "My opponent has all the politicians. All we have is the people. And that is the way I want it. Let him have the men in the big hats. Give me the good, decent, earnest people who work hard for a living and who are on the march in this battle to save their city from my opponent and his wrecking crew."[32] On November 3, 1959, those people chose Collins over Powers by 114,000 votes to 90,000, in what is often called the biggest upset in Boston political history.

But while candidate Collins appealed to the people, Mayor Collins, like his predecessor, appealed to the business community. Rather than seek to increase services, he focused on decreasing spending. "Our first year, he cut the tax rate by 10 cents," recalled Scagnoli, by then the city's chief financial officer. "Now, that didn't mean much to homeowners. But it meant a lot to the business people."[33]

Collins also adopted his predecessor's prescription for how to restore Boston's economic health, declaring, "We must restore, rebuild, and redevelop." Hynes had cultivated the entire business community. Collins concentrated his attention on a small group of the chief executive officers of the city's biggest companies who had recently-formed something called the Boston Coordinating Committee, which was nicknamed "The Vault" because it met at the Boston Safe Deposit Company. "You have to remember that the city was close to bankruptcy back then," Scagnoli recalled. "Collins went to the business community for the same reason that Willie Sutton said he robbed banks, 'Because that's where the money was.'"[34]

By 1960, most of the money in Boston's private sector was in the growing field of professional services. While all those new high-tech companies might have built their "campuses" in the suburbs, they generated a huge demand for the lawyers, accountants, and money managers who continued to work in downtown Boston. That prompted a boom in the construction of new office buildings that Collins did all he could do to accommodate.

Most of the money in the public sector continued to be in urban renewal, so Collins became a convert to that—and organized his administration accordingly. "All the other departments reported to me," recalled Scagnoli, who soon was also named deputy mayor, "but he made sure that the BRA director, along with the police commissioner, reported directly to him."[35]

To serve as BRA director, Collins chose Ed Logue, the former development director in New Haven, Connecticut, who had displayed a remarkable knack for obtaining federal funds.[36] A brash, Ivy League–educated WASP from Philadelphia, Logue was an example of the Kennedy-era generation of public officials David Halberstam later called "the best and the brightest," confident he could fix what was broken in Boston. Collins gave Logue all the tools he needed for his repair work, and for that the new BRA was grateful. "Ed Logue once told me 'John Collins's political views are to the right of Attila the Hun,'" Henry Lee recalled, "'but I revere him because he gave me my head.'"[37]

The Boston Redevelopment Authority was exempt from civil service regulations, so Logue could hire the "professional planners" he wanted. Soon after he arrived, the Boston Planning Board was abolished and its powers were transferred to the BRA, making it one of the only agencies in the country to combine planning and development functions under one roof. That gave the BRA enormous power—and even more to the already powerful mayor.

On September 22, 1960, Collins and Logue showed how they planned to use that power by announcing a staggeringly ambitious "Ninety Million Dollar Development Program for Boston." It called for extending urban renewal to one-fourth of the city and areas that were home to half of Boston's residents.[38] In making the announcement, even the autocratic Collins felt it was necessary to acknowledge the protest and criticism over how the West End urban renewal plan had been carried out. He promised he and Logue would take a different approach. "I would call it planning WITH people," the mayor said, "rather than planning for people."[39]

It was a catchy slogan, but it was hard to imagine two men more temperamentally unsuited to carry it out. "If John Collins thought something was right, he'd do it. He didn't care what other people thought," recalled Scagnoli. "Collins smoked cigars, and when he rolled the cigar in his fingers that meant he was playing with you. But when he was biting on the cigar, that meant you better get out of the room."[40]

As for Logue, he was called at the time a "forceful man who glorifies in political brawls and has a temper as quick as his smile." Later on, he was described as someone who "chafed at the demands of community activists who insisted that all displaced persons in urban renewal areas be allowed to move back into rehabilitated units," and someone who thought "there was something un-American about returning to where you had already been."[41]

As it turned out, it didn't matter what slogan Collins and Logue adopted because the people of Boston came up with their own. It was a modern-day version of the one Paul Revere had used two hundred years earlier. But instead of "The British Are Coming," it was "Remember the West End." As it also turned out, the neighborhood in which Paul Revere had begun his famous ride was the one where that slogan would be used first.

Cut off from the rest of the city by the mouth of the Charles River and Boston Harbor, CHARLESTOWN *had first been settled in 1629, a year before Boston. It had remained a separate town until 1873, when residents approved its annexation by Boston in return for the promise of better city services. Since 1800, Charlestown's economy revolved around its navy yard, which built and repaired ships and which provided first all of the rope used by the U.S. Navy and then all of the chain.*

By 1960, Charlestown was a self-contained, overwhelmingly white, working-class neighborhood of 20,000 people in which many of its families had lived for generations. Thanks to its location, it had little to do with the rest of the city. In recent years, those interactions were not very pleasant. One corner of the neighborhood had been torn down to make way for a public housing development. A whole side was sliced off to make way for the Mystic River Bridge. Now this new threat of urban renewal prompted some residents to question whether the town should have agreed to become part of Boston almost a hundred years earlier.

Charlestown was better prepared for urban renewal than it might otherwise have been, thanks to the efforts of resident Leo Baldwin. In April 1960, Baldwin, who described himself as having "a wife and six kids and two jobs," wrote a series of letters to the local *Charlestown Patriot* newspaper. In the first few, he declared that "Charlestown is in a bad way" and it was "time that all the people and all the organizations got together for common self-preservation." In his last letter, Baldwin suggested residents form a committee to respond to urban renewal. "The people of the West End formed their committee when the West End was doomed," he wrote. "Have you seen the West End lately?"[42]

The question was more than rhetorical, since Charlestown residents could actually look across the water and see the new, luxury Charles River Park high-rise towers rising from where the West End had been. The residents responded by forming the Self-Help Organization of Charlestown (SHOC) and electing Baldwin the new organization's first president.[43] They acted just in time.

That spring, the BRA unveiled its first urban renewal proposal for Charlestown, the "District Plan." It called for tearing down 60 percent of the neighborhood's housing stock, homes the agency said were not worth saving.[44] But the idea of knocking down more than half the town didn't sit well with most of its residents, and in November 1961, more than 400 of them, most of them SHOC members, turned out for a meeting at the local Knights of Columbus Hall to tell that to the BRA.

But Charlestown had learned from the West End. Rather than just say what they didn't want—as the West Enders had done—Charlestown residents told the BRA what they would accept: less demolition, more rehabilitation, and a guarantee that those forced out of their homes would be relocated in the neighborhood. At the end of the meeting, to emphasize those demands, the residents chanted "Yankee Go Home!" over and over again, leaving BRA officials, according to one account, "shaken back on their heels."[45]

Despite their bravado, residents were anxious, remembered lifelong "Townie" Moe Gillen, a no-nonsense, ruggedly built meter reader for Boston Edison who was at the meeting. "During that first go-round, everybody talked about the disaster of the West End. But we didn't know what we could do about it—or if we could stop it from happening to us."[46]

Forced by how effectively SHOC had organized the opposition, Ed Logue ordered his BRA planners to go back to the drawing board. But knowing that organizing can be a two-way street, he also hired Joe Vilemas, who had worked under Saul Alinsky in Chicago, to "counter-organize" support for urban renewal in Charlestown. Vilemas convinced Baldwin and others that since SHOC's membership was only open to residents, it didn't represent all of the neighborhood's interests, and that they should start another group with representatives from local business groups and social, religious and other institutions, as well as from residents.

In January 1962, the Federation of Charlestown Organizations was formed. Its membership was made up of representatives from some 50 neighborhood groups and organizations. Somehow, SHOC was given only one of those slots. In a bid to marginalize the resident-led opposition, the BRA quickly recognized the Federation as the local organization with which it would deal on urban renewal. SHOC was outraged and charged that Collins and Logue were only interested in "planning with *some* people."

"The Federation was made up of the 'establishment' and 'political' types," recalled Gillen, "like the churches, the Longshoreman's union, and the Knights of Columbus that wanted to give urban renewal a shot. SHOC was seen as representing the 'regular people,' who felt that government wanted to destroy their homes."[47] As the two groups competed over which one should represent the neighborhood, a split developed between the "moderates" in the Federation and the "militants" in SHOC—the kind of split that would arise again in again in neighborhoods throughout Boston over urban renewal and other issues for the next twenty years.

In early 1962, the BRA released three "sketch plans" for urban renewal in Charlestown, and the agency spent the next several months discussing them with the groups represented by the Federation. By the fall, a "composite plan" was released.[48] It reduced the housing stock to be demolished to 20 percent and called for rehabilitating the rest, as well as for building 1,400 new units. It also promised that the approximately 4,000 residents who would have to leave their homes would be relocated within Charlestown, into either the renovated or new housing. The plan also called for building two new elementary schools, a new fire station and shopping mall, new parks and playgrounds, and a new arterial street to get traffic off residential streets. Best of all as far as most residents were concerned, the BRA even promised to get the elevated subway tracks that ran down Main Street torn down and relocated, even though this was something that, strictly speaking, was beyond the agency's purview.[49]

After the plan was circulated for a few months, the Federation voted to support it. But SHOC rejected the plan.[50] A public hearing was scheduled to settle the issue. In the weeks leading up to the hearing, residents were pressured to take sides. Some later claimed their employers told them that if they didn't support the Federation, they'd lose their jobs. Others said SHOC members threatened physical harm if they didn't vote against the plan. Because the pastors of local churches did support the plan, SHOC called on residents to boycott the churches, "particularly their collection plates."[51] On the day of the meeting SHOC sent sound trucks around the neighborhood, calling on residents to come to the hearing and "Save Their Homes."[52]

On Monday evening, January 7, 1963, more than 1,000 residents did come out. They packed the auditorium of the Clarence Edwards Junior High School for what turned into a raucous hearing. When Ed Logue tried to present the plan, he was booed. When the chairman of the Federation tried to speak in favor of it, he was drowned out with "hoots and catcalls." When members of the clergy voiced their support for the plan, they "were heard out in silence."[53]

At the end of the evening, BRA board chairman Monsignor Francis Lally, who lived nearby in St. Catherine's rectory, called for a vote on the plan. An overwhelming majority of the crowd voted against it.[54] SHOC had prevailed, one news account said, because "aware that so many urban renewal meetings of 'planning with people' get stacked by the pros, [it] outmaneuvered the maneuverers." [55] Even Logue had to admit, "We were clobbered." [56]

But Logue didn't give up. Although forced once more to send his planners back to the drawing board, he ordered the rest of his staff to step up their counter-organizing efforts in order to "overpower SHOC at the next public hearing." During that time, though, one BRA official admitted that SHOC had "forced us to sharpen our answers about rehabilitation and the plan until those answers began to satisfy people." [57]

It took another two years for the BRA to sharpen its answers sufficiently before it came up with a third plan. The hearing on this one was held on Sunday afternoon, March 14, 1965, when more than 2,500 residents crammed into the Charlestown Armory. Even John Collins came out. Collins rarely attended such events, partly due to his disability, but partly due to his personality. As Alan Lupo later wrote, "he had little patience for those who tried his patience." The mayor's opening "pitch for support" was met by "a barrage of applause interspersed with boos." After he left, the rowdy debate lasted more than seven hours, and, despite the presence of nearly 50 Boston police officers, "threatened to erupt into a donnybrook." [58]

At one point, after Monsignor Gerald Shea of St. Catherine's stood up and made a plea in favor of the plan, he got punched for his troubles. At another, a longshoreman stood up and yelled at Logue, "I don't have to do it. It's my home and that's what I am fighting for. You can stick the money up your ass." [59] It ended when Monsignor Shea suddenly stood up again and asked for a vote, shouting, "All those in favor, stand. Stand for Charlestown, stand!" [60] Pandemonium broke out. Many of those in the standing-room-only crowd dove to the floor. But, since those residents who remained on their feet appeared to outnumber the rest, BRA officials declared victory and hastily adjourned the meeting.

Charlestown residents who opposed the plan didn't give up. On April 27, 1965, more than 400 of them descended on City Hall for a four-and-half-hour hearing described in a front-page *Boston Globe* headline as "the wildest session ever staged in City Hall's Council chambers." Not long after that, 350 residents signed a petition asking the state legislature "to authorize the citizens of Charlestown to form a government completely independent of the City." [61]

Charlestown didn't secede from Boston, and urban renewal did proceed. But it did so in a way that was more carefully thought out. Only 10 percent of Charlestown's housing stock ended up being demolished, far below the 60-percent figure first proposed. Almost all of the 2,000 residents that were displaced—half the number that would have been displaced under the previous plan—were resettled within the neighborhood.[62] Some 700 new units of public housing and 200 new units of private housing were built, and homeowners took advantage of low-interest loans to renovate more than 2,000 additional units, many in Charlestown's historic district. The new schools and other public buildings, parks and playgrounds, streets and sidewalks were all built, and so was the new Bunker Hill Community College. Even the hated elevated tracks along Main Street came down, replaced by a new subway line a few blocks away.[63]

Once it was finished, there were some complaints, mostly over the quality of public housing that was built. But, at least initially, most residents were pleased with the results. They were also proud to have set an example for other neighborhoods on how to fight City Hall, improve on the proposals of professional planners, and make urban work better. Unfortunately, residents of the next neighborhood in Boston to face urban renewal didn't follow that example.

ROXBURY *was founded in 1630 and, like Charlestown, allowed itself to be annexed by Boston in exchange for the promise of improved services. In Roxbury's case, that took place in 1861. But unlike Charlestown, Roxbury was not a homogenous community cut off from the rest of the city. It was a heterogeneous one located in the geographic center of Boston, and it became a "streetcar suburb" and home to successive waves of Irish, Jewish, and, most recently, African American residents.*

By 1960, Roxbury's population was just over 93,000. Approximately half of its residents were white, and most of the rest were African American. But in Washington Park, the area chosen for urban renewal, the population of 26,000 had changed from 70 percent white to 70 percent African American over the previous ten years.[64]

Washington Park was still a largely working- and middle-class community by 1960, but an increasing number of poor families had begun to move into the adjacent Dudley Square area. Residents of Washington Park suspected that the decline in city services they were noticing in the neighborhood had something to do with this recent demographic change. They were persuaded by community leaders that urban renewal might be just the thing to help stabilize the neighborhood and get the city to pay more attention to it.

Two of the leaders who did that persuading were Otto and Muriel Snowden. The son of a career army officer, Otto had grown up in Roxbury, attended Howard University in Washington, DC, and after serving in the military returned to Boston to begin his career in social work. Muriel had grown up in New Jersey and came to Boston to attend Radcliffe College; she had married Otto and gone into social work as well. In 1949, with other middle-class African American professionals, they founded Freedom House, a social service agency with a goal "to centralize community activism in the fight for neighborhood improvement."

With the Snowdens as its directors, Freedom House became a place where the African American community gathered to discuss problems, agree on strategies, and attempt to carry them out. It became so influential, in fact, that it was referred to as Boston's "Black Pentagon." When urban renewal came along, the Snowdens used that influence to convince first Mayor Hynes and next Mayor Collins to designate Washington Park as one of the first areas for the program.[65] Then, even though the Roxbury Community Council had long represented the community, the Snowdens got the newly created Washington Park Steering Committee—whose membership was dominated by Freedom House—designated as the official urban renewal planning committee for the area.[66] "My parents didn't want another West End," explained Gail Snowden years later. "They wanted to create a new model."[67]

In 1960, when the BRA presented its first Washington Park plan, it covered 186 acres, called for demolishing 25 percent of the housing stock, and for displacing some 1,500 families. But unlike in Charlestown, where residents fought to make their plan smaller, the Snowdens and other members of the "black establishment" wanted their new model to be much bigger in Washington Park.

Those other members of the establishment included Elma Lewis, a small, feisty woman born and raised in Boston, the daughter of West Indian immigrants. Lewis pursued her activism through the arts, and turned the small dance school she had started into an important community institution that became the National Center of Afro-American Artists. Another member of the establishment was Melnea Cass, by this time the president of the Boston Branch of the National Association for the Advancement of Colored People (NAACP). The regal "Mrs. Cass," as everyone called her, was born in Virginia in 1896. She moved to Boston with her family five years later, and began her career as an activist as a suffragette in 1919, registering African American women to vote. Since then, she had been involved in every civil rights campaign in Boston and become a mentor to young activists following in her path. Her reaction to the first Washington Park plan was to tell BRA officials, "Let us tell you what we want."[68]

What these leaders said they wanted was a plan that covered 500 acres and called for demolishing 65 percent of the existing housing stock, almost all of it in the lower-lying and lower-income areas of the neighborhood. That was too much, even for the BRA. The agency came back with another plan that, while it did cover 500 acres, called for demolishing "only" 35 percent of the housing stock.[69] It also called for building 1,500 new units of housing, new schools and recreational facilities, a new shopping center, and a new "civic center" in Dudley Square.[70]

The plan called for relocating some 2,200 families.[71] Unlike in Charlestown, spokespersons for the community didn't demand that those families be relocated "within the project boundaries."[72] Some critics would later claim that this was because the Snowdens and other community leaders intended to use urban renewal to preserve Washington Park as a bastion of the middle class. That charge seems to be supported by the fact that only 30 of the new units were to be reserved for public housing.

The biggest contrast between Charlestown and Roxbury came in how the community reacted to the plan. On January 14, 1963, a week after more than 1,000 Charlestown residents had turned out to "clobber" the BRA's plan for their neighborhood, more than 1,200 Roxbury residents packed the auditorium at Boston Technical High School and showed almost unanimous support for the Washington Park plan. Indeed when Monsignor Francis Lally, the BRA's board chairman, called for a show of hands, only four or five people signaled their opposition.[73]

That show of support was somewhat misleading, because some residents—especially those like Dan Richardson, who was a member of the younger generation of emerging activists—were not on board. Born and raised in Lower Roxbury, Richardson's father had been a newspaperman "chased from the South" for his editorials against the lynch laws still on the books there. By the time the Washington Park plan was proposed, Richardson was a self-described "young rabble rouser." Years later he recalled, "Whenever we said something bad about urban renewal, Ed Logue would go to the people who were running things and ask them to shut us up."[74]

With so much apparent community support behind it, the Washington Park plan quickly won local, state, and federal approval. In May 1963, ground was broken on the first phase of the project, Academy Homes, and various labor unions, local churches, and other nonprofit organizations sponsored this one and subsequent phases.

Demolition and construction proceeded quickly in Washington Park. But as it did, criticism began to mount. Although the Boston Branch NAACP continued to support it, the Boston chapters of the Congress of Racial Equality and the Urban League did not. They criticized the neighborhood urban renewal committee for being too heavily influenced by Freedom House and for being composed mostly of middle-class homeowners. They also complained that three-fourths of those being forced from their homes were poor families unable to relocate within the neighborhood.[75]

The Boston Housing Authority objected in May 1966 when a majority of the 75 people attending a meeting at Freedom House voted to remove even those 30 units of public housing from the plan. The BHA's administrator, Ellis Ash, said that allowing so few people to make such an important decision raised "serious questions in terms of procedures of how we function in urban renewal areas." When the BRA's director Ed Logue defended the decision—saying it had been made by "same group we have been dealing with throughout"—he buttressed claims by urban renewal critics that the BRA was once more only "planning with some people."[76]

Much of the Washington Park urban renewal project was eventually completed. It resulted in more than 1,800 new units of housing being built and more than 4,600 units being rehabilitated.[77] But the poor quality of much of the work made it necessary to renovate many of the new housing units within only a few years. Higher than expected maintenance and operating costs led to most of the nonprofit sponsors losing control of many of the housing developments through foreclosure. A new elementary school and a new recreational center were built; so were the new shopping center and the civic center that included a new branch library, a Boys & Girls Club, YMCA, police station, and courthouse. But the shopping center struggled to attract tenants and was plagued for years by poor management and vandalism, and the civic center would be criticized for being made up of "inwardly looking buildings [that] drained the life" from Dudley Square.[78]

Ed Logue later called Washington Park "the most successful of our renewal programs, and the one that caused the least grief."[79] But a 1972 report concluded the project had "not achieved the basic objective of long term residential stability" and that "middle income families have continued to move out and many new and rehabilitated homes have fallen quickly into disrepair." Even Otto Snowden, once the project's biggest backer, admitted to second thoughts soon afterwards. "That's not the way to do things," he told a reporter. "You tell black people to work within the system; when they do, this is what happens." [80] What happened to the residents of the next area targeted for urban renewal, was even worse.

ALLSTON–BRIGHTON *is attached to the rest of Boston only by a narrow strip of land that runs between the Charles River and the neighboring town of Brook-line. Originally part of Cambridge and the site of a cattle market that provided beef for General George Washington's colonial troops, it had become an independent town by the time its residents approved annexation to Boston in 1874, and thereafter developed as another of the growing city's "streetcar suburbs."*

By 1960, Allston–Brighton was a stable, overwhelmingly white and predominantly middle-class neighborhood of just over 60,000 people. Many of its residents lived in single-family homes or in the many large apartment buildings built along Commonwealth Avenue and other major streets. It was a neighborhood with little apparent need for urban renewal.

In 1961, despite that lack of apparent need, the Boston Redevelopment Authority proposed an urban renewal plan for the tiny Barry's Corner area, a working-class enclave of two- and three-family wood-frame houses at the intersection of North Harvard Street and Western Avenue. The plan covered just 10 acres, and called for demolishing 52 homes and dislocating 71 families all in order to build one ten-story building containing 270 "luxury rate" apartments.[81] The sole reason for the plan seems to have been that a development team made up of a judge, his racetrack-owner brother, and a local landlord just happened to want to construct that type of building there.[82]

Residents of Barry's Corner didn't think that was a good enough reason for them to lose their homes, so they fought back. The best account of that fight was written by Marjorie Redgate, the woman who led it. Titled *To Hell with Urban Renewal,* it is a remarkable 300-plus-page unpublished manuscript held together by bobby pins and thread, and what it lacks in polish it more than make up for in passion.

Marjorie Redgate was a small woman who wore her dark hair piled high on her head. She and her husband Al had grown up in Charlestown and had bought their home in Barry's Corner twenty-five years before. Al ran a roofing business from a shack in the backyard, and, after buying the vacant store next door, Marjorie ran the Ready Luncheonette, which soon became the neighborhood gathering place.

According to Marjorie, residents first learned of the Barry's Corner urban renewal plan from a television newscast in October 1961. Not long after, they gathered at a local church to try to figure out how to respond. They invited residents from neighborhoods that had already faced urban renewal to join them at the meeting. One of those who did was Wanda Zachewicz, described back then as "the last resident of the West End." "We didn't really learn about the West End until then," recalled Marjorie Redgate's son, Bernard, who was a college student at the time. "Until after we were attacked." [83]

The Barry's Corner residents formed a group they called Citizens for Private Property. "We were all pretty conservative," Bernard Redgate explained. "Our fight was more over it being wrong to take people's property than the 'we love our neighborhood' aspect." [84] In spring 1962, the group held a series of Saturday morning demonstrations to protest the plan. But because their neighborhood was so far off the beaten path, they picketed instead outside Park Street Station in downtown Boston. For several hours on each of those Saturdays, they carried signs that read, "Fight Urban Renewal!" and "Save Our Homes!"

The Boston Redevelopment Authority finally scheduled a public hearing on the Barry's Corner plan for Wednesday June 27, 1962, at 10 a.m. A *Boston Globe* account published that day provided details of the lively proceedings that followed. [85] Despite the inconvenient weekday time, more than 100 residents of the tiny neighborhood turned out, marching into the Thomas Gardner School auditorium carrying signs that read, "Urban Renewal Profits Only the Real Estate Speculators" and "Urban Renewal Belongs in Russia." Then, for more than hour, they stomped their feet on the bleachers, chanted, "Get out! Get out!" and refused to let BRA officials speak. They stopped only when it was announced that the agenda for the meeting would be changed to allow the "public comment" period to precede the presentation of the plan.

For another hour, speaker after speaker stepped to a microphone and denounced the plan to tear down their homes. One of the speakers was a young woman whose great-grandfather had settled there a hundred years earlier and for whom Heffernan Street was named. Another was Monsignor Timothy Gleason of St. Anthony's Church. He declared, "Barry's corner is not a slum area. These people are good, God-loving people. The word *blighted* means rot and decay. There is nothing rotten, nothing decayed in Barry's Corner."

After the last resident had spoken, BRA officials tried again to make their

Successor to the sign erected on North Harvard Street in Allston on October 27, 1962. Boston Globe Staff file photo.

presentation. But again they were drowned out, this time, as the *Globe* reporter described, by "an incessant chorus of hisses and boos." The meeting was adjourned, and, according to one account, Ed Logue and board chairman Monsignor Francis Lally left the school looking "visibly shaken."[86]

Logue recovered quickly, and vowed to press on. "If the Authority had been persuaded to drop the project by that kind of demonstration," he declared, "it might as well have gone out of business right then and there."[87] That would have been fine with the residents of Barry's Corner. But since the BRA didn't go out of business, the residents tried—unsuccessfully it turned out—to enlist support from the larger Allston–Brighton neighborhood. They fared no better with their elected officials, whom Bernard Redgate described as "useless." Things went even worse when they met with officials at nearby Harvard University, which had begun to buy up property in the area. The residents asked the school to take better care of its buildings, in hopes that might help to forestall the plan. But Harvard responded by shutting off the utilities to the vacant houses and boarding them up in order to hasten their demolition.[88]

On October 27, 1962, forced to rely on themselves, the residents erected an 8-by-16-foot sign in the front yard of Annie Soricelli's home on North

Harvard Street. Its headline read, "TO HELL WITH URBAN RENEWAL" in big, block letters, and it soon became one of the iconic images of this still-growing era of protest in Boston.[89]

For more than two years, residents did everything they could think of to hang onto their homes. On December 29, 1962, a group of 60 residents and their supporters picketed in the snow outside the Jamaica Plain home of Mayor Collins. Some carried signs that read, "Mayor Collins Approves the Theft of Our Homes," and "Turn Out of Office the Politicians Responsible for Urban Renewal," and "Remember the West End — Fight Urban Renewal."[90] Collins was home at the time, but refused to come out or acknowledge the protesters.

In June 1963, the Barry's Corner residents even rented Faneuil Hall for a citywide rally against urban renewal. A few hundred people from across the city turned out, but the Boston media ignored the event. Later that summer, when BRA appraisers and city officials showed up to inspect their homes, residents armed themselves with "brooms, wet mops, sticks, rolling pins," and drove the inspectors away.[91] The local *Allston–Brighton News* ran a front-page photo of the skirmish, with the caption that read, "Allston Minutemen Rout BRA."[92]

Despite the residents' best efforts, the Boston City Council, the state, and the federal government approved the Barry's Corner plan.[93] And, on the day before Thanksgiving in 1964, residents received eviction letters from the BRA informing them that their homes had been taken by eminent domain. By the time school let out in June 1965, more than half of the families had left.

On August 3, 1965, a hot, hazy, Tuesday morning, a caravan of moving trucks, police officers, and sheriff's deputies arrived on North Harvard Street to begin evicting the remaining residents. One hundred demonstrators — residents and their supporters — were there to meet them. The protesters sat down in the street, forcing the moving trucks to halt, until police dragged them out of the way. Four people were arrested, and the demonstration was the lead story on local television that night and made the front pages of Boston newspapers the next morning.[94]

A few days later, the scene was repeated. This time 400 demonstrators turned out, many of them college students just starting to grow their hair long. Once again, the protesters sat down in front of the moving trucks. Once again, the police cleared them away. This time 12 people were arrested. But while everyone's attention was at one end of North Harvard Street, a bulldozer brought in at the other end proceeded to flatten several of the empty houses. Within a few weeks, most of the remaining houses had been demolished. Only a handful, including the Redgates', remained.

The demonstrations and demolitions generated so much bad publicity that even the notoriously stubborn Mayor Collins felt it necessary to call a halt to the evictions. After a group of city planners and housing specialists from Harvard and Massachusetts Institute of Technology wrote an open letter published in the *Boston Herald* denouncing North Harvard Street as "a West End in miniature," Collins felt compelled to appoint a "blue-ribbon commission" to take another look at the plan.[95] Surprisingly, the commission recommended the BRA scrap the original plan, choose a new developer, and that the few houses still standing "be returned to their owners and rehabilitated."[96]

The BRA complied with two out of the three recommendations. It came up with a new plan to build low-cost housing on the site instead of the luxury apartment building. For the new developer, it selected a newly formed group called the Committee for North Harvard, which was made up of representatives from local churches, a synagogue, and other nonprofit organizations. But, because the U.S. Department of Housing and Urban Development said it wouldn't fund the project unless the entire site was cleared, the BRA said the remaining residents and their houses still had to go.

The Redgates and one other family held on for four more years, but on October 29, 1969, the moving vans, sheriff's deputies, and police came for them. Several hundred demonstrators were there to meet them this time. After "a flurry of shoving and fist-fighting," 14 people were arrested. The Redgates had barricaded themselves inside their home. But after some negotiation, they emerged, and Marjorie tearfully told her supporters, "I don't want you or the police to be hurt. We're all finished here."[97]

As soon as the moving trucks left, another bulldozer was brought in and pushed down the last two homes. Five days later a groundbreaking ceremony was held for the Charlesview Apartments. Although it was described as "community-built housing," it was built at the expense of a small but feisty community that was no longer there.

Urban renewal plans continued in Boston throughout the 1960s and into the 1970s. Some neighborhoods—the ones with sufficient political clout—were able to stop the plans for their communities from proceeding after a single show of force.

That was the case in South Boston on October 25, 1965, when more than 500 residents and every local elected official turned out at the Broadway

Theater to back South Boston Citizens' Association president George Sweeney, who told city officials, "We don't need urban renewal. We can do our own rehabilitation."[98] That was also the case in Jamaica Plain on August 27, 1965, when more than 2,000 residents jammed the auditorium of the Mary E. Curley School, interrupted city and BRA officials when they tried to speak, and cheered the Jamaica Plain Action Committee president Edward Dalton when he declared, "We'll have our own renewal program. We don't need outsiders here in Jamaica Plain."[99]

In the more restrained Back Bay, residents didn't have to resort to such public displays of emotion to keep urban renewal out. After the BRA released a plan that called for constructing eight high-rise apartment buildings along Commonwealth Avenue, residents formed the Back Bay Civic Association and Neighborhood Association of the Back Bay, and they hired high-priced lawyers to make the plan go away. But that was not the case in less politically powerful or less well-off neighborhoods, where residents were forced to engage in long-running battles with the city and endless negotiations with the BRA to produce plans they could live with.

Urban renewal was successful in rebuilding the physical side of the New Boston. But its biggest success may have been in rekindling the flame of activism and protest that had gone out some time before. "Looking back," Langley Keyes said, "there had never been anything in Boston like the city-wide engagement of citizens that took place because of urban renewal" — at least not for two hundred years.[100]

CHAPTER 3

Community Organizers
and Advocacy Planners

W HEN URBAN RENEWAL BEGAN, PEOPLE IN THE NEW BOSTON'S
neighborhoods were pretty much on their own in trying to figure out
how to deal with it. That soon began to change when some people in the
nonprofit sector and academic world decided to get involved in the "real
world." They created new kinds of organizations that provided residents
with the kind of help they needed to respond to the city's efforts to rebuild
their neighborhoods—and even to do that rebuilding themselves.

One of the first of these new organizations was Action for Boston Community Development. Founded in 1961, ABCD was initially funded by the
Ford Foundation. It was put together by Charles Liddell, who took a leave
from running a network of social service organizations called the United
South End Settlements, in an effort to set up a similar network for the rest
of the city.

"Originally, ABCD was going to focus on social research and social development," recalled Joe Slavet, its first executive director. But the city and
the Boston Redevelopment Authority (BRA) had other ideas. According
to Slavet, "John Collins wanted ABCD to be the handmaiden of urban
renewal." According to Bob Perlman, who was ABCD's first director of
program development, BRA director Ed Logue wanted "to use our community organizers to build a bridge to the neighborhood people, so that
they would maybe modify or react to his [urban renewal] plans, but in the
end accept them." As a result, according to Stephen Thernstrom in his book

Poverty, Planning, and Politics in the New Boston: The Origins of ABCD, the new agency found itself caught up in the "complex and confusing controversies" in Charlestown and in the "tensions between the Snowdens and other factions" in Washington Park.[1]

But not everyone at ABCD went along with what Collins and Logue had in mind. At one early board meeting, the mayor charged that someone in the organization "was encouraging city residents to protest against lack of physical facilities such as street lamps," and complained that he "did not see it as the role of ABCD to foment dissatisfaction."[2]

But that dissatisfaction only increased and ABCD's role in fomenting it only expanded, when in 1964, ABCD created the South End Neighborhood Action Program (SNAP) to promote social development alongside the physical redevelopment of urban renewal in the South End and Lower Roxbury. Bob Coard was its first director. Born in the West Indies and raised in Texas, Coard had come to Boston to attend graduate school at MIT, then worked briefly for the BRA. But he had a different idea of the role that SNAP should play. "In those days, you have to remember there was a strong feeling of residents wanting to do things themselves in each neighborhood. And we wanted to encourage that feeling."[3]

Coard hired Byron Rushing and Chuck Turner to do some of that encouraging. Rushing had grown up in New York City and Turner in Hartford. Both had come to Boston to attend Harvard and then had gone on to work for the Congress of Racial Equality (CORE) and the Northern Student Movement in other cities, before returning to work at SNAP. "We were full-time community organizers," Rushing recalled. "We walked around and talked to people, and we found out what they wanted but hadn't gotten around to getting."[4]

In the Madison Park area of Lower Roxbury, they found out that what people most wanted was for the park that gave the neighborhood its name to be cleaned up. So they set up meetings between residents and city officials to try to get it done. When that didn't work, they organized a series of very provocative demonstrations. In March 1966, they loaded a truck with trash and garbage from the park and dumped it all on the steps of city hall.[5] That summer, they organized more than 100 residents to come out to the park on a Friday night, gather up even more trash, and light it up to create a bonfire. The Boston Fire Department had been alerted beforehand, so the blaze was quickly extinguished. But the demonstration was front-page news the next day and it produced the desired results.

"On Monday morning, the city sent a DPW crew out and it worked for two weeks to clean up the park," Turner recalled. "They put poles in the ground so contractors couldn't just drive in and dump there anymore. Then, the city added a second trash day for Roxbury, making it the only neighborhood other than Beacon Hill to get more than one a week."[6]

Rushing's and Turner's methods were a little extreme, and both men soon decided it might be better if they found other places of employment. But the roster of young activists who worked with them and followed them at SNAP and ABCD reads like a *Who's Who* of Boston community organizers of that era, and almost all of them continued their organizing work when they moved on to other jobs.

In 1965, ABCD had to pull back from such aggressive community organizing after the organization was designated the City of Boston's official antipoverty agency. However, its primary purpose became receiving and dispensing federal funds to groups and programs that did engage in organizing and in providing direct services. Much of that funding came from the new Office of Economic Opportunity, which had been established the year before as part of President Lyndon Johnson's War on Poverty. One of OEO's primary missions was to support the creation of community action programs that promoted "maximum feasible participation of residents of the area and members of the group served."[7]

ABCD helped support that mission by creating Area Planning Action Councils throughout the city, which were locally based social, human, and educational service programs, many located in public housing developments. "The whole notion of the APACs was built around the activism model," recalled Slavet.[8] In addition to activism, APACs promoted long overdue communication among people from different neighborhoods.

"The neighborhoods in Boston were turf conscious," noted John Gardiner, who worked in Charlestown. "Everybody had that same feeling. 'We're from East Boston, we're from Southie, we're from Charlestown, we're from Roxbury, we're from Dorchester, we're from the South End, we're from Chinatown, leave us the hell alone.'"[9] The APACs helped change that.

"I remember growing up in Boston in the '40s and '50s," said Val Hyman, who worked in Roxbury. "I didn't know anybody in other neighborhoods." Through his involvement with ABCD and its APACs, Hyman met people like "Alice Colbert from Charlestown, Bill Hearles from South Boston, and Joe Smith from Allston/Brighton. All these people, I found, were really very similar to me. They were interested in doing stuff in their neighborhoods, raising their kids, raising their families, creating a nice environment for their families and you got to know them as people . . . I think it really did a lot in bringing people from different neighborhoods together." [10]

But according to Alan Lupo, organizing and bringing people together were not enough—people also needed information and expertise. "Even if you had the best community activists in the world, the kind who turn out all kinds of people to meetings every night and hold demonstrations every week, it's still not a level playing field when it comes to community redevelopment," he explained. "Community activists need partners who know how to get things done. Otherwise, you can have the best plan in the world. But it will go nowhere." [11]

Lupo called his formula for successful community redevelopment "The Four P's. Without the Press, the People can't get the attention of the Politicians. But without the Planners to provide them with credibility, the People can't get the attention of the Press." [12] Fortunately for the People of Boston, two groups of Planners came along at just this time.

One was the South End Community Development, Inc. (SECD), later Greater Boston Community Development (GBCD) and today called Community Builders. Created in 1964, it was funded initially by United South End Settlements and what is today the Boston Foundation, and run by the architect Bob Whittlesey. Its purpose was to show that it was financially feasible to turn the neighborhood's brick row houses into safe, decent and solid affordable housing.

Within two years, SECD converted its first row house on East Springfield Street into five apartments. Within a few more years, when it was known as GBCD, it converted 10 more buildings into more than 80 units. Within ten years, it was helping community groups all over the city to build housing and rebuild their neighborhoods.

The other group was Urban Planning Aid. It was created in 1966 by faculty and graduate students at Harvard and MIT to help Cambridge residents fight a plan to build a highway through that city. Fred Salvucci, one of UPA's founding members, recalled very specifically how the group got started. "A bunch of us were sitting around somebody's apartment when Bob Goodman came. He was waving a copy of Paul Davidoff's book *Advocacy and Pluralism in Planning*, and he said, 'Hey, this is us! This is what we do! Why don't we write a grant?'" [13]

They wrote the grant, got funding initially from the American Friends Service and then from OEO, and UPA quickly assembled a staff of urban planners, architects, traffic engineers, and lawyers. Those professionals provided neighborhood residents and groups with the technical assistance and helped them get the credibility they needed to grapple with urban renewal and other government programs when they had to, and to rebuild their own communities when they could.

Not everyone welcomed the arrival on the scene of these advocacy planners. In 1966, Logue, the BRA's director, denounced them as "academic amateurs" who looked at community development as "an intellectual exercise." He complained that one particular development plan UPA got involved with was "not a plaything or a tinker toy for the M.I.T. faculty."[14] But neighborhood residents were glad for the help. Before the contributions of these planners could be fully put to use, however, another wave of activism and protest arose that was less concerned with rebuilding the New Boston than with making sure some old promises were kept.

A Rekindled Civil Rights Movement

URBAN RENEWAL MAY HAVE REKINDLED THE FLAME OF ACTIVISM and protest in much of the city in the mid-twentieth century, but the civil rights movement being carried out in the South at the time rekindled that flame in Boston's black community. "You can't overestimate how much what went on down there fueled what went on up here," said Hubie Jones years later.[1]

Jones grew up in the South Bronx in New York and moved to the Boston area in 1955 to attend graduate school at Boston University. He and his wife Kathy were among the few African American families who were able to buy a house in Newton back then—but only after a white couple had posed as the buyers as part of a Fair Housing program. Despite the fact that he lived in the suburbs, Jones became a respected leader in Boston's black community, but only, he recalled, after undergoing "the requisite ascension ritual."[2]

Boston has a long and contradictory history when it comes to civil rights. In 1638, the first slaves arrived in Boston from the West Indies. Massachusetts Bay was the first British colony in North America to recognize slavery as a legal institution three years later, but Massachusetts was also the first state in the new union to abolish it in 1785. Boston was a hotbed of abolition and an important stop on the Underground Railroad prior to the Civil War, but it was also the home of textile mill owners (whom the U.S. senator from Massachusetts at the time, Charles Sumner, called the

"Lords of the Loom"), who worked closely with Southern plantation owners (whom Sumner called the "Lords of the Lash"). Boston was also a city where immigrants from Ireland and other European countries competed fiercely with African Americans residents for low-skill, low-wage jobs that were the only ones available to both of those groups.

By the twentieth century, Boston "was socially progressive, but economically backwards" when it came to civil rights, according to the Tufts University professor Gerald Gill.[3] Gill died in 2007, before he could complete what would have been an important book he planned to call *Struggling Yet in Freedom's Birthplace: Race Relations and Black Protest Activities in Boston, 1920–1972.*

During the first half of the twentieth century, the city supported a very energetic civil rights movement. In 1903, William Monroe Trotter, the crusading editor and publisher of the *Guardian* newspaper, led a protest called the "Boston Riot" against the accommodationist policies of the visiting Booker T. Washington. In 1909, when the National Association for the Advancement of Colored People was founded, Moorfield Storey, a white Bostonian, was named its first president. Three years later, the Boston Branch NAACP became the organization's first local chapter. Vigorous campaigns for voter registration and against workplace discrimination were waged right up through the 1940s.

But by the 1950s, according to Gill, the Boston Branch NAACP had become "mostly a social club," Boston's chapter of the Congress of Racial Equality (CORE) "virtually moribund," and its chapter of the Urban League "a job referral agency . . . less than fully effective."[4] Unlike in the South, Boston's black churches didn't pick up the civil rights slack. The historian Robert Hayden recalled one black minister's explanation. "We don't have rummage sales. We take care of our parishioners' souls."[5]

By 1960, a Harvard University study found that "politically, Boston's Negroes are only a shadow of their militant, crusading, sometimes violent past," and that "in no other major city has a Negro been the passive political force he has been in the Boston scene."[6] One reason for this, according to the study, was "the general apathy of the fifties." Another was the "numbing benevolence of 'Curleyism.'"[7]

In this latter case, black Bostonians found themselves in the same boat as whites. As the New York University professor James Fraser later wrote, "what little advantage there was in this effort to secure jobs, housing, or good education usually rested with those who could count on political machines."[8] In Roxbury's Ward Nine, the political machine was run by brothers Shag and Balcolm Taylor. Like their white counterparts in other wards, the Taylors dispensed political favors that were based not on how much noise residents made, but on how many votes they could be counted on to deliver.

A third reason for the decline in the push for civil rights in Boston was the unique makeup of its black community. In 1930, African Americans constituted less than 3 percent of the population, the lowest of any major city in the country. But at the same time, it was composed of both the highest percentage of locally born blacks *and* the highest percentage of "foreign-born" blacks.[9] Many Boston-born blacks were either middle class or aspired to be. According to Bob Coard, who would later direct the antipoverty Action for Boston Community Development Agency, they "manifested a remarkably faithful adherence to certain Brahmin and proper Bostonian values such as the importance of family lineage, pride in local origin and superiority toward outsiders, and political and social conservatism."[10] Many of the foreign-born blacks came from similar backgrounds and had similar aspirations. Not many in the first group, called "Black Brahmins," or the second, called "Turks" because many came from the West Indies, wanted to rock the boat in which they both found themselves floating.

That began to change between 1950 and 1960, when Boston's black population increased by nearly 60 percent to 63,000. Although that was still just 9 percent of the city's population, it now included larger numbers from two new groups. One was a large influx of newly arrived poor and working-class families from the South, and the other a smaller number of middle-class young people drawn to Boston to attend its colleges or begin their careers. The arrival of these two groups, combined with other factors, prompted Coard to write, "there is growing evidence that unless constructive and practical leadership is forcefully exercised by both whites and Negroes, the uneventful slumber of Boston's rapidly increasing Negro community may be drawing to a close."[11]

In February 1960, a sign of that awakening appeared when black and white college students formed the Emergency Public Integration Committee to support the sit-ins being held by black college students to integrate the lunch counter in the Woolworth's store in Greensboro, North Carolina. On March 26, 1960, EPIC sponsored picket lines in front of Woolworth stores throughout the Boston area, and a month later, on April 21, 1960, it held a benefit concert by Harry Belafonte at the Boston Arena to raise money for the North Carolina college students.[12]

By 1962, Cornell Eaton and some other young Boston-born, activists formed the Boston Action Group to address more local civil rights issues. Working out of the St. Mark's Social Center in Roxbury, BAG launched a campaign to use the black community's economic clout to prod employers, beginning with Wonder Bread, to hire minorities as route drivers. One of the young BAG members was Sarah-Ann Shaw.

Shaw's family had moved to Boston from Atlanta in the 1920s, and she remembered her father taking her and her brother to hear civil rights speakers at the Ford Hall Forum. Growing up, Shaw also remembered chafing at what seemed to her to be the too-patient approach to civil rights taken by her elders in Roxbury. They included Melnea Cass, her Girl Scout troop leader; Elma Lewis, her dance teacher; and Judge Elwood McKenney, who supervised the Boston Branch NAACP Youth Council, which was once suspended for a time for its overly aggressive activities. "They wanted us to do more traditional things," Shaw explained many years later, "but we wanted to be *activists*. We wanted to show some *muscle*—and we didn't take direction well."[13]

Shaw called BAG a "little ragtail group" but acknowledged it was where she learned what it took to do community organizing at the time.[14] "If you wanted to have a meeting, you had to put out a flyer. But if you wanted a flyer, you had to get a typewriter and a stencil. Then you had to find an organization that would let you use their mimeograph machine. Then you had to crank out the flyers one at a time." After all that, "Some people would take the flyers and some wouldn't. Some people would say, 'You can't leave those flyers here'—at churches and stores. Some of the older people thought we were going too far. They would say, 'Let the NAACP handle it.' Or 'Let the Urban League handle it.' But we'd say 'They've been doing things their way for a long time and nothing's changed.'"[15]

The BAG campaign did change things. After a month-long boycott, Wonder Bread agreed to hire African American drivers. "Then Hood Milk got in touch with us," Shaw recalled, "and they had no black route drivers until then, either, so it was a two-fold success."[16]

The success by young people and new groups just beginning their activism prodded some older people and established organizations to resume theirs. The Boston Branch NAACP launched an investigation into the mistreatment of women working as domestics in Boston. The local chapter of

CORE moved its headquarters from Cambridge to Roxbury and chose the young Alan Gartner as its new executive director. Gartner grew up in New York City and moved to Boston to attend graduate school. Soon after he joined CORE, it launched campaigns against Sears, Roebuck & Company, Trailways Bus Company, and several Boston banks to get them to hire more minority employees.

"We took up techniques of civil rights movement in [the] South," Gartner said years later, acknowledging that not everyone in the community approved of those tactics. "We negotiated, but, when that wasn't successful, we did non-violent direct action instead. It wasn't all sweetness and light among the organizations. Many thought it was a terrible thing for us to organize the boycott."[17] But CORE's boycott succeeded and persuaded those employers to hire more minority workers.

On May 12, 1963, any friction between the generations in Boston's black community was set aside temporarily when more than 10,000 people—black and white—gathered on Boston Common to show their support for the civil rights campaign being waged at the time in Birmingham, Alabama. Most of the speakers at the rally were members of the black community's "old guard," but they had to call on a young, newcomer to come up on stage and lead the singing of what were described the next day as "Freedom Songs." "I was the only one who knew all the words," explained Julian Houston many years later. A Boston University undergraduate from Virginia, Houston had just learned them a few months earlier at a Northern Student Movement conference in New York City. "That was my identity for a while, 'the college student who knew the freedom songs,'" he recalled. "I wasn't altogether comfortable with that."[18]

But, a month after the demonstration on the Common, friction between generations and between longtime residents and newcomers reemerged when Hubie Jones came up with an idea for an even more ambitious boycott. "It was a Sunday afternoon," Jones recalled, "I was at Dick Rowling's house. He was the head of Catholic Inter-Racial Council. Our kids were playing in the backyard, and we got to talking about how bad things were for blacks in Boston, and I said, 'You know what. We ought to just stop the city for a day!' And Dick said, 'That's not a bad idea,' and that I should run it by Mel King. When I told him I didn't know Mel, he said he'd introduce us."[19]

King, a youth worker in the South End at the time, had already become one of the most respected of the younger, homegrown activists in the black

*STOP Campaign march through Park Square to Boston Common on June 26,
1963.* Globe Staff file photo.

community. He liked the idea of what came to be called the STOP Campaign, a one-day boycott by black residents of work, shopping, and public transportation to protest continued discrimination.

Jones and King shopped the idea around the community. Younger activists—both homegrown and newcomers—were all for it. But most of the members of the old guard were opposed. They argued the boycott's goals were too vague, and that it would be difficult to pull off and siphon energy from other efforts. Jones later maintained they had another reason. "The 'establishment' wanted to control the action, and they resented the fact that a newcomer like me had ginned things up." But the proposed boycott went forward anyway, according to Jones, because "STOP had taken on a life of its own. People were into it."[20]

On Wednesday, June 26, 1963, the STOP Campaign began with a march from the Carter Playground in Roxbury to Boston Common. Several hundred people began the march. Despite the warm temperature, most of the men wore suits and ties, and the women wore dresses and hats. Some of them carried signs that read, "Racial Equity" and "Stop Housing Injustice." As they proceeded down Columbus Avenue and through the South End, many more people joined the march. By the time it reached the Common, the marchers were nearly 1,000 strong.

The Boston Branch NAACP had refused to endorse the boycott and the march, but had devised a way to take advantage of it by sponsoring a simultaneous memorial service on the Common for Medgar Evers, the Mississippi civil rights leader who had been assassinated two weeks earlier. When the marchers arrived, the combined crowd totaled more than 3,000 people. The old guard dominated the speaking program that followed, but they did allow a young newcomer, the Reverend James Breeden, to offer a prayer.

Breeden had recently moved to Boston from Minnesota. Along with the Reverends Gilbert Caldwell, Virgil Woods, Vernon Carter, and some others, Breeden was part of a group of new-to-Boston young black ministers whom Robert Hayden later described as being "organizationally ready for the civil rights movement, and [who] provided a setting and a background and a place for people to talk—and sometimes do more than that." [21]

Some homegrown black ministers—both young and older—were ready to join them. One was the Reverend Michael Haynes. The son of immigrants from Barbados, Haynes was born and raised in Roxbury and served as youth minister at the Twelfth Baptist Church, where, a few years earlier, he had become friendly with a Boston University Theological School student who sometimes served as a guest preacher, Reverend Martin Luther King Jr. After graduation, King tried to get Haynes to go back to the South with him. Years later, Haynes explained why he didn't go. "I was not comfortable below the Mason–Dixon line." [22]

But Haynes was comfortable taking a more active approach to civil rights in his hometown. "There were some things that I was not willing to wait for until I got to heaven," he recalled. [23] With other local ministers, including William Hunter Hester, Walter Davis, and Richard Owens, he joined the newcomers in forming the Black Ministerial Alliance. [24] The group even attempted a "takeover" of the Boston Branch NAACP by running its own candidate, Reverend Gilbert Caldwell, for president. But the insurgency was "crushed" by the establishment in what Hubie Jones wrote was "the last major effort on the part of the black clergy to participate in a major social institution." [25]

Despite this friction between newcomers and longtime residents and between generations, "there was no difference over ideology," maintained the homegrown and then-young activist Dan Richardson. "You couldn't classify Mrs. Cass or Mrs. Lewis as 'moderates.' They were just as 'militant' as we were. But for them to have the access they did, they couldn't do the street stuff that we did. It was kind of like a 'good cop/bad cop' kind of thing. They would say to the downtown power brokers, 'I'll talk to the people who are demonstrating. But you've got to give me this and that.' But that was okay with us, because they had a track record. They had done things and been politically savvy before we were born." [26]

As activists in the black community continued to struggle over how to work together, one issue—how black children were treated in the Boston public schools—emerged over which they were able to unite.

CHAPTER 5

From School Reform
to Desegregation

JUST AS IN CIVIL RIGHTS, BOSTON HAS A LONG AND CONTRA-
dictory history when it comes to public education. Some of the best accounts of this history are contained in *From Common School to Magnet
School: Selected Essays in the History of Boston's Schools,* edited by James W.
Fraser, Henry L. Allen, and Sam Barnes.

Boston was home to a number of educational firsts in the United
States—the first school (Boston Latin, est. 1635), the first public school supported by taxes (the Mather School, est. 1639), and the first free public high
school (The English High School, est. 1821). In the middle of the nineteenth
century, Boston was where Horace Mann began the reforms that became
the basis for the modern American public education system. Through the
first decades of the twentieth century, Boston could boast of operating one
of the best urban public school systems in the country.

But, like the city itself, the schools declined sharply thereafter. By the
1940s and 1950s, according to Joseph Cronin, a former Massachusetts secretary of education, "the Boston public schools weren't so much a school
system as an employment bureau." A report at the time called it a system
"run by politicians . . . failing to spark the imagination or the curiosity of
its pupils, a dull bureaucracy . . . deadly to honest thinking."[1]

Politics was just one reason for the decline, demographics another.
The schools were being abandoned by middle-class parents, who were
either moving to the suburbs or sending their children to the many

private and religious schools that had opened as alternatives to the public schools.

A third reason for the decline of the schools was the lack of involvement by the parents of students who remained. In 1907, a citywide parents organization, the Home and School Association, was established. But by 1960, it was described as "a company-union PTA" and the "Everyone Joins Association, No One Participates."[2]

One of the first modern efforts at school reform began in February 1960, when Dorothy Bisbee, a Beacon Hill resident, founded the Citizens for Boston Public Schools (CBPS). Bisbee, a Republican who had just run unsuccessfully for School Committee, used a stack of stamped envelopes left over from her campaign to invite people to a meeting to form "a school watchdog organization." "I was surprised," she recalled, "at the people I didn't know who showed up."[3]

One of the people who showed up was Herb Gleason. A tall, deep-voiced Brahmin, Gleason had grown up on the South Shore. After Harvard College and Law School and service in the military, he and his wife Nancy settled on Beacon Hill, began a family and careers, and embarked on a longstanding commitment to public service. "I joined CBPS," Gleason remembered, "because I was appalled at what was going on in the schools."[4]

Gleason recruited Paul Parks, who lived in Dorchester at the time, to join the group. The son of an African American father and Native American mother, Parks had grown up and attended segregated schools in Indianapolis. After graduating from Purdue University and serving in the military during World War II, he moved to Boston to begin his career as an engineer. Parks joined CBPS, he recalled, "because I felt guilty at bringing black children into a world where people looked at them as less human."[5]

CBPS had hoped to expand across the city. But according to Gleason, "We got very little response from other neighborhoods, except for the black community. Because of the response and energy we found there, we just sort of slid into being involved with them. Civil rights was happening then. It was exciting and seductive to be appreciated and to find supporters for what we were trying to do."[6]

Boston's history in regard to integrated public education is also a long and contradictory one. While Boston was home to the first public primary school for African American children in the country (the Abiel Smith School on Beacon Hill, est. 1835), it took a boycott by African American residents as well as lawsuits and state legislation before the city's public schools were integrated twenty years later. For almost one hundred years,

Boston's schools offered both a quality education and a comparatively equal education to its students. But in the 1940s and 1950s, when the quality of education declined, so did the commitment to equality.

The campaign to restore both quality and equality in the schools had already begin in the black community. It was led by Ruth Batson, who tells the story of that campaign in a 500-page memoir/scrapbook titled *The Black Educational Movement in Boston: A Sequence of Historical Events, A Chronology.*

Batson was born and raised in Boston. Her mother showed how important she thought education was by returning to school as an adult and graduating from eighth grade at the Edward Everett School when Ruth was a sixth grader there. Batson's commitment to educational equality began in the 1940s, when her three daughters reached school age. In her book Batson described attending a meeting at which she was "amazed to learn that the oldest school buildings in Boston were located in the black communities." Determined to do something about that disparity, she brought her concerns to Lionel Lindsay, then the president of the Boston Branch NAACP. He promptly formed an Education Committee on the Boston Public Schools and asked Batson to chair it. "From that point on," she later wrote, "my life changed profoundly, and I lost all fear of 'important' people or organizations."[7]

Black parents had long suspected that schools in their neighborhoods were shortchanging their children. In the 1950s, it was Batson who helped parents get organized and try to prove it. "My wife used to say 'She gave people spine,'" Hubie Jones remembered.[8]

One of those people was Eva Jaynes, a member of the newly formed Higginson-Ellis Parents Association. "We checked with other school districts, and found wide discrepancies," she recalled. In black school districts, the parents found students confined to overcrowded classrooms in dirty schools. In white school districts, they found that students "went on field trips to museums, concerts; had the latest models in visual and learning equipment; their classes were small with teacher aides in attendance . . . [and] the schools . . . were kept clean." The black parents found few black teachers in any of the schools, no black principals, and found that very few black students were being admitted to the city's three prestigious exam schools.[9] But most of the evidence that the black parents gathered was "anecdotal." To really make their case, they needed facts. That's where CBPS came in.

In April 1960, CBPS produced a fact-filled enrollment study showing that a mostly black school district in Roxbury was alarmingly overcrowded, whereas an overwhelmingly white district in Back Bay and Beacon Hill had 1,300 seats for only 900 students. CBPS tried to follow that up with a study comparing per-pupil spending in the two districts, but the Boston School Department refused to provide the data. "Publicity attending the first study had caused turmoil and an angry reaction from parents," explained district superintendent Dennis Haley. "Many others were asking for figures, and the requests constituted a nuisance." [10]

But on May 22, 1963, CBPS was somehow able to produce another study, this one on spending, maintenance, and enrollment in schools across the city. It showed that schools in black neighborhoods received only 65 percent of the per-pupil funding schools in white neighborhoods received; that only 40 percent of the school buildings in the city were more than fifty years old, but all but two school buildings in the black community were that old; and that although the older schools in black neighborhoods were overcrowded, the newer schools in white neighborhoods had plenty of empty seats. [11]

The CBPS report attracted a lot of attention, and a meeting was held at Freedom House in Roxbury to discuss its findings. The entire Boston School Committee was invited to the meeting, but only one member, Louise Day Hicks, a lawyer from South Boston, chose to attend. Hicks had been one of four newcomers elected to the five-member board in 1961. At the time, it was hoped she might turn out out to be a reformer and someone willing to bring long-overdue changes to the school system.

CBPS members were glad to see Hicks at the meeting. "We thought that if Louise could hear it directly from black parents—from mothers, especially, since there were almost all women in the room—that she would be more sympathetic," recalled Gleason. [12] Hicks seemed to listen attentively, as parent after parent rose to complain about overcrowded classrooms, old books, and the shortage of permanent teachers in the schools that their children attended.

After the meeting, "she said how awful it sounded, and that she was going to do something about it," recalled Paul Parks, who drove Hicks home to South Boston. "But four days later, she called me and said 'I can't do what I said I was going to do.' I asked her why not, and she said that Gillis [Frederick Gillis, the Boston school superintendent] told her that if she supported the black parents she would never be reelected." As Gleason remembers, "I think that was the moment she changed. From then on she gave up any pretense of trying to change things. I think her brother John,

Crowd entering Boston School Committee hearing on June 11, 1963. Photo by Bob Dean/Globe Staff.

who was her closest advisor, saw the political opportunity in her going against the blacks."[13]

The NAACP tried to keep the pressure on by convincing the Boston School Committee to hold a special meeting where the organization could present its grievances. The meeting was held on June 11, 1963, at School Department headquarters, which back then was located at 15 Beacon Street. The meeting began just a few hours after Alabama governor George Wallace had barred two African American students from entering the University of Alabama, and at the same time that President John F. Kennedy was delivering a nationally televised address in which he called civil rights a "moral issue" on which "all men of good will" should be able to unite.[14]

Outside the building, more than 500 NAACP supporters filled the sidewalk and spilled onto the street. Inside on the third floor, more than 100 people squeezed into the cramped, low-ceilinged hearing room. Even the room's layout was oppressive. The five School Committee members sat behind a wooden table that was on a raised platform, while members of the black community who testified had to sit behind a table at floor level and look up at them. The first to speak was Batson. She later wrote about having, even before the meeting had begun, "the distinct feeling that we had gone 'set up.' We had gone into the lion's den, like lambs being led to the slaughter."[15] But she proceeded nonetheless.

"We are here because the clamor from the community is too anxious to be ignored," Batson said, as the sound of the chanting and singing of members of the community outside wafted in through the open windows.[16] Then, after listing those complaints, she yielded the floor to Parks, who cited the CBPS reports that documented the disparity between schools in black neighborhoods and those in white neighborhoods. Other members of the black community testified, then Batson and Parks delivered a list of fourteen demands to the committee.

Nine of the demands were not specific to the black community. They called for improving the curriculum, providing more and better materials, improving teacher training, and increasing maintenance in schools throughout the city. Four of the demands had to do with eliminating the inequality between schools in black neighborhoods and white neighborhoods. The remaining demand—the one listed first—would spark the most controversy. It called for "an immediate public acknowledgment of the existence of De Facto Segregation in the Boston Public School System."[17]

When Batson and Parks finished, Hicks, who chaired the hearing, "politely" thanked them for their testimony, and then she called on Boston school superintendent Gillis to respond. He strenuously denied that schools in the black community received less-favorable treatment. He also rejected the charge of de facto segregation (which occurs when school enrollments merely reflect the residential makeup of the neighborhood around them). Gillis insisted that students in Boston were assigned to schools based on "building capacities, distances between homes and schools, and unusual traffic patterns" and not "by ethnic or religious factors."[18] It was a position that the School Committee and School Department would stick to— despite mounting evidence to the contrary—for the next decade.

June 11, 1963, became the turning point for the black community's efforts at school reform, according to Paul Parks. "Up until then, it was the quality of the schools and fairness when it came to resources that we were after—not desegregation. In the beginning, we didn't care that much about whether our kids were going to school with their kids or not. We just wanted to make sure our schools got the same things as they did, and we wanted them to stop assigning all the drunks to teach in the schools in black neighborhoods." After June 11, the focus of the movement changed. "I don't want to say that education reform was taking a back seat," said Mel King, "but the energy now that was coming out of the black community became focused on desegregation."[19]

To maintain that energy and keep the pressure on the School Committee, Reverend James Breeden proposed a one-day school boycott by black students, like the one he'd witnessed recently in Birmingham, Alabama. The idea, Breeden later explained, "was also a reaction to hearing people on the School Committee say, 'How do we know you represent anybody?' I said 'Let's see if we can get three or four thousand kids to stay out of school. Will that get their attention?'"[20]

Not everyone in the black community immediately embraced the idea. But Ruth Batson, who had opposed the STOP Campaign boycott, was all for this one—and invoked Boston's history of activism and protest to justify it. "From the Boston Tea Party to this present day," she said, "civil disobedience to underscore moral necessity has been in the mainstream of the American tradition."[21]

The boycott came to be called the School Stayout for Freedom, and, although it was Breeden's idea, it was a community-wide effort. "People get the impression that one or two people made it happen," he said years later, "but that's not true." Hundreds of volunteers were needed to pull it off. Jean McGuire, born and raised in Boston and on her way to becoming a teacher, was one of them. She recalled spending long hours at a mimeograph machine—"it was the time of the old purple masters, where you ran things off and got ink all over your hands"—to make flyers, then putting them up "in bars . . . on corners . . . at churches and hair salons."[22]

On June 16, 1963, the school stayout became the first boycott to protest school segregation in Boston since abolition.[23] More than 8,000 African American junior high and high school students took part. But that participation involved more than just skipping school. Students were transported by rented buses to what were called "Freedom Schools" set up for the day at various churches and community centers, where they were taught by volunteers, who used a "protest curriculum" created by Noel Day, the director of the St. Mark's Social Center and a former Dartmouth College classmate of Breeden's. Lectures were also delivered by guest speakers, including Reverend Anson Phelps Stokes, the Episcopal bishop of Massachusetts, and the Boston Celtics star Bill Russell. The day went off without any incidents of violence or delinquency, according to Boston police, and Breeden later called it "a monumental achievement for the entire community."[24]

Despite the success of the stayout and the publicity it generated, the School Committee refused to address the NAACP's other demands or even discuss the issue of de facto segregation. So, for the next few months, demonstrations continued, with black and white protesters regularly picketed outside School Department headquarters. Some carried signs that read, "Will the New Boston Be Integrated?"

These small demonstrations were temporarily suspended at the end of the summer so that residents could take part in a much larger one, the historic March on Washington for Jobs and Freedom. On August 27, 1963, 2,000 members of Boston's black community boarded buses and trains that took them down to the nation's capital, where the next day they marched and heard Reverend Martin Luther King Jr. deliver what came to be called the "Dream" speech. Melnea Cass, who had already spent more than forty years fighting for civil rights, later called the event "the Second Emancipation." [25]

In September, when the campaign against the School Committee resumed, it had a new leader. Tom Atkins was born and brought up in Indiana, where he attended the state university and was elected the first black student body president of a Big Ten school. He had come to Boston the year before to attend graduate school at Harvard, where he had written a paper that described "the organizational failings" of the Boston Branch NAACP.[26] Rather than take offense, the Boston Branch president at the time, Ken Guscott, hired Atkins to be the organization's first executive director.

In dealing with the School Committee, Atkins first tried the "carrot" approach. He announced that the NAACP would drop its demand for the committee to admit the existence of de facto segregation if its members would just agree to develop a plan to do something about it. When the committee rejected that offer, he resorted to the "stick," and led one of the most dramatic demonstrations yet in what was becoming an increasingly contentious New Boston.

On September 5, 1963, at 10:30 a.m., Atkins and approximately a dozen other young NAACP members—the men wearing suits and ties and the women wearing dresses—entered the School Department building at 15 Beacon Street. They made their way up to the third floor where the School Committee offices were, sat down in the hallway, and announced they weren't leaving until the committee addressed the issue of segregation.[27] Boston police soon arrived, but were asked by school officials not to do anything for the time being. For the rest of the day, Hicks and the other members of the School Committee and School Department staff tried to go about their business, as if there was nothing unusual about having to step over the bodies of these well-dressed African American young adults in their midst.

At 5 p.m., when everyone else left the building, the protesters stayed, as did a half dozen police officers and a gang of newspaper reporters, photographers, and local television crews who had by then joined them. Outside the building, hundreds of supporters of the protesters gathered along Beacon Street, chanting and singing the by-then familiar civil rights slogans and songs. At one point in the evening, when the protesters inside got hungry, they fashioned a line from men's belts and women's stockings and lowered it out a window to the parking lot below. Supporters tied a bag of food to the end of the line, and when it was hauled up successfully, everyone on the street cheered.[28]

The sit-in lasted all through the night and all through the next day. That evening, the school committee held its regularly scheduled meeting, and supporters of the protesters, representing both the younger and older generations of the black community, packed the hearing room. Herb Gleason asked Melnea Cass what brought her there, and she replied, "I heard some people might be arrested and I thought I should be one of them."[29]

As things turned out, no one was arrested. The meeting adjourned, everyone else left, and the demonstrators prepared to stay for another night. But soon after, police arrived, announcing they had received a bomb threat and had to clear the building. After huddling, the protesters agreed to end the demonstration that had already gone on for more than forty hours. When Atkins and the others filed out, they were greeted with cheers and applause by hundreds of supporters who were still keeping watch in the street.

The sit-in at School Department headquarters succeeded in further uniting the black community, but it failed to persuade the School Committee to come up with a school desegregation plan. So the NAACP came up with one of its own. On September 12, 1963, it released what came to be called the "Atkins Plan." It was a modest proposal, and could afford to be, since at the time minority students made up only about 15 percent of the school system's 93,000 students, and the NAACP estimated that only about half a dozen of the system's 200 schools were heavily segregated.[30] The Atkins Plan called for reassigning students in just 16 schools to other schools still within their neighborhoods. It did not require any busing, which an NAACP official described at the time as the "least satisfactory way to handle the problem."[31]

The Atkins Plan did contain one element that would later prove controversial—it defined a segregated school as one in which minority students made up more than 50 percent of the enrollment. Not everyone in the black community supported that definition. Paul Parks said later he "had a problem with using such a specific and arbitrary number." As Dan Richardson recalled, "Some of us said that the percentage shouldn't matter, that it should be more about the resources, the quality of the teachers, and the quality of education taking place in the schools. But it was easier to make the numbers argument than the educational argument or the social argument."[32]

As things turned out, no argument could have persuaded the school committee. Its refusal to even consider the proposal was a missed opportunity that would have enormous repercussions. Years later Hubie Jones reflected, "If the Boston School Committee had adopted the Atkins Plan, the course of Boston history would have been very different."[33]

The protests continued. On September 22, 1963, a cold, gray, misty Sunday, more than 6,000 people—black and white; children as well as adults; many wearing their Sunday best and some in choir robes—took part in a "March on Roxbury" that had two purposes. The first was to protest the recent bombing of the 16th Street Baptist Church in Birmingham, Alabama, in which four little girls attending Sunday school had been killed. The second was to protest the continued unacceptable conditions of the schools in the black community and school segregation in Boston.

Marchers converged from three different starting points on the Sherwin School on Sterling Street in Roxbury. The ninety-three-year-old, wood-frame building was chosen, according to the event's organizers, because it represented a "glaring example of educational inferiority in Boston. In addition to its dilapidated physical condition, it had an enrollment of 317 students, all but one of them black."[34] When it came his turn to speak at the rally in the schoolyard, Tom Atkins warned that marches and protests alone were not enough to produce change. "We're not just here to sing songs," he told the crowd. "Don't go complaining about anything until you register and vote!"[35]

The black community did both, thanks to aggressive voter registration drives by established groups like the NAACP, CORE, and Freedom House, and by newer groups like the Boston Action Group and the Northern Student Movement. But the community's small size prevented even its increased participation from producing the desired results.

In the 1950s, Ruth Batson had twice run unsuccessfully for the school committee. In 1961, Mel King had run and lost. The only "reformer" elected that year was Arthur Gartland, but he subsequently found himself on the short end of countless 4 to 1 votes. In 1963, King ran and lost again. Gartland was reelected but finished far behind Hicks and the other three incumbents, who, according to the *Boston Globe*'s political editor, Robert Healy, waged a "campaign of distortion [so] busing was the issue [even though] Negro leaders never asked the school board to bus Negro students to other sections of the city [but only] that district lines be redrawn and new schools located so as to diminish racial imbalance." Even so, Healy warned, "Politically, the sit-ins were dynamite. Obviously the Boston voters rejected the means to gain the ends."[36]

On November 5, 1963, John Collins defeated City Councilor Gabe Piemonte by 108,000 to 73,000 votes to win a second term as mayor, but it was the showing of Louise Day Hicks that got the most attention. The woman who, a few months earlier, had been called "the Bull Connor of Boston" by the national director of the Congress of Racial Equality, topped the school committee ticket and received 20,000 more votes than Collins. Hicks and her three allies (all reelected by an overwhelming majority) were described as having run "with the pledge that there would never be any massive desegregation of Boston's schools as long as they were in office."[37]

In 1965, Mel King ran and lost again. Hicks and her allies were once more reelected. But this time Gartland was defeated by a newcomer, who promised to vote with the other four. The election results were crushing to the black community. "We told them that by voting they could demand their rights," said Reverend Vernon Carter, the pastor of All Saints Church. "Now they feel frustrated. They see that the ballot did not help them. We are afraid they will feel there is no point to voting. I have never seen the Negro community so frustrated before."[38]

"After all the knock-down, drag-out fighting, all the punching and counter-punching between the NAACP and the school committee, all it was doing was getting Hicks and people like her more votes," Hubie Jones said years later. "The black community was just exhausted, physically and psychologically, from a battle that did not move the school committee an inch." At this point, Jones said, "Black residents decided to disengage from trying to change the school committee. The feeling was, 'We've got to find other routes to give kids to get to quality education.'"[39]

Black parents had already discovered one of those other routes, taking advantage of a recently implemented "Open Enrollment Policy" that allowed students to attend any school in the city that had empty seats if their parents could get them to and from those schools. This was a big *if* for poor and working-class parents, especially the many who did not have cars, but they rose to the challenge.

In the fall of 1964, parents at the William Lloyd Garrison School in Roxbury were upset when their children were abruptly transferred to the nearby William Boardman School, which they considered inferior and unsafe. When the Garrison parents found there were enough empty seats at the Peter Faneuil School to accommodate their children, they all chipped in and rented a bus that shuttled their kids between Roxbury and Beacon Hill every day.

Parents at the overcrowded William Endicott School in Dorchester did much the same thing. They organized car pools and chaperoned groups of students on the MBTA so their children could attend the less-crowded Pauline Agassiz Shaw and Roger Walcott Schools not far away. It wasn't easy, admitted Joan McCoy, one of those parents. "Rain or shine, snow or hail, every morning . . . crossing the six lanes of 8 a.m. traffic on Blue Hill Avenue, with baby on hip and these little third and fourth graders running every-which-way. Getting over to the other side to Franklin Park to catch the MBTA bus down to Morton and Norfolk Streets. . . . Then going back at dismissal time and reversing the trek and juggling our own schedules, etcetera . . . every single day." [40]

In the summer of 1965, a group of black parents created Operation Exodus to take advantage of the Open Enrollment policy on a much larger scale. The group was led by Ellen Jackson and Betty Johnson. Both had grown up in Roxbury and had previously worked as parent coordinators for the Northern Student Movement. Jackson later explained the reason Exodus was created: "The days of boycotting and marching, of protesting physically are over. We were using ourselves up." Johnson said she was "tired of the paddling, of teachers pushing children against the walls, of temporary teachers and poor buildings. We were quite convinced that children in these crowded Roxbury schools weren't learning as much as those in other schools." [41]

Operation Exodus was a massive undertaking. Working out of a storefront at 378 Blue Hill Avenue that was donated by the building's owner and fixed up by their husbands, the group of women first had to find where the "empty seats" were (the list had to be "stolen" from an uncooperative School Department, according to Jackson [42]). Then they had to assign students to appropriate schools, coordinate schedules, create routes for the fleet of rented buses and vans, hired taxis, and borrowed cars, and recruit volunteers to chaperone the children.

They had to do all this in the face of fierce resistance by the school committee and School Department. At one "receiving school" a hostile principal ordered unused chairs and desks to be unbolted from the floor and taken out of the classrooms. When the black students arrived, he turned them away, claiming there was no room for them. "When Ellen Jackson found out about that," recalled Exodus volunteer Henry Allen, "she went out and forced her way into the school, then she demanded that the chairs and desks be put back and the kids allowed in. The School Department had to back down. That was just too blatant—even for them."[43]

Finally, the parents had to figure out a way to pay for the whole thing, which they did by holding bake sales and fashion shows, soliciting donations from local businesses, and getting performers like Harry Belafonte, Eartha Kitt, and Odetta to perform benefit concerts.[44] "We had nothing to do with it," admitted Ken Guscott, the Boston Branch NAACP president at the time. "The parents planned it all. In fact, at first we didn't even think it was such a good idea, because we didn't think it could be successful."[45]

The Harvard sociologist Robert Coles accompanied some of the students to their new schools and marveled at the whole operation. "For poor people, many of the men jobless, the women on relief, a good number without high school degrees, to accomplish such tasks so quickly and efficiently came frankly as a surprise to me. These people had guts. They had more initiative and more perseverance than I expected. A crisis had brought them together, enabling dormant strengths in them to appear, furnishing a direction for their energies and hopes."[46]

In its first year, Operation Exodus enabled nearly 400 black students to attend better, less crowded schools throughout Boston. It grew each year thereafter, and within four years was serving more than a 1,000 students. By January 1969, when parents just couldn't keep it going any longer, Exodus was no longer needed. Its example spurred officials in communities around Boston to make thousands of empty seats in suburban schools available to minority students from Boston. They created the Metropolitan Council for Educational Opportunity, a much larger program than Exodus, which they got the state to pay for, and which continues to this day.

The black community also tried another route, one that involved starting up their own schools. Funded by contributions from residents and grants from foundations, a handful of the so-called Freedom Schools sprang up in Roxbury and Dorchester over the next few years, staffed by underpaid teachers and administrators as well as volunteers. One was the New School for Children, which was formed by the parents of children who attended the Gibson School in Dorchester, until Jonathan Kozol, a substitute teacher at the time, was fired for teaching a Langston Hughes poem to his fourth grade students. (Kozol went on to write *Death at an Early Age: The Destruction of the Hearts and Minds of Negro Children in the Boston Public Schools,* a searing portrait of the conditions from which black parents were trying to spare their children.) Eventually, however, the burden of running these Freedom Schools proved too much. All of them closed within a few years.

A third route taken by the black community ran through the state legislature. In 1963, state representative Royal Bolling Sr. of Roxbury filed a bill that came to be called the Massachusetts Racial Imbalance Law and required the state to take action against school districts with segregated schools. The original bill didn't define what constituted such "imbalance," but it subsequently used the figure in the Atkins Plan and defined it as occurring whenever more than 50 percent of the enrollment was made up of minority students.

The bill was defeated in the first year it was filed, and again in 1964. But that year Governor Endicott Peabody appointed a Racial Imbalance Advisory Commission to study the issue. In 1965, the commission released a report that found 55 "racially imbalanced" schools in Massachusetts, 45 of them in Boston. The report proposed remedies that school districts could take to relieve this imbalance. They included redistricting and "mutual transfers" between schools "relatively close together [so that] no extensive cross-city transportation is involved." [47] Finally, the report said that the state would be willing to pick up a substantial portion of the cost of these remedies. [48]

The Boston School Committee responded to this report in the same way it had responded to earlier reports and proposals by CBPS and the NAACP—it refused to even discuss it. This refusal and the refusal of the Massachusetts legislature to pass the bill prompted one of the most "singular" demonstrations in the New Boston so far.

On April 28, 1965, Reverend Vernon Carter began a one-man picket line in front of the Boston School Department headquarters, which he vowed to continue until the Racial Imbalance Law was passed. For the next 114 days—often alone, sometimes with a handful of supporters, and sometimes with hundreds—the diminutive, bespectacled, beret-wearing minister walked back and forth on the sidewalk outside 15 Beacon Street. He ate meals brought to him by friends or strangers while walking. He slept for a few hours each night in the back of a van that was parked nearby.

On June 21, 1965, when some 300 ministers, priests, and rabbis joined him for the day, Carter told them, "For years, we have operated behind the stained glass windows of our churches. We now must step from behind those walls."[49]

On August 18, 1965, after the legislature had finally passed the bill, Reverend Carter ended his vigil when Governor John Volpe signed the Racial Imbalance Law. The new law made Massachusetts the first state in the country to outlaw segregation in its public schools. It also forced the Massachusetts Board of Education to try to do something that Boston's black community hadn't been able to—get the Boston School Committee to address segregation in the Boston public schools.

The fourth and final route that the black community had taken to try to do this had been initiated a few months earlier. On April 20, 1965, the Boston Branch NAACP filed a class action suit in U.S. District Court charging that the Boston School Committee and School Superintendent "have established and are perpetuating a racially segregated school system." The NAACP hadn't wanted to pursue this route. Lawsuits are expensive and can drag on for years. Court rulings—and court remedies—can be unpredictable. In filing the suit, NAACP's president, Ken Guscott, admitted that the organization had "reluctantly yielded to the urgings of the parents of the city of Boston."[50] It was this route that would eventually threaten to tear the city apart. But that tearing apart would not take place for another ten years.

Meanwhile, in the spring of 1965, even as the black community was pursuing these other routes in its campaign to bring change to the Boston schools, the city witnessed two of its largest demonstrations yet as part of Boston's rekindled civil rights movement.

The first began on March 12, 1965, when some 200 demonstrators began a sit-in inside the federal courthouse at Post Office Square to protest the murder in Selma, Alabama, three days earlier of the Reverend James Reeb. Reeb had moved to Boston with his wife and four children less than a year earlier to run a housing program for the American Friends Service. He had been beaten to death after taking part in the historic voting rights march over the Pettus Bridge.

Most of the protesters inside the courthouse were college students, and they occupied the eleventh-floor hallway of the building outside the office of the U.S. attorney W. Arthur Garrity. They vowed to stay until President Johnson agreed to send federal troops or marshals to protect civil rights demonstrators in the South. One of the leaders of the demonstration was Julian Houston, the Boston University student who had been enlisted to lead the singing of "freedom songs" at the Boston Common rally two years earlier.

At one point during the sit-in, Houston was called into Garrity's office to take a phone call from President Johnson's civil rights advisor, Morris Abrams, who said, "'Look, we're doing everything we can, but your demonstration isn't helping,'" Houston recalled. "I told him we weren't leaving until they sent marshals to Selma, and just as I'm saying that, I can hear people in the background singing 'We Shall Not Be Moved.'"[51]

The demonstrators weren't moved for the next day and a half. Ironically, when they were moved—at 11 p.m. on Saturday night—it was by federal marshals, who had been called in to assist the Boston police. As the protesters were dragged from the building, they were cheered by hundreds of supporters who had been keeping a vigil for them in Post Office Square. The next day, 20,000 people—black and white—marched from Roxbury and from various college campuses to Boston Common to mourn Reverend Reeb's death and to demand that federal marshals be used to protect civil rights marchers in the South, not eject protesters in the North. The Johnson administration eventually complied with that demand.

On April 23, 1965, an even larger demonstration took place. Called the "March on Boston," it was held to show support for the civil rights movement in the South and to continue to push for more progress in Boston—and it was led by Dr. Martin Luther King Jr. himself.

At 8 a.m., two hours before the march was to begin, a large crowd had already gathered at Carter Playground in Roxbury, its starting point. Reverend Virgil Woods, who headed the Boston chapter of the Southern Christian Leadership Corps, recalled how excited residents were that Dr. King had come back to Boston to lead the march. "They said, 'We have to clean the streets.' And they went and mopped the street where the march was going to start. I realized later that it was cathartic for them."[52]

Some 5,000 people began the march, but many more joined it along the route. As the column made its way down Columbus Avenue, it stretched for more than a mile, and by the time it reached Boston Common, the crowd had swelled to more than 25,000 people. Despite the drizzling rain, people stood patiently and listened to the various speakers. Dr. King spoke last. A day earlier, he had been taken on a tour of Roxbury and been shown run-down tenements that he called "deplorable" and "an outrage to society." In his remarks Dr. King said, "I come to Boston, not to condemn, but,

Dr. Martin Luther King Jr. speaking at March on Boston rally on Boston Common on April 23, 1965. Photo by Joseph Runci/Globe Staff.

instead, to encourage this great city." But in closing, he declared, "the vision of the New Boston must extend into the heart of Roxbury." [53]

After the rally Dr. King went to City Hall for a scheduled meeting with Mayor Collins, who had expected it to be a private discussion. But Dr. King brought a dozen Boston civil rights activists with him, including Reverend Woods, with whom Collins had refused to meet just a few weeks earlier. Dr. King insisted that the local activists take part in the meeting, and at the end of it they presented the mayor with a "bill of particulars" demanding improvements in social services, housing, employment, and the public schools. [54] It was clearly Dr. King's way of trying to make sure that the vision of the New Boston extended as far as he thought it should.

CHAPTER 6

The Conflict over
the Vietnam Conflict

For many young people in the New Boston in the 1960s, it wasn't urban renewal, civil rights, or the Boston schools that spurred them into activism or paying more attention to the world around them—it was U.S. involvement in a small, until then obscure country halfway around the world.

In the 1950s and early 1960s, some of their parents may have paid a little attention when presidents Eisenhower and Kennedy sent U.S. "military advisors" to Vietnam to try to keep the corrupt but democratically elected government in the South from falling to nationalists backed by the Communist government of the North. In doing so both men were subscribing to the so-called domino theory, which held that if all of Vietnam were to become Communist, it would fall under the sway of the Soviet Union or China, and other Southeast Asian countries would follow. But in 1965, after President Johnson began to send combat troops to Vietnam, young people themselves began to pay attention to Vietnam—because that's when many of them became eligible to be drafted and sent there to fight.

U.S. involvement in Vietnam produced an ideological split that divided the entire country. At its most basic level, that split pitted two groups against each other. One group thought America had no business engaging in a civil war in a country that wasn't vital to U.S. interests. The other group either thought citizens had a responsibility to support their government's decisions, no matter what, or that fighting the spread of Communism was in America's interests. In the New Boston, demographic changes contributed to this ideological split playing out as a class split as well. Two of the best books on the subject are *Working-Class War: American Combat Soldiers and Vietnam* by Christian G. Appy, and *Confronting the War Machine* by Michael S. Foley.

Between 1950 and 1960, Boston may have experienced a dramatic *decrease* in its overall population, but it experienced a sharp *increase* in the number of young people—residents and nonresidents, alike. This was the result of the national post–World War II population explosion called the "baby boom" and the economic prosperity that accompanied it. The combination produced a record number of young people and a record number of parents, many new to the middle class, who could afford to send their children to college. Boston's many colleges and universities were glad to expand their enrollments to accommodate this increased demand, and the city became—more than it ever had before—a "college town."

Full-time college students were exempt from the draft that supplied many of the troops sent to Vietnam. But many young male college students were not enthusiastic about the prospect of interrupting their lives after graduation to fight in a far-off war based on a questionable theory. These young men, their families, and their friends made up the core of the antiwar movement, at least in Boston.

But Boston was still predominately home to poor and working-class families. Many of the young men from these families did not attend college, and they didn't see military service as an interruption so much as a worthy and worthwhile next step in their lives. These young men, their families, and friends made up what came to be called the "silent majority" supporting U.S. involvement in Vietnam—although, early on, some weren't so silent, and, later on, they may not have made up a majority.

Much of the early antiwar activity in Boston consisted of small "teach-ins" on college campuses or in churches. It wasn't until October 16, 1965, that the first sizable demonstration took place when approximately 3,000 college students marched from Harvard Square and Boston University to Boston Common. Some carried signs that read "End the Bloodshed" or "Get the Troops Out."

The split over U.S. policy in Vietnam manifested itself at the climax of the demonstration. After the two groups of marchers merged into one at the Common, it found itself confronted by an even larger group. Some of the counter-demonstrators carried signs that read, "Stay in Viet Nam," or "Draft the Pinkos." In the face-off that followed, the first group chanted,

"We want peace," but they were drowned out by the second group, who chanted, "We want victory."[1]

A Harris poll taken at the time revealed the latter group better represented national sentiment. It showed that Americans opposed withdrawal from Vietnam by a more than 10 to 1 margin, and that 9 out of 10 thought protests against the war only produced "a firmer resolve . . . to continue the fighting until we can negotiate on our own terms."[2]

Nonetheless, the protests continued throughout the country. In Boston, many of the protests took place on college campuses. At Harvard, many were generated by the school's chapter of Students for a Democratic Society. Founded in 1962 as a "New Left" version of an "Old Left" group, SDS would later be described as the "undisputed leader of an anti-war movement that was growing far more rapidly than anyone had anticipated."[3] It also represented the militant side of that movement, since its members not only opposed U.S. military involvement in Vietnam but also adopted a Marxist criticism of U.S. government and society in general.

Michael Ansara was one of the leaders of the Harvard SDS chapter. He had grown up in Cambridge and Brookline, taken part in anti-nuclear and civil rights demonstrations since high school, and by now adopted the bearded, long-haired, fatigue-jacket look that became almost a uniform for many antiwar radicals. Ansara later admitted that Harvard's chapter had only about 25 members at the time. "Our strategy was 'organize, educate, and polarize.' Every time we held a demonstration, it would provoke an overreaction by the school, and we'd get a few more students to take our side."[4]

On November 7, 1966, the group successfully employed that strategy when SDS members and other students surrounded a car carrying Robert McNamara, the U.S. secretary of defense, who had just delivered a speech at the Kennedy School of Government. The crowd refused to let McNamara leave until he climbed up on the roof of the car and answered some of their questions. "It was our largest demonstration by far," recalled Ansara. "I think about 600 students turned out. And even though something like 2,300 students signed a letter apologizing for what we did afterwards, it resulted in a massive debate that got more students on our side."[5]

Harvard's SDS group was much less successful when it tried to spark that debate off campus. Earlier in the year, on March 4, 1966, Ansara and some others had tried to pass out leaflets titled, "Why Should You Pay for the Vietnam War?" to meatpacking workers at Newmarket Square in Roxbury. The workers, about equally divided between blacks and whites, were either not interested or downright hostile to what SDS had to say. After a few hours of this less-than-warm welcome, the group left—with one of the students muttering, "So that's the proletariat." [6]

Residents of one neighborhood not far from Newmarket Square were particularly not interested in SDS's message.

SOUTH BOSTON, *located on a peninsula in Boston Harbor, had been part of Boston since 1804. For years the area had attracted few settlers, prompting the historian Walter Kilham to write that the failure of fashionable Bostonians to flock to "the breezy hills of South Boston with their splendid marine views is one of the unsolved questions in Boston's history."[7] Immigrants did, however, eventually, flock there. Most came from Ireland, but a substantial number came from Poland and other Eastern European countries as well.*

In 1960, South Boston had 48,000 residents; 99 percent were white, and most were poor or working class. Many of the men worked on the docks or in local industries. Many of the women were "at home," raising large families. "Growing up in Southie, you went to school and you played sports," recalled Tom Lyons, who was born and raised on O and Second Street. "The war wasn't something we thought about on a day-to-day basis. It was more 'Who are we playing today?'"[8]

At the time, South Boston was still home to a U.S. Army base, which was where young men had to report for their pre-draft physical examinations. On March 25, 1966, members of the recently formed Committee for Non-Violent Resistance, based in Cambridge, set up a picket line outside the gates of the army base. They chanted antiwar slogans, passed out leaflets, and tried to prevent buses carrying young men from entering the base. The protesters soon found themselves confronted by approximately 300 longshoremen and local teenagers, who first heckled and then allegedly attacked them. When police arrived, they arrested a dozen people. In what seemed to be a clear indication of which side of the debate the cops were on, only protesters were arrested.

Those arrested were arraigned a week later at the South Boston Court House, and they had announced they would burn their draft cards on the courthouse steps. When they arrived, they were met by a crowd of about 250 South Boston teenagers including Tom Lyons, then a junior at South Boston High School. "It wasn't like we wanted to get them," he later explained, "so much as we wondered, 'Who the heck are these people?'"[9] Some of the teenagers did attack the protesters, though, and when police arrived this time they allowed the protesters to take refuge inside the building.

By 1967—at least on and around college campuses—Boston had become a hotbed of the national antiwar movement. That spring, the Boston Draft Resistance Group was formed in Cambridge as the local chapter of a national group known as The Resistance. According to Michael Foley in *Confronting the War Machine,* BDRG ended up collecting more draft cards from young men refusing military service than any other chapter in the country, except for the one in San Francisco. The group was made up mostly of Harvard students or recent graduates, except for Harold Hector of Roxbury, who was described as bringing "a much needed blue-collar background to the organization."[10]

This class split over U.S. involvement in Vietnam even manifested itself within the South Boston army base. Pre-draft physicals were conducted twice a week, on Tuesdays and Thursdays. Somehow, draft counselors at BDRG, the American Friends Service, and other groups told college students to report on a Tuesday if they weren't interested in military service. On that day, the lines moved slowly from station to station because so many of the young men came armed with letters from doctors describing why they weren't fit for service. Of the many who reported that day, few were chosen.

That left young men like Tom Lyons, who actually wanted to serve, to report on Thursdays. In June 1967, Lyons and seven of his buddies, recently graduated from South Boston High, enlisted in the Marines—even though, he later acknowledged, "We knew that meant we would automatically go to Vietnam."[11]

In the summer of 1967, while Lyons and his friends were getting ready to report for basic training, Dr. Martin Luther King Jr. and the pediatrician Benjamin Spock came to Boston to take part in a door-to-door campaign called "Vietnam Summer," an effort to broaden sentiment against the war beyond college campuses.[12] But progress toward that goal was slow. On October 16, 1967, 5,000 people did gather on Boston Common for the city's largest antiwar demonstration yet, but most were college students. One of the speakers was Boston University professor Howard Zinn. A bombardier during World War II, Zinn would become a fixture at such rallies. He would also write *A People's History of the United States,* a book that presented "history from below," examined in the context of "the tumult of social movements in America in the 1960s and 1970s."[13]

On this day, however, Zinn sounded less like a 1960s radical than a 1770s revolutionary. He told the crowd, "Ever since governments were first formed, people have felt the need to gather from time to time . . . to declare the rights of conscience against the inhumanity of government." [14]

It wasn't until 1968 that sentiment against U.S. involvement in Vietnam really began to broaden and grow—but that wasn't because of protests or campaigns here, but because of what Americans saw going on over there. In January 1968, Communist nationalist forces launched the Tet Offensive, a series of coordinated attacks against cities, towns, and villages all across South Vietnam. Tet wasn't a military success for the Communists. But it served them well as propaganda, bringing grisly scenes of pitched battles into American homes night after night on the television news. A Gallup Poll taken soon after showed support for U.S. policy in Vietnam among Americans had dropped to 32 percent.

Tom Lyons didn't have to watch Tet on television—he was in the middle of it. He was an eighteen-year-old who had never been outside Massachusetts before, spending a year with the Third Marine Division along the Demilitarized Zone.[15] But despite the fact that so many U.S. soldiers came from similar backgrounds, according to the *Boston Globe* reporter Michael Kenney, it wasn't until the fall of 1968 that many in Boston's antiwar movement came to "the realization . . . that the only kids who were going to Vietnam were working-class kids." [16]

That realization led those in the Boston antiwar movement to show more support for returning soldiers who had come to oppose the war. In October 1968, the *Boston Globe* reported that more than 1,000 Boston University students kept a 24-hour-a-day vigil inside the school's Marsh Chapel with an eighteen-year-old Army private seeking sanctuary there. But that realization didn't lead to a greater show of support for returning soldiers who had just done their jobs. As Michael Ansara later admitted, "There was the idea that the antiwar movement treated returning veterans horribly," although he claimed that in SDS, "We didn't." [17]

In 1969, when Lyons returned to Camp Pendleton in California, he was shocked by how much the country had turned against the war—and hurt and angry at how many citizens had turned against those who had been sent to fight it. "A lot of our peers called us 'suckers' and 'baby killers.' A lot of the World War II guys blamed us for being the first Americans to lose a war. So there we were, in the middle of the worst nightmare we could ever experience. That's tough for a nineteen-year-old to handle." [18]

But Lyons recalled that he and his friends got a different reception in South Boston. "The community never looked down on us," he said, suggesting that this was because military service was a long and proud tradition among its families. Then he acknowledged, "It was probably harder for kids from Newton or Wellesley who had been in Vietnam." [19]

In 1969, while Lyons and other returning soldiers tried to get on with their lives, militant college students in Boston's antiwar movement tried to kick the U.S. military off their campuses. On April 9, 1969, approximately 70 members of SDS and an even more radical offshoot, the Progressive Labor Party, entered University Hall in Harvard Yard and ejected the faculty and staff. After being joined by more than 100 other students, they chained the doors shut and announced they wouldn't leave until the university agreed to end its Reserve Officers' Training Corps (ROTC) program. Ansara, one of the leaders of the protest, charged the university with supporting an immoral war and the faculty with having "blood on [its] hands." [20]

A poll of Harvard students, who were described at the time in the *Boston Globe* as "moderates," showed most didn't support either the building takeover or the demand to get rid of ROTC. That changed, however, after the state police roughly ejected the students from University Hall early the next morning and after the school threatened to expel the protesters. A few days later, some 10,000 students, faculty, and staff gathered in Harvard Stadium and released a list of demands, including one to end ROTC. Then they went on strike until the university agreed to end the program a week later. [21]

In the next few weeks, similar demonstrations on other campuses in and around Boston led to similar results. The only two schools who held onto their ROTC programs were MIT, which was heavily involved in Defense Department–funded research, and Northeastern, back then a largely working-class commuter school.

While these protests against ROTC were confined to college campuses, the growth in sentiment against U.S. involvement in Vietnam wasn't. John Bassett grew up outside New York City and then went to Harvard, where he had been involved in the antiwar movement. By 1969, however, he was a carpenter on union construction jobs. "More and more of the guys I was working with had changed their minds about the war," he recalled. "Some of them came out against it because it was costing too much in lives and money. Some because they'd come to believe it was wrong. But more and more of them had turned against it." [22]

Just how many people in and around the city had turned against the war became clear on October 15, 1969, when a crowd of 100,000 turned out

National Vietnam Moratorium demonstration on Boston Common on October 15, 1969. Photo by Joseph Runci/Globe Staff.

on Boston Common for what was called the "National Vietnam Moratorium." It was the largest antiwar demonstration in the country that day and the largest in Boston history. Just as noteworthy, the crowd was no longer primarily made up of college students. A Boston businessman who happened by marveled at the large number of "ordinary" people—adults and families—who took part. "If I hadn't been here," he said, "I would not have believed this."[23]

But just as sentiment against the war was rising, the ranks of the antiwar movement were suddenly depleted—literally overnight. The sudden drop resulted from the Pentagon's decision to change how it obtained the troops to fight the war. During the four years that it had been operating, the draft was criticized for being unpredictable, since it left the decision as to which young men were called up to some 4,000 local draft boards. It was criticized for being interminable, since it kept draft-eligible young men in limbo from the time they turned nineteen until they turned at least twenty-six, and sometimes even thirty-four. And it was criticized for being unfair, since by granting deferments to full-time, undergraduate college students, it drew disproportionately from among the poor and working class.[24]

On December 1, 1969, however, much of that changed when the Pentagon introduced the first draft lottery since World War II. Under the new system, young men were called up in the order that their lottery numbers—which were based on their birth dates—were drawn from a clear, plastic drum. Young men were called up only during the first year they became draft-eligible, and only enough were called to meet the military's current manpower needs. Because President Nixon had ordered the beginning of a drawdown of U.S. troops in Vietnam six months earlier, only young men whose lottery numbers were among the first third drawn were likely to be drafted from now on.

The new lottery system did continue to grant deferments to college students, however, so in that respect it was no fairer than before. "It really was a working-class war," recalled Tom Lyons ruefully more than forty years later, "and the draft made it that way." [25]

Lew Finfer was a Harvard undergraduate at the time. He had grown up on Long Island, and he had been active in both the civil rights and antiwar movements since high school. The day after the first draft lottery was held, the results were posted on the bulletin board in Finfer's dormitory. He wrote a note that he tacked underneath the list of the birth dates in the order they had been drawn. "My note said the new system was still unfair because most of us still could get out of the draft thanks to our student deferments, and the issue of the war shouldn't be over just because some of us might have gotten a high number in the lottery." Evidently, not all of Finfer's classmates agreed with those sentiments. The next day, when he passed by the bulletin board, he saw that someone had scrawled "Fuck You" over his note. [26]

With the number of male college students concerned with the draft reduced so dramatically, antiwar activity in Boston began to ratchet down. Demonstrations became less frequent and smaller; they lacked the energy of previous protests; some were marred by violence. Some 50,000 people did turn out on Boston Common on April 15, 1970. But that was half the number that had come out six months earlier, and the crowd was described as including "far fewer older people and family groups" and lacking "the spirit and fervor" of previous protests. Afterward, several hundred of the demonstrators, many of them members of SDS, smashed windows, looted stores, and set fires in Harvard Square during what was described as "the most extreme disorder in Cambridge history." [27]

Two weeks later, demonstrations did break out on college campuses throughout Boston and across the country—including those in which students were killed by National Guard troops at Kent State University in Ohio and Jackson State University in Mississippi—after President Nixon ordered U.S. troops to invade Cambodia. But the national student strike that followed seemed to sap even more energy from the antiwar movement. After students returned to their campuses in the fall, no big demonstration was held in Boston that season. Some 25,000 did turn out on Boston Common for the annual spring demonstration on May 5, 1971, but that was half the number of the year before. The fall demonstration was canceled again because organizers feared a low turnout.

Fewer than 500 people turned up on Boston Common for the annual spring demonstration on April 29, 1972, which was described as "listless." One of the speakers that day was John Kerry, a leader of the Vietnam Veterans Against the War. He told the crowd that "talking and marching and striking and sloganeering . . . are not going to end the war," and they should turn their activism toward electoral politics.[28]

Among those in the crowd that day were Jim and Peg Canny. Their presence showed that, while the antiwar movement might be losing momentum, antiwar sentiment was spreading into Boston's working-class neighborhoods. Both Jim and Peg had grown up in South Boston. After getting married, they had moved a few blocks away to Dorchester and were raising a family that by this time included three young sons. "When we first started going to demonstrations, it was like being in a different world down there, with all those hippies and radicals," Peg recalled. "But then we saw priests there, and rabbis, and doctors, and that let you know that you weren't the only normal people against the war."[29]

Among the Cannys' neighbors was a group of former Harvard SDS members, including Michael Ansara, who had recently moved there, Ansara recalled, "because Dorchester was the biggest blue-collar neighborhood in Boston, and we wanted to organize more people who were paying the highest price for the war and suffering the most from inequality." Jim Canny was president of the newly revived Columbia/Savin Hill Civic Association, and Ansara and the others persuaded him to invite Howard Zinn to speak at one of the group's meetings. "Hundreds of people on both sides of the issue showed up," Jim recalled, "but Howard charmed everybody. He didn't talk about Vietnam that much. Instead, he talked his own experiences in World War II, and what any war was like. It was good for the neighborhood. It calmed things down for a while."[30]

Things calmed down even more in 1973, when the United States withdrew the last of its troops. The "conflict" in Vietnam—it was never officially declared a war—finally had ended, at a cost of more than 58,000 American lives and the lives of countless Vietnamese. Once U.S. troops were gone, the government of the South soon fell to that of the Communist North—but neither Vietnam nor any other Southeast Asia country fell under the control of the Soviet Union or China as the "domino theory" had predicted. In the United States, the conflict over the conflict in Vietnam left wounds that took a long time to heal.

In 1978, Tom Lyons and some of his fellow veterans began to try to heal some of those wounds—at least in South Boston, which had lost 25 of its sons in Vietnam, one of the highest per capita losses of any community in the country. They decided to put up a monument in memory of those men. After going to the city and getting no help, they went ahead and did it themselves. They put collection cans in stores and bars throughout the neighborhood, and held a "time" at nearby University of Massachusetts Boston that was attended by more than 1,000 current and former South Boston residents. Eventually, they raised enough money to get it done.[31]

On September 13, 1981, the families of the 25 men, some 200 local Vietnam veterans, and several thousand South Boston residents attended the dedication of the memorial at M Street Park. Made of black marble and designed by South Boston artist and Vietnam veteran Harry Carroll, the monument is inscribed on the front with the names of the men who never made it back from Vietnam and the message, "If you forget my death, then I died in vain."[32] But for Tom Lyons, the most important message is the one on the back of the stone. It reads, "Welcome home."[33]

———— ◄○► ————

The Media and the Protest Movements

T HE PEOPLE OF BOSTON HAD BEEN PROTESTING FOR ALMOST a decade, but until the protests against the Vietnam War came along local media hadn't seemed to be paying much attention. "There were a lot of young reporters at the *Boston Globe* back then," recalled Bob Turner, who was one of them, "and they had a sympathy for the antiwar movement that eventually that led to a connection with neighborhood activism."[1]

Given the history of Boston journalism's support for dissent, it shouldn't have taken that long. *Publick Occurrences: Both Foreign and Domestic* (est. 1690) was not only the first newspaper to be published in the British colonies, but also the first to be banned in Boston. The town's Puritan fathers shut it down four days after the first edition appeared for publishing "sundry doubtful and uncertain Reports." The *Boston Gazette* (est. 1755) and the *Massachusetts Spy* (est. 1770) played an integral part in the American Revolution by making their pages available to activists of the era such as James Otis and Samuel Adams. Boston was the home of *The Liberator* (est. 1831), the leading abolitionist paper of the day. Published by William Lloyd Garrison, its goal was to lift "the standard of emancipation in the eyes of the nation, within the sight of Bunker Hill, and in the birthplace of liberty." It was also the home of *The Guardian* (est. 1901), published by William Monroe Trotter, and the progressive *Women's Journal*, in which Trotter wrote in May 1903 that the city "is the home of abolition, of equal rights. It leads in these principles the rest of the country. Reaction is setting in. Any compromise in Boston will doubly damage the cause."[2]

By 1960, however, like so much else in the city, Boston's tradition of crusading, activist journalism had faded. The *Boston Post*, long the city's leading Democratic newspaper, had folded in 1956. *The Guardian*, kept going by Trotter's family, had followed suit a year later. The last issue of the *Boston Chronicle*, which called itself "New England's Largest Negro Weekly Newspaper," appeared in 1960. By then, there were only a handful of newspapers struggling to stay open on Boston's "Newspaper Row" along upper Washington Street, where once more than a dozen had thrived. None were very enthusiastic about upholding what the nineteenth-century Chicago newspaper columnist Finley Peter Dunne had called journalism's responsibility to "comfort the afflicted and afflict the comfortable."

"Up until the mid-1960's, Boston newspapers were of the 'rah rah' variety, boosters for the city's business interests. They didn't provide a platform for anyone who wasn't part of the establishment," recalled Tom Mulvoy, a former *Globe* managing editor who had grown up in Dorchester and, as a kid, caddied for Mayor Hynes. "The *Herald* under Bob Choate and then Harold Clancy wasn't about to let people who didn't wear ties into their newspaper. The *Record* was only interested in printing 'the number.' The *Globe* didn't take a stand on anything because it didn't want to offend anyone."[3]

In 1965, that attitude began to change, at least at the *Globe*, when Tom Winship succeeded his father as editor. "Winship instituted a youth movement that opened up the *Globe*'s front page and op-ed pages to Lefties, especially to people in the antiwar movement," confirmed Mulvoy.[4] But it would take a little longer for its pages to be opened up to activists of other stripes. "Winship was still a top-down guy," recalled a former *Globe* reporter who wanted to remain an unnamed source. "For him, politics started at the White House, worked its way down through Congress, the State House, and City Hall—and stopped there."[5]

Indeed, under Winship, the *Globe* was a big supporter of urban renewal. In fall 1966, the paper ran a series of articles on the state of the city's neighborhoods, titled "Blight in Boston," that was little more than an extended advertisement for "slum clearance." Six months later, the paper published a progress report on urban renewal with an introduction by Winship. Its boldface, all-caps headline proclaimed, "THE MOST ATTRACTIVE CITY IN AMERICA IS OUR GOAL, AND WE WILL MAKE IT."[6]

But the clamor made by residents against urban renewal, for civil rights, and over the Boston schools and other issues soon grew too loud for the *Globe* to ignore—especially if other newspapers didn't. The fiercely competitive Winship was notorious for leaving clippings from other newspapers on the desks of editors and reporters accompanied by scrawled notes that read, "Why we no have?"[7]

"Tom Winship hated not to know something," recalled the former *Globe* reporter Ken Hartnett, "but, when it came to local issues, he compensated for it clumsily. If he wanted to find out what was going on in a certain part of the city, he would talk to the Irish Catholics, or the Italian Catholics, or the Jews that worked at the paper. But a newspaper has to be able to do more than that—it has to have people who knew the neighborhoods."[8] Eventually, Winship hired them.

One of the first of those hired was Alan Lupo, a genial, moon-faced man who had grown up in nearby Winthrop, attended the University of Massachusetts and the Columbia School of Journalism School, and after stints as a reporter in New York and Baltimore was brought back home by Winship to head the *Globe's* new "Urban Team." It was a perfect job for Lupo, and a godsend to the long-ignored residents of Boston's neighborhoods. "Because I grew up in a family and in a neighborhood that had no voice," he later wrote, "I have tried in some small way to be a voice for those whose feelings are too rarely heard, or even expressed."[9]

"In the tumultuous 1960s, most of the media concentrated their attention on the civil rights revolution and the anti–Vietnam War protests," Lupo also wrote, but "what the media too often missed was an equally significant uprising among white working stiffs . . . an awakening among ethnic Americans that they, too, had rights being trampled upon, concerns being ignored, and problems being unaddressed by those in power."[10] First at the *Globe,* then at other newspapers, radio, and TV stations in Boston, Lupo became the champion of "working stiffs" of every race, creed, and color.

But Lupo bristled when what he and others did was called "advocacy journalism." "Journalists who report on activism aren't advocating anything, they're just telling the other side," he explained years later. "It's the other journalists, the ones who just report the 'establishment' side of things, who are the real 'advocacy journalists.' When the governor calls a press conference, it's all set up with lights, electric outlets, press releases, the whole bit. The press knows what's expected of them, they show up and report what they're told. When a neighborhood group calls a press conference, there is nothing set up. The press doesn't always show up, and when they do they do they don't know what it's all about. That's unequal access, and that's something some of us tried to do something about in the 60s and 70s."[11]

In the summer of 1967, Lupo and some of the other young *Globe* reporters produced a much different series of articles on the state of Boston neighborhoods than the one the paper had run a year earlier. Instead of an advertisement for urban renewal, it was an indictment of the city for failing to provide residents with the services they deserved and for implementing programs that failed to "renew" the neighborhoods as they were supposed to do. Each article's headline featured the name of a different neighborhood followed by a subheadline that served as an accusation—for instance, "Brighton–Allston: The Warning Signs Are Up," "Jamaica Plain: Area of Sharp Contrasts," or "Charlestown: Proud and Neglected."

It was in the final article of this series that Lupo first called the New Boston "two cities." He described one as a "city of activity and progress, of a dramatic two billion dollar public and private renewal program which has greatly stimulated the job and money markets and has given corporate Boston new self-confidence." He described the other as "a city of many neglected neighborhoods, of people alienated and often untouched by the New Boston. . . . To these people, and to the poor, the New Boston of high-rise office buildings and revitalized business districts has little meaning."[12]

Lupo was not the first or only journalist of the era to pay attention to Boston's neglected neighborhoods. Others at the *Globe* included Elliott Friedman, Bill Fripp, Ken Hartnett, Robert A. Jordan, Anne Kirchheimer, Robert Levey, Viola Osgood, Janet Riddell, and F. B. Taylor. Jack Driscoll, who succeeded Winship as editor, contributed greatly by starting up a community media committee that regularly met with neighborhood leaders and groups from all over the city. Reporters at other daily papers on the "neighborhood beat" included Bob Hannan, William Lewis, and Barbara Rabinowitz at the *Boston Herald* and Luix Overbea at the *Christian Science Monitor.*

Weekly newspapers and local radio and television stations also began to increase their coverage of neighborhood issues. In 1965, Mel Miller provided Boston's black community with a replacement for the *Boston Chronicle* when he began to publish the *Bay State Banner* and hired activist Bryant Rollins as its first editor. In 1968, WGBH, the public television station, began to air *Say Brother,* a weekly news and public affairs show "of, by and for the black community," and hired activist Sarah-Ann Shaw as a reporter.[13] A year later, Shaw was lured away by WBZ-TV to become the first African American reporter on a nightly television news show in Boston.

Shaw later admitted she sometimes had a hard time separating her past role as activist from her new one as journalist. "When I first started at Channel 4, I was less circumspect as far as giving advice to demonstrators. If they were having a press conference, I would suggest ways for them to get attention. I used to tell them 'Don't let reporters get you off your topic.' And when I used to get sent to events where they wanted me to interview the mayor or governor, I'd tell the demonstrators, 'Keep at it. Don't be disappointed.'"[14]

In 1970, WGBH-TV established the gold standard for local news coverage when it hired Lupo to anchor *The Reporters*, a nightly news show with a team of veteran, neighborhood-oriented reporters including Joe Day and Diane Dumanowski. They not only provided in-depth coverage of a handful of local stories each night, but also followed up each story on subsequent shows until the issues were resolved. "*The Reporters*' and WEEI radio did the best local coverage," Shaw agreed in an interview years later. She then praised Dexter Eure, "who had the ear of the Taylors who published the *Globe* and of its editors, Tom Winship and Jack Driscoll, who were very committed over there."[15]

Competition, as much as commitment, drove the increased coverage of neighborhood news. The competition with what we today call the "mainstream media" came from what were dubbed back then "alternative" newspapers. With circulations of more than 50,000 readers, *Boston after Dark*, the *Cambridge Phoenix*, and the *Real Paper* were weekly tabloids that eschewed objectivity for the "new journalism," which allowed reporters to side with the underdog.

"We were saying things that the 'straight media' wouldn't say. We were covering things that they wouldn't cover. And we were admitting things they wouldn't admit," recalled Paul Solman, the *Real Paper's* first editor.[16] These papers also served as a proving ground for young journalists like Solman, who brought their experience of activism and advocacy with them to the establishment media as they continued their careers.

There was even new competition within Boston's neighborhoods for coverage of local issues. Almost all neighborhoods had long supported local, weekly newspapers, yet they tended to steer clear of controversy, printing press releases from City Hall and relying on birth, death, and wedding announcements as well as local sports stories to maintain their readership. But now they found themselves competing for readers with new "community newspapers" springing up in neighborhoods. The young activists who staffed these papers jumped eagerly into any and all controversies, enthusiastically siding with neighborhood "Davids" against "Goliaths," a category that included local landlords, outside developers, big institutions, and city and state government.

At one point, there was even a short-lived attempt to try to pull these community newspapers into some kind of citywide coalition. "We had one or two meetings with people from the other community newspapers," recalled Renée Loth, then editor of *East Boston Community News.* Loth, who had grown up in Port Chester, New York, and come to Boston in 1970 to study journalism at Boston University, had since found a way to combine her politics and chosen line of work. "But like everybody in what we called 'the movement' back then, we couldn't agree on anything and we were never able to pull it off." [17]

For quite a while, though, the Boston media did seem to agree that all this activism and protest going on in New Boston was worth covering—and by providing that coverage, they helped to encourage even more of it.

CHAPTER 8

◄○►

Mothers for
Adequate Welfare

"Activism comes from a group getting a sense of its own dignity and worth and of being deserving of better treatment," Mel King said not long ago.[1] In the mid-1960s, one of the groups to develop a sense of its own dignity and worth was made up of women on welfare. At the time, despite all the claims of progress being made in the New Boston, approximately 150,000 residents, one-fourth of the city's population, were categorized as "poor," and 40,000, most of them women and children, received welfare—twice the number of residents who had been on "relief" during the Great Depression.

Those unfortunate enough to qualify for assistance were doubly unfortunate because they found themselves entangled in what was undoubtedly the worst welfare system in the country, although even calling it a "system" is a stretch. Massachusetts was the only state in the country in which each city and town was responsible for operating the four major programs that "welfare" comprised—Aid to Families with Dependent Children, Disability Assistance, General Relief, and Old Age Assistance.[2] The result, according to the *Boston Globe*, which published a series titled "The State of Welfare," was "an uneven river of local busibodiness and red tape uncommon even for welfare, which is the Land of Red Tape."[3]

Rules and regulations varied from one municipality to another. Allotments were low and caseloads high. Policies discouraged families from staying together and kept recipients from looking for work.[4] Taking a low-paying job meant losing health-care coverage. Worst of all, recipients charged, was the suspicion with which they were looked at and the lack of respect they were shown. "One of my mother's sorority sisters was a welfare worker," recalled Val Hyman of Roxbury, "and she used to have to go out on midnight raids on welfare mothers to see if a man was living in the home."[5]

Welfare in Massachusetts was not only complicated, counterproductive, and demeaning, it was also expensive. It cost the state more than $200 million a year and the cities and towns another combined $50 million. It also did not work. As the *Globe* series concluded, "The welfare program in Massachusetts is giving the poor a handout without giving them a hand."[6]

In 1964, a dozen African American women on welfare who had met at the Dudley Street Area Planning Action Council decided to try to do something to fix the so-called system in which they found themselves trapped. They formed a group, which they named Mothers for Adequate Welfare (MAW), and they elected Doris Bland its first president.

Born in Canada and now a resident of Dorchester, Bland had left school after the ninth grade and now found herself a single mother of five children. Her first brush with activism had come a few years earlier, when she and some of the other women on her street staged a rent strike against their landlord for not providing their apartments with sufficient heat.[7] "Doris was an extraordinary woman, as were so many in that group," recalled Laura Morris, whose job at the time was to train psychiatrists and social workers in community mental health and who became a mentor and friend to Bland.[8]

Once formed, MAW decided it needed to recruit more members, which it did by putting out flyers with a somewhat misleading come-on: "If you want $27 worth of free food, come to a meeting." Bland later admitted, "The sign was a lie ... but people came, and we found that they were interested not just in surplus commodities, but in other problems, too."[9]

"Initially," according to Morris, "MAW's focus was not so much on changing the system as just getting the benefits available to women, and on figuring out how to not be awed by the system." The latter was a particularly tough challenge. "The mothers were very well spoken when we'd talk with them in their homes," recalled Marcia Butman, then a member the Education Research and Action Project of Students for a Democratic Society, which was trying to help the mothers organize. "But when we went to the welfare offices with them, we saw they had a difficult time talking with their case workers. It wasn't just because a lot of the recipients were poor, uneducated, and black and almost all of the caseworkers were better educated and white. It was that the caseworkers were just very difficult people. They would have been difficult for *anyone* to deal with." [10]

In support of its members, MAW established a "buddy system" so that whenever a new recipient had to undergo an intake interview, a MAW member would go with her. "It irritated the bureaucrats," recalled Morris, "because there was a sense that they [the MAW members] were women you couldn't ignore." Soon, the organization began to grow, and, although its core group never exceeded more than 200, it developed a mailing list containing the names of more than 1,000 of the approximately 13,000 women on welfare in the city. But according to Doris Bland, it wasn't until MAW began to hold demonstrations that "a new organization was born." [11]

One of the its first demonstrations took place in the spring of 1965, when some 50 MAW members showed up outside Mayor Collins's office at City Hall to demand that the city speed up its distribution of surplus food. When their demand wasn't met, they staged a sit-in at the city's Welfare Department Headquarters at 43 Hawkins Street. The slowdown ended and the food was handed out.

Viola Osgood, a young reporter at the time, covered a number of the MAW protests. "I always used to ask them, 'Where are your kids?' and 'Why are you doing this?'" she recalled. "And they had the best answers. They'd say 'My mother'—or my sister, or my oldest daughter—'is watching my kids.' And 'I'm doing this *because* of my kids. They need to eat. They need clothes.'" Once they began demonstrating, Morris explained, MAW members set up "telephone and door-knocking trees, because some of the women did not have telephones, to make sure their children were cared for if they had to stay late at meetings or if they got arrested at demonstrations." [12]

"None of us knew our rights, what we could and couldn't do," Bland said a few years later. But with help from Morris, SDS members, and others, the group soon learned all that. "We got a copy of the State Manual of Welfare," Bland recalled. "All hell broke loose when we got hold of that." [13]

MAW even established connections with similar groups around the country. On June 30, 1966, it participated in what was described as "the first national demonstration ever staged to demand a better welfare system," which included protests in various cities. In Boston, some 50 women—black and white, some accompanied by their children—marched from the South End to Boston Common. There, Bland presented a list of demands to William Lally, the commissioner of Boston's Welfare Department, while

MAW members surrounded the pair and waved signs that read "Lally Don't Dally." [14]

Some of MAW's demands were for increased benefits. "You can't find a broom closet in Boston for $49, and that's what I get each month to pay the rent for myself and my daughter," complained member Gertrude "Nicky" Nickerson. A single mother who lived in the South End, Nickerson later explained that she had ended up on welfare by making one mistake: "I picked the most irresponsible creature alive to be Andrea's father." [15]

But most of MAW's demands were to improve the "system" itself. The group called for more and better daycare, so women could go to work; for interviews with social workers to be conducted privately; and for publishing all the various rules and regulations in one, clearly written document so recipients could understand what they could expect and what was expected of them. [16]

After MAW presented its demands to the welfare commissioner on Boston Common, the members marched to the State House to lobby for them. Just by chance, they encountered Governor John Volpe as he was stepping out of an elevator. The governor spent a considerable amount of time right there in the State House corridor listening to the women, and when their conversation ended, they applauded him for his courtesy.

But MAW was not nearly as cordial toward Attorney General Ed Brooke, the first African American elected to a statewide office in Massachusetts history. MAW members were already annoyed with Brooke because they had invited him to their rally on the Common and he had chosen not to attend. When they marched to the door of his State House office, the women were told he was not in, so they sat down in the hallway and said they'd wait. But when they began to sing, "We Shall Overcome," a flustered aide ushered them into a meeting room and served them refreshments. Ten minutes later, Brooke appeared and met with the group. [17]

On the following day, a newspaper reporter writing of MAW's protest declared, "The State House has never seen anything remotely like it." [18] A year later, another MAW demonstration generated something that the city of Boston had never seen.

On May 26, 1967, MAW held a sit-in to protest conditions at the Grove Hall Welfare Office at 515 Blue Hill Avenue in Roxbury. The Grove Hall office was the busiest in the city, and even its layout seemed designed to demean those required to use it. Every day, more than 100 women, many with small children, had to sit for hours in straight-back chairs along a hallway and wait under the bored gaze of a police officer, sometimes for hours, to see their caseworkers. When their turn finally came, the women had to squeeze into tiny, low-walled cubicles and, with no privacy at all, answer the most personal questions imaginable. Doris Bland called the Grove Hall office "a snake pit." Jessie Herr, a social worker there, admitted it was "terrible for us and worse for the clients." One of her colleagues had recently quit, but not before predicting, "Grove Hall is going to explode." [19]

Grove Hall didn't explode that day, and MAW continued its sit-in all through the night. It didn't explode the next day, when the women finally left, after what was described as "a silent, frustrating session" from which they "got no satisfaction." [20] But Grove Hall did explode a week later.

On June 1, 1967, a Thursday, at about 10 a.m., approximately 30 MAW members returned to the Grove Hall Welfare Office and presented another list of demands. As with the previous list, some were for increased benefits, but most for improvements to the system itself. One merely asked that recipients be treated with "politeness and respect." [21] Then the women sat down on the floor and announced they weren't leaving until their demands were met.

The MAW members sat there all day, as welfare workers tried to go about their business. At the end of the day, when the workers left, the women chained themselves to radiators and pipes to discourage the Boston police officers from trying to remove them. As they had done the week before, the MAW members stayed the night in the Grove Hall office, with a few police officers watching over them.

On Friday, MAW continued its vigil. By late morning, as news of the demonstration got around, MAW supporters began to gather outside the building. Most were African American residents from the surrounding neighborhood, but early in the afternoon a delegation of white college students showed up as well. So did reporters, photographers, and television crews. At some point during the day, someone taped a sign on the outside of the building that read, "Help Us Kick Off Welfare Month and Kick Off This Lousy System."

At 4 p.m., as the welfare staff prepared to leave the office for the weekend, the MAW members huddled. Then they announced they wanted city welfare director Daniel Cronin to come out to Grove Hall to meet with them—and that no one could leave the building until he did. [22] With that, some of the women chained the doors of the building shut from the inside, while some of their supporters did the same from outside. [23] With some 50 welfare workers now trapped inside, the sit-in had turned into something more akin to a hostage situation. [24]

*Mothers for Adequate Welfare occupation of Grove
Hall Welfare Office on June 2, 1967.* Photo by Dan
Sheehan/Globe Staff.

Outside, the crowd had grown to more than 700 people, almost all of
them African American.[25] Soon, more police arrived, many in riot gear.
For about an hour, the situation was a standoff. But when one of the welfare workers inside the building fell ill, the police were ordered to move
in. The helmeted, bullet-proof-vest-clad officers pushed their way through
the crowd, reached the doors of the building, and cut the chains holding
them shut. Once inside, they brought the sick woman out first, and then
the other welfare workers. The police then ordered the MAW members
out and, when the women refused, cut the chains that held them to the
radiators and pipes and began to drag them out—and that's when Grove
Hall exploded.

Doris Bland later claimed that she and other MAW members were
"beaten, kicked, dragged, abused, insulted and brutalized."[26] According
to a timetable of events published in the *Globe,* the police said they were

"set upon by demonstrators . . . [and] were assaulted," and the media reported that some in the crowd—mostly young men—began throwing rocks and bottles at the police and overturning parked cars.[27] Some of them chanted "Black Power." Some chanted antiwar slogans.[28]

The police were able to clear most of the crowd away from the front of the building fairly quickly, but that only pushed the violence up and down Blue Hill Avenue, which by 10 p.m. was described as looking like "a battlefield." A veteran police officer said, "I've worked in Roxbury for years, and I know CORE, the NAACP, and the other Negro welfare organizations. I've been at a lot of their protests, and they have always been passive resistance affairs. But this was a different type of group. This wasn't passive resistance. It was active resistance."[29]

It was more than that—it was a riot, the kind Los Angeles, New York, Philadelphia, Cleveland, and Chicago had already experienced in recent years, and which were called "race riots" at the time. Now it was the New Boston's turn to experience one.

For the rest of that night and for the next three nights, roving bands of neighborhood residents—mostly young men—smashed windows, looted stores, and set fires along a fourteen-block stretch of Blue Hill Avenue. "It was wild. It was all happening right outside the Roxbury Multi-Service Center," recalled Hubie Jones, who by this time had become the center's assistant director. "People were on the rooftops shooting at firemen and police. They were burning buildings across the street."[30]

Jones and his staff kept the center open around the clock to provide refuge for residents and a place where they could receive medical care and food. Other activists, working out of the nearby Operation Exodus office, "tried to help police quiet the crowd [but were] shouted . . . down" by the rioters. Some of those activists, including Byron Rushing, Chuck Turner, and Tom Atkins, were arrested for their troubles, and Atkins was beaten. "It could have all been avoided," he said later, adding, "I have never witnessed such a disgusting and stupid display of officialdom."[31]

The riot resulted in millions of dollars in property damage to one of the main business districts in Boston's black community. No one was killed, but 68 people were injured, and more than 50 were arrested. The riot left a physical scar along the black community's major boulevard that would last for years and an emotional and psychological scar on the city that would last just as long. The riot also set in motion a remarkable series of political events that played out over the next few days.

On Saturday morning, MAW held a press conference, at which Doris

Bland deplored the violence but defended the demonstration that had set it off. "We're sick and tired of the way the Welfare Department—and especially Grove Hall—treats us. We're tired of being treated like criminals, of having to depend on suspicious and insulting social workers and of being completely at the mercy of a department we have no control over."[32]

On Sunday, Mayor Collins held his own press conference, at which he called for an end to the violence and announced creation of a committee to recommend ways to improve the welfare system.[33]

On Monday, a MAW representative delivered a new list of demands to City Hall. One was that Collins come out to Roxbury to meet with the group. Collins refused, characteristically declaring, "The mayor of Boston conducts the city's business in City Hall."[34] MAW appeared to give in and agreed to have some of its members meet with the mayor in his office at 10:30 a.m. the next day.

But on Tuesday morning, the MAW members failed to show up at City Hall for the scheduled meeting. Collins waited for twenty minutes, then he hastily convened another press conference and abruptly announced that he would not run for reelection that fall.

That evening, in a television address, John Collins defended his legacy as mayor, particularly his emphasis on urban renewal. "Our critics are quick to say that we used the bulldozer too often. I don't agree. In my recollection the only thing this administration ever bulldozed was the graveyard of indifference and indecision in which Boston was mired. In doing so we built the foundation upon which the New Boston stands today." Collins also took aim at MAW specifically and at other increasingly fractious activists in general. "I shall continue to be available at City Hall to meet with any responsible group at any time. However, I feel I must repeat again that disorderly protests will not and cannot be tolerated in Boston."[35]

John Collins never admitted these disorderly protests convinced him to leave office, and his deputy mayor, Henry Scagnoli, later denied they did. But the historian Thomas O'Connor later wrote, "The activism took Collins by surprise. He saw mothers chaining themselves to radiators and people dumping trash outside City Hall in protest. . . . He just couldn't understand this kind of behavior. It came as a revelation to him that suddenly politics was different. . . . If this was the politics of the future, Collins was having none of it; he wasn't interested."[36]

Collins "pushed the 'New Boston' of high-rises and a financial services industry," wrote Alan Lupo, but "his insistence on cutting taxes year after year left the neighborhoods feeling abandoned when it came to city services, and hot button issues of race and class would help convince him that the mayor's office was not worth in 1967 the power and glory it had offered when he first ran."[37]

But the mayor's office did still offer enough power and glory to entice others, and very quickly, a large number of candidates stepped forward to run for it. Three candidates in particular offered the people of Boston the choice of dramatically different new directions that the New Boston could take.

One of those candidates was Ed Logue, who tried to put the best possible light on his tenure as director of the Boston Redevelopment Authority. On August 10, 1967, when he stepped down to run for mayor, Logue released a "farewell report" that predicted what the New Boston would look like in 1975, once all its urban renewal projects were completed. "Boston's residential neighborhoods are renewed," the report claimed. "Their schools and other public services have reached the quality level of the better suburbs and the exodus of families has halted, neighborhoods are secure about their future because for one thing, they had a lot to say about it." The report even predicted that "the Boston Redevelopment Authority will vote to dissolve, its work completed" and stated that the people of Boston would "not only . . . enjoy governing themselves, but they do it rather well."[38]

The second of those three candidates was school committee member Louise Day Hicks, who sought to promote an angry and divisive brand of populist politics. Hicks would later be remembered for her campaign slogan "You Know Where I Stand," a not-so-subtle reminder of her staunch opposition to school desegregation. But her first slogan, reported by the *Globe* in May 1967 when she entered the race, was "Boston for Bostonians!" During her campaign, she called for urban renewal "with a heart instead of a bulldozer." She also charged, "Mayor Collins lost contact with the people and they knew it. He too often turned deaf ears to them. What the people wanted was to be heard by City Hall, but they found that he belonged to big business and special interests."[39]

The third of those three candidates was Kevin White, then the Massachusetts secretary of state. White's criticism of Hynes, Collins, and Logue was more muted than that of Hicks. "All urban renewal plans must be based on close consultation with the affected neighborhoods," he declared. "The last two administrations have laid plans and in part constructed great new buildings." Then he continued, "But the truth is that a great city is not only a place in which to work, it is also a place in which to live and to raise a family, and it is precisely here that we have failed."[40]

White's campaign manager, Barney Frank, later said, "The 1967 Boston mayoral campaign presented a polarization. Louise Day Hicks represented angry white people. Ed Logue was seen as the representative of the establishment. Kevin White fell between the two poles. Previously, the idea had been that the way to make the city prosperous was to improve the overall value of the city. But in 1967, that got rejected. What people were saying was, 'What do I care what's going on downtown, when I'm getting screwed.' Kevin White put together a synthesis of the two sides." [41]

White himself represented something of a synthesis in terms of his background and style. He had grown up in West Roxbury and was descended from a long line of Irish Catholic politicians, but after graduating from Williams College and Boston College Law School, and becoming a lawyer, he had moved to Beacon Hill and adopted a button-down Brahmin affect, one that didn't always square with his more mercurial Celtic personality.

In the preliminary election on September 26, 1967, Logue finished fourth and out of the running. Hicks finished first and White second to earn the right to face each other in the final. On the day of the final election, November 7, 1967, White defeated Hicks by 102,000 votes to 90,000 to be elected mayor. But according to John Sears, the Republican state representative from Beacon Hill who had finished third in the preliminary, White's victory had less to do with any synthesis he represented and more to do with the threat that Hicks did. "We all thought that Louise would wreck the town and [we] did try hard to help Kevin after the preliminary." [42] The people of Boston seemed to agree. While they may have felt—in Barney Frank's words, that they were "getting screwed"—the majority showed that they didn't want to be pitted against one in another in the process.

Even before taking office, Kevin White was able to get rid of the last headache that his predecessor had faced. Thanks to MAW's efforts, a bill had been filed in the Massachusetts legislature that called for the state to take over responsibility for administering the welfare system. For various reasons, the bill was stuck in committee, but Kevin White found a way to get it unstuck. He discovered that, legally, he could continue as Massachusetts secretary of state even while serving as mayor, and threatened to do that if the welfare bill wasn't passed. Since politics is, more than anything, a game of musical chairs, and since White's exit from his state job would allow a number of members of the House of Representatives to move up in the ranks, the legislature, Barney Frank recalled, was persuaded "to see the wisdom of the takeover." [43]

The upcoming takeover of the welfare system by the state didn't stop MAW from continuing its organizing. But now it found itself with competition. The National Welfare Rights Organization had recently established a Boston chapter, and it began to reach out to recipients in a way that MAW did not appreciate. "NWRO hired professional organizers to come in and work with the women," recalled Laura Morris, "and they acted as if nothing had been here before."[44]

Lee Staples was one of those professional organizers. He had grown up in Fairhaven, graduated from the University of Massachusetts and Boston College Law School, and after becoming a conscientious objector had been assigned to the Volunteers in Service to America program (VISTA), where he began working with NWRO. Staples later agreed with Morris's criticism. "We basically went 'underneath' MAW, and our attitude was one of disrespect for what was there."[45]

MAW and NWRO found themselves working with different groups of recipients. In August 1968, groups affiliated with both organizations held several weeks of demonstrations in Boston-area welfare offices to try to influence the new regulations being drawn up by the state. The demonstrations had seemed to produce their desired results, when Robert Ott, by now the state public welfare commissioner, agreed to include recipients on the local committees that would recommend the guidelines for the new system. MAW considered that a victory and ended its demonstrations, but an NWRO-organized group refused to end its occupation of the Mission Hill welfare office, which undercut MAW's bargaining position.

Initially, MAW had tried to keep this split between their own home-grown "amateur" organizing efforts and the one by the "outside professionals" quiet. "We figured if we ignored them they'd hang themselves," said one MAW member at the time. "Now they're hanging us with them." Eventually, the split became public. Writing in the MAW's newsletter, "Nicky" Nickerson blasted NWRO for coming "to Boston uninvited and completely unneeded, to organize what was already organized!" Eventually, according to Staples, NWRO's efforts in Boston "kind of fell apart as quickly as it formed. Folks just didn't want new organizing."[46]

MAW continued its old organizing. It had taken years of work, a riot, some political machinations, and a dust-up with outside organizers, but this small group of women had succeeded in creating a brand new welfare system. And if it didn't work, Doris Bland would be there to fix it—she was one of the dozen people named to the new board that would implement it.

The Illusion of Inclusion
and Assault by Acronyms

"KEVIN WHITE UNDERSTOOD THAT TIMES HAD CHANGED, and that they called for a different style, so he went out into the neighborhoods with his sleeves rolled up and his jacket slung over his shoulder," recalled the historian Thomas O'Connor. Then he added, "Of course it was a Brooks Brothers jacket, but that didn't matter."[1] Fittingly, one of the best books on White and his administration is *Style versus Substance: Boston, Kevin White, and the Politics of Illusion* by George V. Higgins.

A few weeks after taking office, the new mayor proclaimed that these changed times called for bringing city government "closer to the people," and he had the front doors of Boston's Old City Hall swung open and promised to keep them open 24 hours a day, 7 days a week, so that residents could come in with questions and complaints.[2] A few months later, White announced he was going to set up "Little City Halls" in every neighborhood so residents didn't have to go all the way downtown with those questions and complaints.

Mayor John Lindsay of New York City had come up with the idea of establishing little city halls a few years earlier. In Boston, according to Andy Olins, whose first job in the White administration was to find people to staff them, "Little City Halls were a response to a problem that Kevin inherited. People felt city government was all about downtown under Collins, and Kevin felt he had to do something dramatic to change that perception." Eighteen were eventually opened in various neighborhoods throughout the city, and Olins called them "an early alert system [that] let us deal with the problems before they blew up on us. In the beginning, they were quite clean. How much tending to friends and ignoring enemies . . . that increased as time went on."[3]

In the beginning, Little City Halls were popular with residents, and so was another new, neighborhood-oriented initiative, the Boston Community Schools, which kept school buildings open after school hours to provide educational, social, cultural, vocational, and recreational programs for young people and adults. The community schools program was a particularly good fit for the times, since residents were allowed to run each site themselves, through locally elected councils.

But reaching out to the neighborhoods "did not come naturally" to Mayor White, according to Herb Gleason, who had by now become the city's corporation counsel. "Kevin's heart was never with the community groups. He was very smart politically, and he knew that the wave to ride was community action, and that it was the only way to stay in charge. But his approach was pretty elitist. Rather than deal with the 'real activists,' he dealt almost exclusively with the 'establishment' in each neighborhood, people with whom he was more comfortable. In Roxbury that meant Mrs. Cass and Elma Lewis; in Chinatown it meant the Chin family; in Charlestown, he dealt with his relatives and in West Roxbury his in-laws. He was not a neighborhood guy."[4]

"Kevin White wanted to stabilize the neighborhoods," said *Boston Globe* reporter Ken Hartnett years later. "He wanted to avoid conflict. He wanted to make them safer. But he wasn't interested in sharing power with them or transforming them. Mel King described what Kevin did best—'the illusion of inclusion.'"[5]

On April 4, 1968, after just two months in office, White's desire to stabilize the neighborhoods was severely tested in Boston's black community by the assassination of the Reverend Martin Luther King Jr. The news of King's murder prompted several nights of sporadic vandalism and looting along Blue Hill Avenue. But the violence in Boston wasn't nearly as serious as in other cities at the time or as serious as the violence that had taken place in Grove Hall the year before, and part of the credit for that was due to Mayor White, who reached out and went out to the black community.

Part of the credit, though, was also due to neighborhood activists who donned white armbands, patrolled the streets, and passed out leaflets asking residents to "cool it." Foremost among them was Tom Atkins, who had just become the first African American to be elected at-large to the

Boston City Council. He recorded public service announcements asking residents to "stay at home" and "keep your children off the streets," and, according Alan Lupo, worked closely with the mayor and the police commissioner to keep things calm. "Last year Tom Atkins was clubbed, beaten across the face, and cut up," noted South End activist Marty Gopen. "This year, he was telling the mayor how to run the show. The community knew they could get in touch with anybody they wanted to get in touch with."[6]

In the days after Dr. King's assassination, the generation and ideological gaps between activists in the black community were suddenly reopened. On the morning of April 8, 1968, the moderate side was in evidence when a crowd of 30,000 people—made up of both blacks and whites—gathered on Boston Common for a memorial service for Dr. King. That afternoon, it was the militants' turn when a crowd of 5,000 people—all of them African American because no whites were allowed—gathered at White Stadium in Franklin Park.

The Franklin Park event was sponsored by a new group, the Black United Front, which announced a list of demands that could hardly have been more extreme. One called for all white-owned businesses in the black community to close "until further notice, while the transfer of the ownership of these businesses to the black community is being negotiated"; another for public schools in the black community to "have all-black staff, principals, teachers, and custodians . . . [and] be renamed after black heroes"; a third for "all public, private, and municipal agencies that affect the lives of the people in this community" to be turned over to the control of the black community; a fourth for the "white community at large to immediately make $100,000,000 available to the black community."[7] The moderates at the Boston Branch NAACP responded by releasing their own list of sixty-eight "recommendations," which included calls for the city to create more housing and jobs in the black community.

Faced with a choice between the two lists, Mayor White opted for the second one, describing the NAACP's recommendations as "a worthy basis for serious implementation."[8] He also dusted off some old programs and initiated some new ones to try to make things better in the black community. Unfortunately, some of these programs ended up doing more harm than good.

One of these was called the Boston Urban Rehabilitation Program. Launched in the final days of the Collins administration, BURP promised to create some 2,700 units of "instant housing" for low-income minority residents. It was going to do that by steering federally backed low-interest construction loans and mortgages to a small group of private developers who agreed to renovate some 150 apartment buildings scattered throughout Roxbury. The federal loan program had been created in the wake of the urban riots of a few years earlier, but had been criticized for moving too slowly and costing too much. In Boston, to speed things up, the city had quietly recruited the developers, and to keep costs down, the developers had secretly bought up the properties to be renovated.[9] But when news of the stealth program got out, activists were outraged because the black community had not been consulted, because all of the developers were white, and because no provision had been made to promote hiring minority construction workers.

On December 4, 1967, Housing and Urban Development secretary Robert Weaver, the first African American to serve as a cabinet member, came to Boston to publicly announce BURP at a luncheon at Freedom House. But as he started to speak, Weaver was interrupted by activist Bryant Rollins, now an organizer with the New Urban League. Rollins denounced the program as a "travesty" and "a robbery of the Roxbury people" and repeated those other criticisms. When Weaver finally got his turn to speak, he defended BURP as a "controlled experiment."[10]

It soon became apparent, however, that while BURP might be an experiment, it was anything but controlled. Tenants forced out of buildings so work could be done were given no help in finding temporary housing and no guarantee they could return once their former apartments were renovated. Work that was supposed to take six months took two years. Tenants who moved into the renovated units found that much of the work was either unfinished or been done so poorly it had to be redone.[11]

BURP tenants responded by forming the Tenants Association of Boston. TAB started with 100 members but grew quickly to include more than 2,000. According to TAB's president, Eva Curry, its goal was "to salvage the BURP, despite its clumsy beginning, because of the community's desperate need for decent housing."[12]

TAB began its salvage operation by compiling a list of grievances and submitting it to federal officials. Then, after months of negotiations, TAB signed what was described as a "landmark agreement" with the developers on January 24, 1969. The agreement included a "model lease" that spelled out the responsibilities of both sides and the establishment of community advisory boards to settle landlord-tenant disputes.[13]

Unfortunately, the developer/landlords failed to hold up their end of the agreement and conditions remained unchanged. TAB responded by submitting a long list of housing and building code complaints to the Federal Housing Administration.[14] When that didn't do anything, its members started to withhold their rent. On August 1, 1969, TAB demonstrated outside the FHA regional office in the JFK Federal Building to demand that the agency bring the BURP buildings up to the "FHA's own standards." During the protest, Curry said the group's biggest fear was that "in a few years these buildings will be back to their original state and people will be pointing to us and say 'The tenants tore them down.' We want people to know these buildings were never finished in the first place."[15]

BURP did turn out to be a failure — not because of anything the tenants did, but because the program itself was structurally flawed. Since all the profits came from tax shelters, rather than from payments received once tenants moved into the renovated buildings or rents that were generated afterward, the developers had no incentive to make sure the renovation work was done properly or that the properties were subsequently maintained. Most of the developers just walked away from the properties soon after and left the federal government holding the bag, a reluctant and inept landlord.

By 1979, the Department of Housing and Urban Development had been forced to foreclose on 1,781 of the original 2,100 units.[16] As many activists in Boston's black community had predicted, BURP's promise of "instant housing" turned out to be too good to be true.

The same held true for the promises made by the Boston Banks Urban Renewal Group program. Originally created in 1961 as a response to complaints by civil rights groups of racial discrimination in mortgage lending, B-BURG was an agreement by local banks to make mortgage loans to minority homebuyers that had never been implemented. By the time it was resurrected by Mayor White in the wake of Dr. King's assassination, it included some twenty Boston banks and lending institutions that pledged to make available more than $20 million in federally guaranteed mortgages to minority home buyers.

In relaunching the program on May 13, 1968, Mayor White proclaimed that B-BURG combined "private capital and expertise, governmental coordination and planning, and self-directed economic development by the poor."[17] But as Hillel Levine and Lawrence Harmon showed in their book

The Death of a Jewish Community: A Tragedy of Good Intentions, it proved to contain none of the those ingredients—something that the residents of one neighborhood in particular would soon find out.

Mattapan is located in the southernmost part of what had been the separate town of Dorchester. Its name is derived from an Indian word for "a place where evil is spread about," a reference to the various diseases brought by the first European settlers that proved so devastating to the Native American population. Originally an early Colonial industrial area, Mattapan was the site of the first grist, paper, and chocolate mills in the United States. After 1870, when it joined the rest of Dorchester in allowing its annexation to Boston, the area developed into one more of the growing city's "streetcar suburbs."

By 1960, Mattapan was a largely working- and middle-class area of 44,000 residents, 99 percent of them white and most of them Jewish. It was a stable, almost suburban neighborhood, with rows of well-kept homes lining the streets that ran into Blue Hill Avenue, the major boulevard that ran from Roxbury in the north to the suburb of Milton in the south.

Mattapan was chosen to "host" the B-BURG program for three reasons. First, it shared its northern border with Roxbury, which was fast becoming a predominantly African American neighborhood. Second, like so many neighborhoods chosen for so many programs at the time, it lacked political clout. Ward boss Samuel "Chief" Levine, had looked after Mattapan in the Old Boston, but neither he nor anyone like him was around any longer to protect it. Third, it was the center of Boston's Jewish community, and because of that, according to new BRA director Hale Champion, was seen as being "more willing to accept the problems of minorities."[18]

But because B-BURG was so flawed, the residents of Mattapan never got a fair chance to show just how accepting they really were. The program's major flaw had to do with how the boundaries for the program were drawn—and the fact that they were drawn at all.

On August 15, 1968, Carl Ericson, a vice president at the Suffolk Franklin Bank who had been selected to run the program, stepped up to a map in a conference room at the Boston Five Cents Savings Bank and drew those boundaries. In doing so, he created a diamond-shaped area whose edges included slices of Roxbury, Dorchester, and Jamaica Plain, but which had Mattapan at its center. There is some question whether Ericson used a red or a yellow marker to draw the lines, but there is no question about their effect. "By forcing blacks with home-ownership aspirations to compete in a limited geographic area," Levine and Harmon wrote, "the B-BURG bankers created an eruption of panic selling, blockbusting, street violence, and rage." [19]

B-BURG also created a land rush, as unscrupulous real estate agents raced ahead of minority families to buy up homes from the white residents of Mattapan, using despicable tactics to drive the prices they paid far below market value. In an article titled "Confessions of a Blockbuster," an anonymous real estate agent admitted, "We were told, you get the listings any way you can. It's pretty easy to do; just scare the hell out of them! And that's what we did." Mattapan resident Janice Bernstein reported that one of those agents said to her, "Do you want your child knifed or killed by those colored hoodlums? Sell now, you can still get your price." [20]

Bernstein, her husband, and some 600 residents tried to fight those despicable tactics and save their neighborhood by forming The Mattapan Organization. The group held meetings, tried to combat bad rumors with good information, and discourage panic selling. Most of all, it tried to hold onto longtime residents even as it tried to welcome newcomers.

But the tide of so much mortgage money flooding into just one neighborhood proved to be too powerful to resist. Not only were the longtime homeowners victimized, but the new buyers were as well. The real estate agents who bought low turned around and charged them high prices for the privilege of buying their first homes. Then the banks and Federal Housing Administration took turns making things even worse. Since the FHA backed the mortgage money, the banks didn't adequately screen the new buyers; many of them would never have qualified for conventional loans. Once the mortgages were granted, the FHA inspectors made only cursory "drive by" inspections of the homes and didn't make sure that necessary repairs were made prior to the sales. Once the new owners moved in, the banks refused to give them home repair loans because, unlike the mortgages, such loans weren't FHA guaranteed. Then, when the new owners fell behind on their payments, the banks initiated "fast foreclosures," got their money back, and left the FHA with ownership of the properties, just as in the BURP program.

While the banks and the federal government were creating this financial calamity, the social tensions between the longtime residents and the newcomers became unbearable. White youths threw stones at cars driven by black families who cruised the neighborhood looking for homes to buy. Black youths mugged elderly residents along Blue Hill Avenue. Arsonists set synagogues on fire. On June 27, 1969, when Rabbi Gerald Zelermyer answered a knock at the door of his home on Glenhill Road, he found two young black men standing on his front steps. They handed him a note demanding that he "lead the Jewish racists out of Mattapan," then threw acid in his face and ran away.

"It was a horrible thing those banks did," recalled the former activist, attorney, and future judge Lawrence Shubow. "To take two populations and pitch them against each other . . . two populations at their most sensitive and naked edges being rubbed together. . . . They made it impossible to have an integrated community." Residents didn't just blame the banks. They also blamed the city and the larger Jewish community. "The powers that be ignored us," said Murray Reiser, a lawyer for the B'nai B'rith's Anti-Defamation League.[21]

Mayor White, who was running for governor at the time, later admitted, "I didn't know the neighborhood was dying. I wouldn't have let that happen." But then he tried to shift some of the blame to the victims. "The Jewish community was not making noise. Such swift change and they were not making noise. I missed this completely like you would a child off to the side in a large family."[22]

If Boston was a large family, it was one whose composition soon changed dramatically. Within five years, Levine and Harmon wrote, almost all of Mattapan's 40,000 Jewish residents were gone. It was bad enough that B-BURG had driven these original families out of their neighborhood. It was even worse that the program swindled the new families it had lured in. By 1974, half of them had lost their homes through foreclosure.[23] Many of those homes fell into disrepair, were abandoned, and torn down, leaving the once stable, middle-class neighborhood pockmarked with vacant lots. "We didn't plan to move here and have it become a slum or a ghetto," said Willie Mae Allen, president of the Mattapan Civic Improvement Association. "We've put everything we've got into our homes." B-BURG created such a scandal that a U.S. Senate subcommittee came to Boston and held hearings to investigate what went wrong—and concluded that an attempt to promote minority home ownership had turned into a "ghetto enlargement" program instead.[24]

Kay Gibbs, a housing activist and someone who served as an aide to several of the leading public officials in the city and state, later summed up what happened. "A common misunderstanding about Roxbury is that it has been a slum ever since the whites moved out. In fact, Roxbury boasted a sizable middle-class black community—sizable, that is, until the federal government moved into town. First there was HUD Urban Renewal. Then BURP. And then came B-BURG. Roxbury was under assault by acronyms."[25]

If the black community felt like it was under assault, other neighborhoods felt ignored. "Kevin White governed Boston for [his first] three years largely as a means to boost his gubernatorial prospects," wrote the *Boston Globe* reporter Chris Wallace at the time. But after losing that race in 1970, White "was forced to return to an administration he never planned to complete." Even Barney Frank, who left the administration in January 1971, had to admit, "The city is relatively better off for having had White as mayor than somebody else, but it is not that much better off in absolute terms."[26]

Despite the fact that the city was not much better off and that the neighborhoods felt under assault or ignored, White won reelection on November 2, 1971, in a rematch with Louise Day Hicks, this time by 110,000 votes to 70,000. Once again, though, the results seemed less a vote of confidence in what the incumbent had done than a rejection of what the challenger might do.

CHAPTER 10

A New Threat from
Newcomers — Gentrification

JOHN HYNES HAD THE VISION TO EMBRACE URBAN RENEWAL.
John Collins had the administrative skill to implement it. Kevin White allowed it to run its course. By this time, residents had gained the confidence
and skills that enabled them to spar with the city and negotiate with the
Boston Redevelopment Authority (BRA) planners in order to make urban
renewal work better. But now they found themselves faced with a new
threat — gentrification, which hit one of Boston's most diverse and contentious neighborhoods particularly hard.

Today's SOUTH END *was created in a mid-nineteenth-century attempt at
urban renewal. Built on "made land" in what had been Boston's South Bay,
the area was developed into one of brick bow-front houses on small squares
crossed by broad boulevards and built to try to keep the middle and upper-
middle classes of the era from fleeing the city before the waves of arriving immigrants. But the "New South End" (the original one was located in today's
downtown) quickly lost the competition for that demographic to the even newer
Back Bay.*

*After its first inhabitants, in the words of the novelist William Dean Howells,
"discovered too late that the South End was not the thing," the new row houses
were carved up into small apartments and rooming houses to shelter those immigrants after all. This went on for the next hundred yeas. By 1960, the South End
was home to a mostly poor and working-class population of just under 35,000*

residents from more than 40 ethnic and racial groups, a quarter of whom were African Americans. It was also home to more lodging houses and more bars than any other neighborhood in the city.[1]

"The South End was a point of entry for people into Boston, and many of them left as soon as they could," explained lifelong resident Clare Hayes some years later. "A lot of the buildings were owned by absentee landlords, who were pulling money out of the houses and not putting any back in."[2]

Like other neighborhoods, the South End wasn't chosen for urban renewal just because of its run-down condition, but also because of its close-to-downtown location and lack of political clout. "It was not exactly a hotbed of voters," recalled Clare's husband, Chris, who lived his whole life on West Canton Street. Chris was one of seven children born to Irish immigrant parents "who were community activists long before it was fashionable," and he followed their example. After serving in the Army, returning home to start a family, and going to work as a truck driver for the Hood Milk Company, he became a volunteer at Lincoln House, where Mel King was a youth worker. "I drove the bus that took the kids and their parents on day trips to Nantasket Beach and Whalom Park. While I was up front, Mel was in the back, organizing the parents."[3]

The South End was better prepared to deal with urban renewal than most neighborhoods because, years earlier, the various settlement houses that had since joined to form the United South End Settlements (USES) had helped form dozens of small neighborhood groups and block organizations. In 1961, representatives of more than two dozen groups sent delegates to the new South End Urban Renewal Planning Committee (SEURC), which was supposed to respond to the city's proposal.[4]

In April 1962, the BRA presented three separate "sketch plans" to the SEURC for its consideration. All three called for building new schools, streets and sidewalks, and housing. But they differed in how much of the existing housing stock should be demolished, proposing 15, 20, and 30 percent, respectively. One resident, Richie Hall, later called it "Ed Logue's 'Goldilocks strategy.' It was supposed to give us the chance to pick the one we thought was 'just right.'"[5]

But the committee didn't think any were just right for two very good reasons. First, all three called for demolishing a strip of buildings along Shawmut Avenue to create a "green belt" running the length of the neighborhood.[6] Although this would have provided some badly needed open space, it would also have split the neighborhood in two—one half slated to have "low-income housing projects for families and the elderly" and the other to become a more upscale residential area and the location for new "community facilities."[7] And second, because all three sketch plans called for building 2,500 units of public housing, all of it south of Massachusetts Avenue, thus further separating the "haves" from the "have-nots."[8]

Val Hyman described residents' reactions to the plans and its growing understanding of the Boston Redevelopment Authority. "We were really pissed. We thought the BRA was out to destroy our neighborhood. It wasn't until later that we realized that wasn't the real problem—the real problem was that the BRA just didn't know what the hell it was doing."[9]

After sending the three-in-one plan around to the various individual neighborhood groups for their comments, the SEURC rejected it. "The committee was absolutely shocked at the first plan," recalled David Sprogis, one of its members, "and when we told that to Ed Logue at a meeting, he made this grand gesture of tearing the plan down from the wall, and saying 'All right. We're going to start all over.'"[10]

Sprogis and his wife Doe were not lifelong South End residents but were part of the first trickle of newcomers who back then were described—and sometimes described themselves—as "urban pioneers." While the BRA was starting all over and developing another plan, this trickle became a stream.

Unlike the poor immigrants who had been drawn to the South End a hundred years earlier in search of any kind of shelter, this new wave of newcomers was made up of middle-class professionals, including a sizable number of homosexuals, from the suburbs or other parts of the country drawn to the New Boston. They were drawn to this particular neighborhood by its proximity to downtown, its diversity, its acceptance of various lifestyles, and the prospect of buying a rundown row house for a song and then restoring it to its intended former glory. In spring 1964, the *Boston Globe* ran a series of articles titled "South End Begins to Stir," which described the arrival of these newcomers with headlines that read, "Discriminating People Moving In," and "South End Destined for New Splendor."[11]

Some longtime residents resented these newcomers and saw them as pretentious and condescending. But others, including Chris Hayes, welcomed them. "For one thing, these new people gave people who had grown up here a chance to sell their houses and move out to the suburbs themselves. For another, most of that first wave of newcomers worked hard. They joined neighborhood organizations and sent their kids to the neighborhood schools."[12]

That's what Herb and Ann Hershfang did. Both had grown up else-where and come to Boston to attend college, Herb at Harvard and Ann at Wellesley. They bought a boarded-up townhouse in the South End, Herb explained, not just for its low price and architectural charm, "but because it offered the chance to create a neighborhood we hoped for along the racial, ethnic and economic lines that we believed would better serve society." Like many newcomers to the neighborhood, their idealism would be tested often, and, in the Hershfang's case, early. "Three days after we moved in, our house was broken into," Herb recalled. "The robbers had stolen the TV, the Victrola, and the three suits that I owned. And when the police got there, they said to Ann 'What do you expect—living in this neighborhood?'"[13]

"There were high negatives—crime, drugs, prostitution, and trash," Ann recalled. "But there were also high positives—the energy, working with neighbors, getting to know people you wouldn't have known otherwise. I consider myself to have been very brave. After the break-in the first week we were living here, I was terrified for years, basically. I didn't feel comfortable until after I had my children, and I started pushing them around in a baby carriage and people didn't bother me."[14]

In April 1964, as the neighborhood continued to undergo this demo-graphic shift, the BRA released its second plan for the South End. Called "The Concept," it relinquished the notion of creating a green belt and backed off the proposal to so drastically divide the neighborhood into areas of "haves" and "have-nots." But the plan was still very ambitious. At just over 600 acres, it was the largest urban renewal plan in the country, and it called for demolishing over 5,000 units of housing and displacing 3,500 "house-holds." Just over half of these households were made up of single people, mostly white men, who lived in the many rooming houses. Just under half were made up of families, most of them with low incomes and most of them African American, who rented flats in tenements or townhouses.

The plan reduced the number of proposed new public housing units to 1,800 scattered throughout the neighborhood, and called for building 2,500 new units of private housing. It called for renovating more than 3,000 of the existing row houses by making low-interest loans available to their owners. Like the first plan, it also called for building new community facil-ities, schools, playgrounds, streets, and sidewalks.[15]

After a year of review by the various neighborhood and block organi-zations, the SEURC endorsed the plan and it received strong support at a public hearing at the Mackey School on August 23, 1965. "I can't say there was a groundswell of people against it," recalled Gene Boehne, whose job at USES was to go around and explain the plan to residents. "Everybody knew about the West End, and they would ask me about that. And I would tell them that it wasn't going to be like that—that what happened in the West End was wrong." [16]

With the community apparently behind the plan, it was quickly approved by the BRA, the city council, and the state and federal government. But in spring 1966, the plan ran into opposition from a group that had recently been formed by Mel King and others. This group, called the Community Assembly for a United South End (CAUSE), criticized the plan for promoting the interests of homeowners (many of them white, middle class, and newcomers), at the expense of tenants (most of them black and poor or working class). CAUSE charged that if low-income residents were relocated to make way for all the construction and renovation, they would never be able to afford to return to the South End, and demanded that all relocation stop until an additional 7,000 low-income housing units were built within the neighborhood. CAUSE also demanded that more tenants be named to the South End Urban Renewal Committee.

A split developed in the neighborhood between the militants of CAUSE, who opposed the plan, and the moderates of the SEURC and the South End Federation of Citizens Organization (SEFCO), a homeowners group, who supported it. CAUSE held a series of demonstrations to dramatize its demands. At one, on July 5, 1967, some 30 CAUSE members picketed in front of the BRA's South End site office on Warren Avenue. During the protest, Mel King injected a racially charged element into the debate when he declared, "The B.R.A. means Blacks Running Again."

On January 15, 1968, SEFCO responded by holding its own demonstration at City Hall to protest an attempt by Boston city councilor Tom Atkins, who was chairman of the council's urban renewal committee, to suspend the South End plan. SEFCO issued a statement criticizing CAUSE for "attempting to isolate black members of our community as well as provoking added tensions between tenants and landlords and between the city and its citizens." [17]

"CAUSE had some valid points," Clare Hayes later admitted, but the ideological split resulted in what she described as "a sad schism between activists, one that was nourished, that didn't allow for compromise, and that lasted for years." [18]

Initially, the militants seemed to gain the upper hand. On January 25, 1968, Hale Champion, Ed Logue's successor as director of BRA, told a standing-room-only crowd of 700 people at the Mackey School that the agency would "consider the right of the people of this area to continue to live here after renewal a fundamental obligation of a good redevelopment project." But that wasn't good enough for CAUSE. The group next called for the current plan to be scrapped completely and for the SEURC to be replaced by an urban renewal committee elected by residents. To dramatize these latest demands, CAUSE members held a series of "occupations" of the BRA South End site office on Warren Avenue. After taking over the office on April 25, 1968, the group refused to speak with Mayor White or Champion when the two men arrived at the front door, or to even let them into the building.[19] The next day, CAUSE staged another demonstration, and this one captured the attention of the whole city.

At 7 a.m. on the cold and drizzly Friday morning of April 26, 1968, some 40 CAUSE members led by Mel King set up a picket line around a parking lot on the corner of Columbus Avenue and Dartmouth Street. The parking lot was on a parcel of otherwise vacant land that had once been the site of homes in which 100 poor and working-class families had lived. Under the current South End plan, the parcel was to become the site for new market-rate housing and a parking garage.

The picket line stopped cars from entering the lot. The protesters handed flyers to the drivers, which read: "Dear Parker. This paper is an attempt to tell you why this parking lot has been closed by CAUSE. It is simple, South End people want to live in decent homes at reasonable rent. No housing has been built. People have been moved, of course. Housing should be built on this land, so your cars will no longer park here."[20]

Not all the parkers took kindly to being turned away. One tried to drive his van through the demonstrators. In the melee that followed, King was knocked to the ground and the van's windshield was smashed. The disturbance quickly attracted a crowd of more than 1,000 onlookers. When police arrived, they arrested King and 22 of the other protesters.[21] They were taken to court, arraigned, and released on bail or personal recognizance that afternoon.

On Saturday morning, though, the demonstrators were back picketing at the parking lot. Now they were joined by several hundred supporters — white, black, and Hispanic; male and female, young and old. Once again, police arrived. But before they could make more arrests, the police received word from the parking lot owner, who was also Boston's fire commissioner, that the protesters "can be my guests for the weekend."[22] What followed was one of the longest and most festive demonstrations the New Boston had yet experienced.

As the day wore on, the crowd occupying the parking lot swelled to several thousand. The demonstrators erected signs that read, "People, Not Cars" and "This Is a Place Where Homes Should Be Built."[23] To feed all the demonstrators, local churches sent over potato salad and fruit salad. The Boston Celtics star Bill Russell, who owned a share of a South End restaurant at the time, sent over soul food. To entertain themselves, some of the demonstrators had brought musical instruments. As day turned into evening, the protest turned into "an impromptu urban fair" with "rhythms and tones of bongo drums and saxophones" filling the air. At the end of the evening, having decided to keep the occupation going, many of the demonstrators spread out sleeping bags on the pavement. Only men were allowed to spend the night, according to a *Boston Globe* article, "to minimize the possibility for scandal."[24]

The demonstration was the lead story on local television news that night, and it was the front-page story in the Sunday newspapers the next morning, when the demonstrators got even more creative. To dramatize the need for affordable housing in Boston, they built a dozen plywood shacks and set up even more tents. That led to the site being christened "Tent City."

The demonstration continued Sunday night and through the next morning. But on Monday afternoon a large contingent of Boston police arrived and announced that they had orders to clear the site and arrest anyone who did not leave. CAUSE members huddled. Then a spokesman asked everyone to leave, explaining, "We're not prepared to carry on further demonstrations at this time that could be guaranteed to be peaceful."[25] Many of the demonstrators were disappointed at the decision. But in the three-plus days it lasted, the Tent City protest not only captured the attention of the whole city, but also produced a number of results — immediate, intermediate, and long-term.

The immediate results came a few days later, when BRA director Champion announced a temporary halt to all demolition in the South End urban renewal area and the creation of what was described as a "crash" program to build new housing that would allow almost 900 low-income families to remain in the neighborhood.

The intermediate results began a few weeks after that, when the city council voted for a proposal to create an elected urban renewal committee

Tent City demonstration near Copley Square in April 1968. Photo by Bill Brett/Globe Staff.

to replace the current one. Reluctantly, Mayor White agreed. But the debate over how the committee should be elected, its makeup, and its powers dragged on for more than a year.

CAUSE and other militants argued that since tenants made up a majority of the residents in the South End, they should hold a majority of the seats on the new committee. They also argued that the committee should have veto power over all aspects of the urban renewal plan. SEFCO and other moderates opposed making any distinctions between tenants and homeowners on the committee and were content for it to continue to play an advisory role. With the two sides unable to agree, the South End was treated to the spectacle of two elections being held for one urban renewal committee in the summer of 1969.

From June 28 to July 3, 1969, an election for what was called the People's Elected Urban Renewal Committee (PEURC) was held in local churches and social service agencies. All South End residents aged sixteen and older were eligible to vote and just over 3,000 did, electing 35 tenants and 7 homeowners. PEURC's first action was to send out letters to all South End residents that urged them not to take part in the "official" election a month later.[26]

From July 26 to July 28, 1969, that election for the South End Project Action Committee (SEPAC) was held in local schools and public housing developments. Residents age twenty or older were eligible to vote, and just over 2,000 did, electing 18 homeowners and 17 tenants.[27] Despite grumbling from the militants, SEPAC became the official urban renewal committee recognized by the city and the BRA as representing the wishes of the neighborhood.

The South End urban renewal plan began to be implemented. It included construction of a new school, a community center, a branch library, parks and playgrounds, and what Dick Garver, a BRA official, later called a "monumental investment" in new streets, sidewalks, street lights, and water and sewer lines that "served as a platform to attract new, middle-class homeowners."[28] Those new homeowners took advantage of low-interest loans to renovate some 4,000 units of existing housing, turning thousands of brick row houses from the run-down tenements and rooming houses they had become back into the stately single-family homes that they had originally been. The most controversial element of the project was and would continue to be over the 2,700 new units of housing that were supposed to be built—and for whom they were to be built.

While moderates controlled SEPAC, the controversy simmered. But in 1973, when militants won a majority of seats on the committee, it came to a boil. On November 28, 1973, the newly reconstituted SEPAC voted for a resolution sponsored by tenant activist Doug Zook calling for 75 percent of the new units to be "affordable" (25 percent for low-income residents and 50 percent for those with moderate incomes), and only 25 percent to be market-rate.[29] The so-called Zook Resolution sparked an outcry from a third constituency made up of more recently arrived—and more conservative—residents.

David Parker, a young carpenter, was one of them. He and his wife, a schoolteacher, had moved to the South End three years earlier, after buying a townhouse that they were renovating themselves. "I didn't do it to make a political statement," he recalled. "I bought it because I had no cash." Getting involved in what he called various "crime and grime" campaigns convinced Parker that the neighborhood had quite enough affordable housing. "Anthony Lukas came and talked to me when he was writing *Common Ground*," recalled Parker. "I took out a map of the South End, and every place they had built subsidized housing, I put a red dot. It looked like the neighborhood had measles. Then I asked Lukas 'Don't you think that's wrong?' And he said 'No.'"[30]

But Parker and Herbert Zeller, an architect, did think it was wrong, so they formed a new neighborhood-wide group called the Committee of Citizens for a Balanced South End. The "Balance Committee" called for a different formula for all new housing, under which only 50 percent would be affordable and 50 percent market-rate. According to Parker, when the amendment was put in front of SEPAC, it was "voted down in a minute, and we were absolutely assaulted as racist for proposing it."[31]

Undeterred, the Balance Committee called for an "immediate moratorium" on building any more new low-income housing in the South End on December 11, 1973, and mounted a campaign for it. This campaign didn't rely on protests and demonstrations, but on lawsuits and lengthy appeals of government decisions, which, although less colorful, seemed to be just as effective. In April 1975, when the BRA announced it would no longer give priority to building affordable housing in the South End, it was an apparent victory for the South End's neoconservatives.[32] But the victory proved to come too late, according to Parker, "because the housing wars ended at the end of the 1970s, when the federal money dried up."[33]

Long term, it was hard to describe the completed South End urban renewal project as either a "success" or a "failure." Unlike in the New York Streets, the West End, and tiny Barry's Corner, where whole neighborhoods had been demolished, most of the buildings in the South End had been saved. But unlike in Charlestown, where most of the residents remained for some time afterward, the population of the South End changed dramatically almost immediately as a result of its "renewal."

Between 1960 and 1980, approximately 25,000 residents were displaced. Most were poor and working class; many were children or the elderly; many were African American. During that same period, an estimated 19,000 new residents moved in. Most were middle class; many were adults; many were white.[34] If buildings make a neighborhood, it can be said that the South End was preserved. But if people make a neighborhood, an argument can be made that it was replaced.

Some twenty urban renewal projects were eventually completed in Boston. After the first two, almost all of them turned out much better than they would have otherwise, thanks to the protests and participation by the residents of those neighborhoods. As a result, urban renewal clearly improved the physical side of the New Boston. But it may have made an even bigger contribution to the human side by sparking an activism in the New Boston that quickly spread into so many other areas of city life.

"The New York Streets and the West End were the catalysts for folks in other parts of the city to demand urban renewal committees and develop CDCs [community development corporations]," Mel King maintained. "People understood they could take on City Hall and the BRA and create change. A successful coalition got created made up of people in different neighborhoods, of community organizations, and of some of the newcomers. One part of the success came because we were righteous, and one part came because we had the numbers. But the righteousness is what allowed us to get the numbers."[35]

CHAPTER 11

———◄◦►———

Do-It-Yourself Community
Development

AFTER SPENDING SO MUCH TIME AND ENERGY IMPROVING
the urban renewal plans drawn up by professionals, activists in the New
Boston gradually came to the conclusion they could do a better job themselves. Aided and abetted by those advocacy planners who had appeared on
the scene in the early 1960s, they took advantage of a new kind of organization to do just that.

Community development corporations (CDCs) are nonprofit, neighborhood-based organizations funded by both public sources and private
investors. They were originally created to build and renovate housing but
have gotten involved in economic development, job training, and social
services as well. The first CDC in the country was the Bedford-Stuyvesant
Restoration Corporation in Brooklyn in 1967.[1] The first CDCs in Boston
were formed soon after in Chinatown and in the Madison Park area of
Roxbury.

But the first CDC in Boston to actually get something built was formed by
an unlikely group in the South End made up primarily of recently arrived
residents from Puerto Rico. Its story is more fully told by Mario Luis Small
in *Villa Victoria: The Transformation of Social Capital in a Boston Barrio.*

In the early 1960s, Boston was home to only about 6,000 Hispanic Americans. Most of them were Puerto Ricans, and many of them had come to
New England to perform seasonal work in rural areas; then, rather than

return home where jobs were scarce, they had moved into the region's largest city to look for work.[2] Many of these new residents gravitated to the
South End because of its supply of rooming houses and still-cheap apartments in tenements and brownstones. Once they got themselves somewhat
settled, they were generally more interested in such immediate concerns as
keeping a roof over their heads and putting food on the table than in more
long-term and abstract concerns like community activism.

But that began to change in 1963 with the arrival of Reverend William
Dwyer as pastor of St. Stephen's Episcopal Church on Shawmut Avenue. A
New Jersey native who had learned Spanish at Princeton and activism in
his first parish on New York City's Lower East Side, Dwyer found a congre-
gation made up of "a few old Yankees, a handful of blacks, a small group
of middle-class Cubans, who were political refugees, but mostly of poor
and working-class Puerto Ricans, who were economic refugees. In the beginning, as we helped them to organize," he reflected. "We just looked for
some small victories."[3]

One of those small victories came after a rent strike against a West Newton Street landlord succeeded in getting him to "seal leaky faucets, patch up
walls, refurbish doors, and unclog toilets."[4] Another came after a campaign
to clean up a vacant lot on West Brookline Street, which included a demonstration by residents who held a mock funeral and carried a coffin with a
sign on it that read, "Death to the Junkyard!"

"It was an exciting time," recalled one of those demonstrators, Jovita
Fontanez, a single mother with two small children. Fontanez had come to
Boston ten years earlier and quickly became involved in her new neighborhood. "There were all kinds of things brewing. It was hard *not* to be
involved, even though I had little kids. I think my kids knew how to say
'meeting' before they learned to say 'mama.'"[5]

In the spring and summer of 1967, fortified by their small victories, the
residents took on a much bigger campaign. The South End urban renewal
plan had identified the area in which most of them lived as Parcel 19. The
plan called for dislocating all the residents, demolishing the four-story row
houses in which they lived, and building new, market-rate housing.[6] With
help from Reverend Dwyer, seminarian Richard Lampert, and a few longtime residents, the newer residents began a door-to-door campaign to organize against that part of the plan.

One of those longtime residents was Helen Morton, a veteran social
activist and the great-great-granddaughter of a Massachusetts governor.
Morton later described her first impressions of her new neighbors. "The

men were always working out of doors in any empty lot on their cars, and . . . their women folk were shut up indoors, maybe rather wistfully looking out of a window." While she was not personally a "devotee of 'Women's Lib,'" Morton said, she derived "some satisfaction [in] liberating the housebound women" as a result of the campaign.[7]

One of the women to emerge as a leader was Dona Paula Oyola, a widowed mother of five who had arrived in the South End in 1961. Despite the fact that she had left school after the second grade to help out on her family's farm in Puerto Rico, Lampert later described Oyola as the "godmother" of the community and "like E. F. Hutton in that old television commercial—when she stood up at meetings and spoke, people listened."[8]

Oyola and the other residents came up with a slogan for their campaign—"No nos mudaremos de la Parcela 19!" (We shall not be moved from Parcel 19!)—and had it printed on badges, which they wore every day. They also drafted a document they called a "Statement of Hope" that declared their opposition to the proposal to build market-rate housing and called for building "housing . . . that we can truly afford" instead.[9]

They took their biggest step on October 27, 1967, when more than 400 residents turned out for a meeting at the South End Little City Hall and voted to form a community development corporation, which they called the Emergency Tenants Coalition. Over the next few years, ETC's membership would grow to more than 1,500 members, approximately 1,000 of them Spanish-speaking.[10]

But forming a CDC was one thing. Coming up with a plan and getting it implemented was quite another. Fortunately for ETC and the other CDCs that followed, Urban Planning Aid had been created a few years earlier and was there to provide the technical assistance they needed. UPA connected ETC with John Sharratt, a young architect who, he later recalled, "was getting tired of designing dormitories for fancy prep schools and wanted to help people solve problems instead."[11] By this time, ETC had hired Israel Feliciano, a young, charismatic army veteran from Chicago, to be its first executive director. Feliciano insisted that Sharratt go with him to Puerto Rico to see the type of neighborhood the residents wanted to build in the South End.

"We couldn't go to San Juan or the other big cities," Sharratt explained, "because Israel said they were 'too American.' We went to the small towns instead. We'd go into the village square, and I'd take notes and measurements, and the plan we came up with reflected those plazas, with little streets and rows of townhouses."[12] It called for renovating the existing brick row houses on Parcel 19, creating a central plaza like those in the Puerto Rican villages, and surrounding it with different kinds of housing that would be affordable to the people who already lived in the neighborhood.[13]

Israel Feliciano proved to be extremely adept at gathering support for the plan, taking it around to every church, community organization, or public official imaginable. "Israel could charm anybody," Sharratt recalled, "old ladies, young blacks, white bureaucrats, gang members. He even went to the real estate investors, and to the 'New South Enders.'"[14] Jorge Hernandez, who would later succeed Feliciano, described those days as like something out of the "the wild, wild West," and recalled hearing stories of angry residents laying their guns on the table before they began meetings.[15]

In dealing with city hall, Feliciano used both the "carrot" of increased voter registration and turnout at the polls and the "stick" of protest demonstrations to sell the plan. "ETC learned early to play the political game," recalled Andy Olins, who by this time was Mayor White's housing advisor, "and they played it well."[16]

ETC played it so well that, on December 11, 1969, at a meeting at St. Stephen's Church, the Boston Redevelopment Authority designated the group to be the developer of Parcel 19. Asked afterward how such a decision had come to pass, the new BRA director John Warner answered, "I think we've had too much arguing with neighborhood groups. When we all sat down together, we found we had the same objectives."[17]

ETC rebuilt the neighborhood in stages. First, it renovated the row houses. Then, it built a mid-rise building and a high-rise building for the elderly. Then it built some 200 townhouses, all painted in pastel, Caribbean colors, around a central plaza. There were setbacks along the way. At one point, Feliciano disappeared, allegedly with some of the group's funds. But ETC persevered. Recognizing it now had less need for a community organizer than for a reliable administrator, it hired first Liz Cuadrado and then Jorge Hernandez to run the growing organization, and it was able to continue its progress.

The new community that ETC built came to be called Villa Victoria ("Victory Village"). Today it includes more than 800 units of affordable housing, and has its own childcare center, credit union, closed-circuit television network, and arts center. Residents would later describe the community as "a new barrio thousands of miles from the Island of Enchantment." That new barrio has attracted visitors not only from the Caribbean but from all over the world, who have come to see how a small group of immigrants—with a little help from some friends—built a new home for themselves in the New Boston.

While this small group of new residents was able to build its own community in the South End, a small group of longtime residents was able to do something similar on Mission Hill. But to do so, it had to persuade an even more formidable institution than city hall—Harvard University—to give it the chance.

MISSION HILL *is that part of Roxbury squeezed between the Fenway and Jamaica Plain neighborhoods and the adjacent town of Brookline. Originally an area of Yankee estates and small farms, Mission Hill began to attract a large number of German immigrants just after the Civil War who came to work in the local breweries that were located along Stony Brook. Those immigrants built the imposing Mission Church from Roxbury puddingstone quarried in the neighborhood. But they eventually ceded the hill and surrounding flatland to Irish immigrants, who were joined just after World War II by African Americans, most of whom lived in the two public housing developments built at that time on the flanks of the hill.*

By 1960, Mission Hill was a predominantly working-class neighborhood of 18,000 residents, 80 percent of whom were white and 20 percent nonwhite. Many of these residents worked in the hospitals that were located on or around the hill or in the adjacent Longwood Medical area. Many of these hospitals were affiliated with Harvard University. Over the years, a love/hate relationship developed between residents and Harvard. While they appreciated the jobs generated by the university, residents resented it when Harvard-related institutions regularly gobbled up residential property in what appeared to be an insatiable need to expand.

As the protest-filled 1960s proceeded, one of the earliest large demonstrations took place on December 17, 1964, when 3,000 Mission Hill residents—men, women, children—gathered on Boston Common and marched on the State House to protest a plan to demolish some 30 homes in their neighborhood so that the Harvard-affiliated Massachusetts Mental Health Center could build a new facility there. The marchers were led by the Reverend Vincent Kelly, the pastor of Mission Church, who had earlier declared, "We are not going to take this lying down. People in this area are living under some form of terror. If urban renewal just drives people out of the city, it's a horrible failure." His curate, Reverend Edward McDonough, added, "The city planners can build beautiful buildings, but they can't build cohesive neighborhoods."[18]

With those two priests and local elected officials leading the way, residents—who were asked to refrain from chanting or singing—marched four abreast into and through the state capitol "like an army of silent soldiers . . . through every floor of the building." A veteran State House observer called it "the most impressive demonstration ever conducted beneath the Golden Dome."[19] It was also one of the most effective, since it persuaded the Massachusetts legislature to withhold its approval and kept the project from going forward.

But institutions like Harvard don't stop, they only wait. Four years later, after secretly buying up some 20 acres of property on the "flat" of Mission Hill north of Huntington Avenue, the university announced a much bigger expansion plan. It called for building a 900-bed hospital that would combine seven teaching hospitals into an "Affiliated Hospitals Complex" composed of three, connected, twenty-three-story buildings.

A hospital newsletter breathlessly described it as "more than a dream . . . more than we ever hoped . . . the Free World's Foremost Teaching Hospital."[20] But the plan was more of a nightmare for the 182 families who received eviction notices in March 1969, because their homes would be demolished to make way for the giant new hospital.

Initially, most of those families didn't see any other option but to pack up and leave. But that changed after a trio of Harvard students found their way to Mission Hill from Cambridge. The three had been among the 10,000 students, faculty, and staff who had gone on strike in the aftermath of the takeover of University Hall by antiwar protesters, which had resulted in a list of demands being presented to school officials. Although most of the demands had to do with the school's relationship with the U.S. military, one stated that "no black workers housing be destroyed at the site of future expansion of the Harvard Affiliated Hospitals in the Mission Hill section of Boston."[21] The three Harvard students had decided to try to make sure that demand was met.

One of the three, Doug Levinson, was a serious young man who had grown up in Boston suburbs. "All of us were trying to do find openings in the university to do something constructive instead of just making some big political statements," he recalled. The other two were Jeanne Neville, an intense Radcliffe student, and Hayden Duggan, described by Levinson as the most "laid back" of the three. When they got to Mission Hill, they began to knock on doors and found that the neighborhood was more diverse than they had imagined. They also found that, with a little encouragement, residents might be willing to fight to hang onto their homes.[22]

One of the first doors the students knocked on belonged to Bob and Theresa Parks, who lived with their four young children in a house on Francis Street. "They asked Bob what he planned to do," Theresa remembered years later, "and he was kind of like 'If Harvard owns the property, they can do what they want.' Remember, this was back when everybody still respected authority. But then they asked me, and I told them, 'I'm going to call a meeting and get everybody together.' And they said, 'Oh, you're a community activist.' And I said I didn't know what a community activist was, but that's what I was going to do." [23]

With "the Harvard kids," as she called them, her sister Anna Adams, and neighbor Betty Powers, Theresa spent the next few months knocking on every door in the neighborhood trying to persuade residents to fight their eviction. At first, many were reluctant. "They'd say 'Are you whacked out?'" Theresa recalled. "Harvard is the most powerful institution in the world. You can't fight it.'" [24]

Eventually however, a small group of residents began to meet and discuss how to proceed. Initially, they met in one another's homes. When word of the secret meetings got out, Harvard's property manager threatened residents who hosted them with immediate eviction, so they began to meet at places like the Mission Church rectory instead.

The group decided to call itself the Roxbury Tenants of Harvard, and it was able to get most of the residents to sign a petition saying that they wouldn't leave their homes, and that Harvard should find another place for its new hospital. RTH tried to meet with university officials to discuss the proposed plan. When they refused, the group began to hold demonstrations outside university buildings. One of their protests even made it onto the nightly local television news.

The demonstrations and bad publicity persuaded Harvard officials to meet with RTH, and shortly afterward the university announced a new plan. It called for construction of a smaller, 680-bed hospital to include just three of the university's teaching hospitals, which meant "only" 49 families would lose their homes. The new plan also called for building more than 1,000 units of housing on the nearby site of a former convent, and, although the housing was primarily intended for hospital employees, Harvard said it would be made available to any residents displaced by construction of the new hospital.

This second plan was a big improvement over the first one. But now that it had gotten organized, RTH decided that it wanted more say in what got built in its own neighborhood. Just as ETC had done, RTH contacted Urban Planning Aid and was connected with the architect John Sharratt. After meeting with the group, Sharratt had two reactions. "My first was that it wasn't fair what Harvard was doing to these people. But my second was that Harvard's power could be used for them to build something really special here."[25] With help from Sharratt, the "Harvard kids," and a newly formed group of students, staff, and faculty called the Harvard-Radcliffe New University Conference Committee on Harvard Expansion & Community Relations, RTH put out two reports to try to secure a role in building something special.

The first report documented Harvard's failings as a landlord, and listed scores of housing and building code violations in the Harvard-owned properties in which the residents now found themselves living. Harvard initially ignored the report. But after a demonstration outside Harvard Medical School on December 17, 1969, in which residents were joined by more than 100 Harvard students, faculty, and staff, the university agreed to make the repairs, freeze rents, and halt any evictions until the proposed new housing was built.[26]

The second report was an eighty-six-page document titled "The Relationship of Harvard Medical School and Affiliated Institutions to the Neighboring Community: Its Problems and a Solution." Despite its prosaic title, the report's soaring prose read like a "Declaration of Inter-Dependence Between Town and Gown."

The report began by describing Mission Hill as "a rare working multiethnic group composed of white, black and Spanish-speaking residents [who desire] a place where our children can grow up and where we can grow old with safety and independence." It continued by acknowledging that Harvard had made the area "the medical capital of the world," but that many of its facilities were now "old and overcrowded" and that the university needed "new research facilities to attract the bright scientists who would otherwise go elsewhere." Then it argued that while "every other university has turned its back on its responsibility to its neighbors, Harvard has the opportunity to set a precedent of cooperation." The report concluded by declaring Harvard could seize that opportunity by making RTH a partner in rebuilding the neighborhood.

Six weeks after receiving the report, Harvard agreed to the proposed partnership with only "minor exceptions," according to Bob Parks. "We were shocked," recalled Levinson. "I mean, we had no leverage whatsoever.

But, after that, the agreement *became* our leverage. I'm sure, looking back, that Harvard must have decided it was easier and more cost effective to work with the community and avoid a big fight."[27]

The new partners came up with a new plan. It covered 13 acres, included the scaled-down hospital, and called for preserving and renovating almost 300 units in the existing wood-frame and brick buildings. It also called for building another 500 units of new housing in high-rise and mid-rise buildings and townhouses, almost all of which would be affordable to low-paid Harvard support employees and to the poor and working-class families of Mission Hill. In fact, it would be the largest single addition to Boston's low-income housing stock in more than a decade.[28] Best of all, from RTH's perspective, the plan would enable most residents to stay in their homes and all of them to stay in their neighborhood.

The new development was to be called Mission Park. It would be owned by Harvard but run by RTH. And just as RTH had predicted in the "Relationship Report," when the plan was announced it was hailed as landmark partnership between an institution and the neighborhood in which it was located and expanding.

Everything seemed to be going smoothly. But before the plan proceeded very far, one of the partners had a big surprise for the other. In August 1972, Harvard announced another plan that called for building what would be the largest, privately owned, power plant in the country across the street from the proposed new hospital. Called the Medical Area Total Energy Plant (MATEP), it was to use oil-fed, diesel generators to provide electricity, heat, and air conditioning to the new hospital, to other Harvard-affiliated hospitals, and to Mission Park.[29]

Harvard announced that MATEP would employ the latest technology to control emissions from its 300-foot smokestack. But the notion of building a power plant in the middle of such a densely packed residential/hospital area outraged residents of Mission Hill, the Fenway, Jamaica Plain, and the town of Brookline, as well as environmentalists throughout the Boston area. Everyone seemed to be against it—everyone, that is, but the Roxbury Tenants of Harvard.

RTH had decided not to oppose construction of the power plant after Harvard had convinced the group that the only way for that housing in Mission Park to be affordable would be if the power plant provided it with free electricity, heat, and air conditioning. "I don't think it was contrived," recalled Michael Lerner, who had recently become RTH's first executive director. "I saw the capital cost that it would save us to not have to build our own plant."

That was why, when the public hearing was held on the proposed plant and critics turned out by the scores to oppose it, RTH members turned out by the hundreds to support it. Many of those RTH members carried signs Lerner made for the occasion that showed cartoon drawings of Mission Park and the power plant. "I took a black magic marker and I drew this tunnel between them, and in big letters I wrote BRING POWER TO THE PEOPLE."[30]

With RTH's support, the plan to build the power plant was approved. "You've got to give Harvard credit," said Charlotte Ploss, a Mission Hill resident whose family had been thrown out of the West End when she was a girl, and who was one of the leaders of the NO-MATEP coalition. "Harvard took its toughest opponent and turned it into a lobbying arm of the university." RTH's support for the power plant ended up causing hard feelings among neighbors that lasted for a long time. Years later, Bob Parks defended the group's decision. "Giving 2,500 people a place to live seemed more important than a fight over a power plant."[31]

The power plant was eventually built, although lawsuits filed by opponents kept it from going on line until years later. The new hospital, which came to be called Brigham and Women's, was built, too. But so was Mission Park.

In 1977, the first building to open was named Flynn House after the RTH member Henry Flynn, whose motto was "Give 'em hell!"[32] But the next three buildings were named Levinson Tower, Neville House, and Duggan House after the three "Harvard kids" who had helped the Roxbury Tenants of Harvard to get organized. Hundreds of townhouses were also built, as was the Bob and Theresa Parks Community Center, which offered a group—that once had to meet in secret—a place where it could meet openly anytime it wanted.

Years later, Mission Park would be described as "an enigma—at once a symbol of the neighborhood's cohesiveness and its deepest, most bitter divisions [one that] depending on whom you talk to represents either the crowning victory of Mission Hill over Harvard expansion or the sellout of the neighborhood to the university and its medical affiliates."[33]

ETC and RTH are just two examples of the many CDCs that sprang up all over the New Boston. Much appreciated by residents, they were not always warmly welcomed by their elected officials. "The CDC movement caught the politicians unawares," John Sharratt said years later. "Kevin White in particular felt threatened by them. He didn't want anybody working for the people. After he saw what was going on with CDCs, he put neighborhood planners into the BRA site offices and the Little City Halls to try to co-opt the community development movement." [34]

For their part, CDCs appreciated all the help they got from those advocacy planning groups, but sometimes CDC members found themselves on a different page when it came to strategy decisions. According to Dan Richardson, a member of the Madison Park CDC, "some of the planners at Greater Boston Community Development would say 'You can't do that' when we wanted to demand more from the city, or investors, or development partners. But some of the people at Urban Planning Aid were even too radical for me. I came to realize that, for a lot of those people, we were a big experiment, an academic exercise. But at end of the day, they could go back home. This *was* our home—we couldn't leave. We had to do what made sense for us." [35]

Some two dozen CDCs would spring up in Boston over the next three decades. They not only helped residents rebuild their neighborhoods, but also helped many of them remain in the New Boston, when they otherwise would have been forced to leave.

CHAPTER 12

Public Housing on Trial

Residents who lived in public housing also struggled to remain in the New Boston. Even though they depended on government for the roof over their heads, public housing residents, too, joined the rising wave of activism and protest. Since its inception, government-supported public housing has always played a particularly important role in Boston, one documented by Lawrence J. Vale in his book *From the Puritans to the Projects: Public Housing and Public Neighbors.*

Boston was home to the first federal public housing development in the United States, the Mary Ellen McCormack development in South Boston, which opened in 1938. It was built and operated by the Boston Housing Authority (BHA) created three years earlier. Most of the city's subsequent public housing developments were built in two phases, federally supported units constructed between 1938 and 1942, and federally- and state-supported units between 1949 and 1954.[1]

During its first phase, most of the public housing built in Boston and in cities across the country went to defense workers during World War II and returning veterans afterward.[2] Many of these individuals and families were working class on their way to becoming middle class, and public housing was a temporary stop before they could own their homes. That changed with passage of the 1949 Housing Act, which required poorer families—including those displaced by urban renewal—be given priority for public housing. Coupled with funding cuts that led to a decline in maintenance, the act gradually transformed public housing into a place reserved primarily for the poor who had no place else to go.

By the mid-1960s, Boston had the largest per capita public housing program of any city in the country. Its 14,500 units of public housing were home to more than 45,000 residents.[3] Approximately 85 percent of those residents were white, but over the next few years, minorities—primarily African Americans—would make up an increasingly larger percentage of the population of public housing.[4] One thing all of these residents had in common was poverty. But although they might have been poor in body, they weren't poor in spirit, and a growing number of them began to organize and speak up.

Some of the first residents to do this lived in the Columbia Point development, a drab cluster of yellow-brick, high-rise buildings stuck on an isolated peninsula in Dorchester Bay that was also where the city's garbage dump was located. For years, residents had complained not just about the smell from the dump, but the danger from the scores of garbage trucks that daily sped up and down Mount Vernon Street, which ran through the middle of the development. In 1962, when one of those trucks ran over and killed a six-year-old girl, residents responded by demonstrating in that street every day, and they didn't stop until the city agreed to close the dump.

In 1963, the residents at the Bromley-Heath development in Jamaica Plain took their turn to protest. Tired of their children being forced to play in the busy streets around the development, 15 mothers—with 30 of their children in tow—marched into the downtown offices of the state housing board and demanded that tot lots and playgrounds be built within the development. In short order, they were.

More demonstrations by residents in other developments followed. One involved senior citizens who lived in Orchard Park in Roxbury, who marched on the State House to protest how poorly their development was managed. According to Lawrence Vale, public housing in Boston was so badly managed because, "to a degree unequaled elsewhere in the country, the Boston Housing Authority of the early 1960s was a public housing agency entirely operated by its Board."[5]

The five board members, it appeared, cared much more about the perks that came with the job than doing the job. Each board member had a private secretary and an office in the agency's downtown headquarters. The chairman had two secretaries and use of a chauffeured limousine. Massachusetts was one of only five states in which public housing board members received a stipend, and the one paid in Boston was five to ten times higher than any other city in the country. The BHA administrator was supposed to be responsible for day-to-day operations. But according to Vale, he had been "progressively stripped of power," and when he died in 1960, the board didn't even bother to name a replacement.[6]

"Public housing in Boston back then wasn't so much about housing as patronage. Jobs were given out by board members to people sponsored by politicians, and vacancies were divided up among them to fill," explained Doris Bunte years later. Born in New York City, Bunte had dropped out of high school, moved to Boston at age twenty, and earned her diploma at night school. She subsequently found herself, as a divorced mother of three, living in Orchard Park—the kind of place, she told a *Boston Globe* reporter, "Where, when you plug the tree in at Christmastime, all the lights go out."[7]

Public housing was not high on the list of priorities during the building of the New Boston. "John Collins was not very interested in public housing," maintained Barney Frank, who served as liaison to the BHA for the mayor's successor. "Collins's view was of the city, not of people. He was fundamentally very conservative. He did not want to make it easier for poor people. He wanted them to move out, wanted them to move away."[8]

In 1963, however, after the Boston Branch NAACP and the local chapter of Congress of Racial Equality brought complaints against the BHA for practicing racial segregation, Collins was forced to get involved. Without consulting the board, he named Ellis Ash as acting BHA administrator. Vale described it as a case where "an Irish Catholic mayor bravely—if half-heartedly—bucked three decades of precedent and installed a Yankee reformer in the BHA's midst."[9]

"Ash was a man before his time," according to Doris Bunte. "He thought residents should have a say in all aspects of public housing, and that, if they did, they'd feel like they had some control over their destiny." Under Ash, according to Vale, the BHA developed a tenant selection and assignment procedure that satisfied both the local civil rights groups and the federal department of Housing and Urban Development. Ash also created tenant task forces in developments around the city to give residents more input in how they were run. One of those residents was Inez Middleton, who noted, "People are anxious to get their teeth in things."[10]

In 1968, when he became mayor, it appeared that Kevin White would become more involved in public housing. A month after taking office, he took the first of what he promised would be more "get acquainted" tours of the city's 36 developments.[11] A few months later, a group of residents held a sit-in at a BHA board meeting and demanded that the 60 patronage jobs "directly" controlled by the mayor and the board (30 by the mayor and 6 by each of the 5 members), go to residents. White and Julius Bernstein, the one board member White had been able to appoint so far, agreed to give "their" jobs to residents. But the other board members refused to follow suit.

Bernstein, the head of the city's Jewish Labor Committee, showed himself to be out of step with his fellow board members again when he suggested, "Tenant organizing should be encouraged." The BHA's board chairman, Jacob Brier, ridiculed the idea as being comparable to "saying you ought to have a student on the Harvard Board of Overseers." Bernstein also backed Ellis Ash when the administrator announced he was going to hold hearings in developments across the city so residents could have a say in how the BHA should spend the federal modernization funds for which it was applying. One of other board members derided that idea as "gobbledygook." [12]

Public housing residents didn't think the hearings were gobbledygook. Nearly 3,000 of them turned out for the chance to be heard. When Boston was subsequently awarded $8 million, the largest per capita grant in the country, Ash said it was "because we convinced them that ours is to be a genuine tenant participation program." [13]

On March 2, 1968, thousands of public housing residents turned out again, slogging through snow to vote in the first citywide election in BHA history for a Tenants' Association Policy Council. Ann Stokes of Columbia Point, a mother of eight and grandmother of five, was one of those who turned out to vote and explained why. "Nowadays, I don't care what race it is, people want things to be changed. They want self-determination." [14]

After being elected secretary of the new council, Doris Bunte recalled how excited she was at the prospect of being a part of that self-determination. But she soon found not everyone at the BHA shared her excitement. "We would go to meetings at the BHA office downtown," Bunte recalled, "and the secretary wouldn't let us go past a certain point in the offices. She said it was because 'we want to keep them clean.'" [15]

In February 1969, Massachusetts governor Sargent gave that self-determination a bigger boost when he used his one appointment to name John Connolly, a resident of the Mary Ellen McCormack development in South Boston, to be the first public housing resident ever to serve on the BHA board. Connolly was a Harvard undergraduate who worked part-time for Action for Boston Community Development. Edward O'Neil, president of the new tenants council, praised his appointment. "We feel that only a tenant really knows a tenant's needs. You have to live in public housing to know what public housing is—to know the needs, the problems, the desires, and hopes of people in public housing."[16]

The tenants council and other community groups then put pressure on Mayor White to follow the governor's lead. A few months later, he did, naming Bunte to be the second tenant and first African American woman to serve on the board. "I thought I had died and gone to heaven," Bunte recalled. But once again her excitement was quickly tempered. One of her neighbors at Orchard Park was a man who, she knew, applied every year for a job with the BHA, but never even received an interview. "When I got on the board, I asked to see his file, and when they brought it out, I saw that written on it in big letters were the words 'NON-WHITE.' That was why his application had never gone anywhere. Racism at the BHA was like an onion. You lifted layer after layer and sometimes it made you cry."[17]

In September 1969, when Bunte joined Connolly and Bernstein, newspaper stories hailed the first "pro-tenant majority" in BHA board history. But that didn't stop residents from continuing to organize. A week before Christmas, a group from Columbia Point walked into a BHA board meeting and deposited "gifts" from BHA buildings on the table in front of the board members and administrator. They included a small Christmas tree decorated with a half dozen dead mice and glass jars filled with cockroaches, some still wriggling. Then the residents presented a Christmas card that contained a list of demands for better maintenance.

But the newly reconstituted BHA board rose to the challenge. In what was described as "an unprecedented response," it directed administrator Dan Finn, whom Mayor White had recently named to replace Ash, to come up with "a program for immediate action," and to meet with the residents the next day to begin carrying it out. The pro-tenant board's stock soared with residents, but it plunged with the mayor. According to Vale, White was trying to increase the power of his new administrator and "rein in the progressive tendencies of the Board, especially regarding the limits placed on patronage."[18]

The board didn't take well to this attempted reining in. "We kept coming up with new resident-oriented policies," recalled Bunte, "but nothing was getting done. Finally, we decided the problem was Dan Finn. We went to the mayor and told him that he needed to tell Dan that he had to step down." But the mayor refused, so the BHA board voted to fire Finn by a 3 to 2 margin. Andy Olins was by this time Finn's deputy. He recalled

"Trial" of Doris Bunte in Boston City Council chambers in May 1971. Photo by
Charles Carey/Globe Staff.

that Mayor White took the firing "as a personal offense, and the amount
of energy that went into dealing with that was energy lost to the effort of
improving public housing." [19]

White's first response to Finn's dismissal was to ask Governor Sargent to
remove Connolly from the BHA board due to what newspaper accounts
described as trivial infractions of the agency's rules and regulations. [20] When
the governor refused, the mayor called on the city council to dismiss Bunte
on charges that included "excessive out of city travel," receiving income
"in excess of the maximum allowed for a tenant in public housing," and
interfering in BHA procedures. [21] Bunte denied the first two charges. The
third stemmed from the fact that she had helped her mother transfer from
a development intended for families into one reserved for the elderly,
something the woman was perfectly entitled to do. But, as *Boston Globe* reporter Fred Pillsbury wrote at the time, "from the beginning it was obvious
that the real issue here is who controls the Housing Authority, the mayor
or the BHA." [22]

When the city council refused to dismiss Bunte, White demanded that
the council implement a procedure called for in the city charter for dis-
missing a commissioner. It was reportedly the first time in municipal
history that the procedure was used, and amounted to a trial, the likes of

which Boston had not seen since the witchcraft trials of the seventeenth century.

The "trial" began on April 29, 1971, and convened first in the Eagle Room, next to the mayor's office. But in order to accommodate the crowds of public housing residents and the media who showed up to observe, it had to be moved into city council chambers. Bunte was the "defendant," of course. Mayor White was described as the "administrative judge." Herb Gleason, the corporation counsel, served as "prosecutor." ("It was not among the favorite roles that I was ever asked to play," he later said.) The city council served as the "jury" — although at one point in the proceedings, Councilor Joe Timilty objected to being forced to participate in what he called a "kangaroo court," and at another, Councilor Tom Atkins reminded the mayor "this is a joint hearing in which you are one member, not king." [23]

The trial/hearing lasted for thirteen days and produced more than two thousand pages of testimony on such arcane subjects as HUD reimbursements limits for parking fees, car mileage, and telephone use.[24] But the fact that the trial was being held at all outraged public housing residents and activists across the city. The Boston Public Housing Tenants Policy Council declared Bunte was being "unjustly accused." [25] Other activists signed a statement saying that if the mayor persisted with the trial, "he will harm not only the black community of Boston, but all the poor of the city." [26]

Once all of the evidence was in, according a *Boston Globe* editorial, it showed Bunte "has in fact worked long, hard and effectively in her job"[27] But somehow the power of the mayor's office proved more persuasive than the evidence. On July 12, 1971, the city council voted — by a 5 to 4 margin — to dismiss Bunte from the BHA board.

A real court — the Massachusetts Superior Court — soon overturned Bunte's "conviction," however. On March 1, 1972, she made her return to the board a memorable one by casting the deciding vote for what was described as a "revolutionary" new lease for BHA tenants. The first of its kind in the country, the lease spelled out not only the responsibilities that residents had as tenants, but that the BHA had as landlord. It also created a hearing panel (which included residents) to resolve disputes, allowed residents to deposit rent in escrow accounts when the agency failed to make necessary repairs, and required the BHA to keep all its developments in "decent safe and sanitary condition." [28]

Bunte didn't remain on the BHA board for very long, however, because on November 7, 1972, she and fellow activist Mel King were elected to the Massachusetts House of Representatives. But before she left, Bunte cast another deciding vote. On December 20, 1972, the BHA board — by another 3 to 2 margin — turned responsibility for running the Bromley-Heath development to the Bromley-Heath Tenant Management Corporation.[29] It marked the first time in Boston and one of the first times in the country that public housing residents were given this authority, and marked a high point in what had been a more than decade-long fight by residents for greater self-determination in their lives.

CHAPTER 13

◄○►

The Tenants' Movement
and Rent Control

Aₛ the 1960s continued, the "renewal" of the New Boston proceeded unevenly. Some neighborhoods benefited from long-overdue attention, and some continued to suffer from neglect. But the chronic shortage of decent, affordable, privately owned housing all over the city only made things worse for the tenants. A newspaper headline summed it up best: "Renewal So Far: High Rents Replace Low." [1]

It was estimated that the city needed to add another 50,000 new units to its supply of housing just to meet the existing demand. [2] But since that wasn't happening, unscrupulous landlords were able to take advantage of the situation by neglecting properties, raising rents, or both. Tenants—many of them elderly, sometimes on their own and sometimes with help from community organizers—had no choice but to fight back.

On May 1, 1964, more than 20 families who lived on or around Waumbeck Street in Roxbury, supported by the Boston chapter of the Congress of Racial Equality, engaged in what was described as "the first major rent strike of its kind in Boston." The tenants hadn't wanted to take such drastic action. Previously they had gotten city inspectors to come out to their buildings and write up more than 150 sanitation, building, and fire code violations. [3] Then they had met with their landlord, Joel Rubin, to try to get him to address the complaints. Only when he refused did they begin to deposit their rent checks in an escrow account set up by the Reverend James Breeden. And only after that did they began picketing outside their landlord's office on Warren Street, carrying signs that read, "Get rid of rats, roaches and Rubin."[4]

More rent strikes and protests by more tenants against more landlords all over Boston followed. Thanks to the increased and often sympathetic coverage from the Boston media, the tenants' movement began to build momentum. "Both sides, the tenant activists and the landlords, would try to steer you in their direction," said the then *Globe* reporter Viola Osgood years later. "My policy was not to get too friendly with either side because I wanted to be objective. But when you ask a landlord, 'Why are the stairs falling down?' and he won't answer, well . . ."[5]

The South End became a particular hotbed for tenant activism, thanks in large part to the organizing done by Ted Parrish. Born and brought up in North Carolina, Parrish had come north to attend Brown University, then moved to Boston to become a youth worker for the United South End Settlements (USES).

In May 1968, Parrish helped tenants who lived in some of the more than 40 buildings in the neighborhood owned by three brothers, Joseph, Israel, and Raphael Mindick. Initially, the tenants took what soon be-came the usual steps to organize. They formed themselves into a group called the South End Tenant Council (SETC). They got city inspectors to come out and write up hundreds of housing code violations. They began to hold demonstrations, first outside the Mindicks' office and then outside their homes.

But it wasn't until SETC planned to hold a demonstration outside the Dorchester synagogue where one of the brothers was a cantor that it got results. When Rabbi Judea Miller, chairman of the Social Action Committee of the Massachusetts Board of Rabbis, heard about the plan, he went out to see some of the Mindicks' properties for himself and found them "disgusting."[6] Instead of demonstrating outside the synagogue, Miller suggested the tenants take their grievances to court—but it wasn't just any court that he had in mind. He proposed they appeal to the local Rabbinical Court of Justice.

Rabbinical courts were established in Europe during medieval times, and normally dealt with religious, social, and contractual disputes between Jews.[7] When the rabbinical court in Boston agreed to mediate the dispute between the tenants and the Mindicks, it marked "the first time in U.S. history that a Rabbinical Court . . . entered a social problem of such magnitude." On August 5, 1968, after three months of negotiations, the court brokered an agreement that spelled out the responsibilities of both the tenants and their landlords. Both sides signed it, and afterward Parrish was jubilant. Holding the agreement up as an example for other faiths to follow, he asked, "How can Catholics, for instance, sit back now?"[8]

Unfortunately, the Mindicks themselves sat back. After waiting in vain for six months for the promised repairs to be made and heat to be supplied, the tenants began another rent strike on February 14, 1969. A few weeks later, the Rabbinical Court of Justice fined the Mindicks for failing to live up to the agreement.[9] Tired of the aggravation and, no doubt, the embarrassment within their community, the Mindicks sold most of their property to the Boston Redevelopment Authority (BRA).

But the tenants ended up prevailing. With the assistance from the United South End Settlements and Greater Boston Community Development, the tenants in SETC set up their own community development corporation, which they called the Tenants Development Corporation (TDC). Then they persuaded the BRA to turn over 56 of the former Mindick properties to TDC, which renovated them into 285 units of affordable housing.[10] What started out as a rent strike by tenants against their landlords ended with the tenants becoming their own landlords.

Those South End tenants had been forced to turn to the rabbinical court primarily because the regular courts in Boston were unable to handle the mountain of housing complaints they were receiving from tenants in neighborhoods across the city. In Dorchester, for example, tenants had been trying for years to get George Wattendorf and his family to maintain the more than 250 apartment buildings they owned in that neighborhood. But the Wattendorfs, unlike the Mindicks, weren't likely to be shamed into living up to their responsibilities. In fact, George's son-in-law, Joe Tibbets, had once bragged to a reporter, "So I'm a slumlord. But I'm going to be the best of the slumlords. That's what I'm going to prove."[11]

The city's housing and building inspectors weren't living up to their responsibilities, either. Newspaper exposés regularly featured photos of them sleeping in their cars, hanging out in bars, or leaving work early to go to second jobs on city time. But even when tenants were able to somehow get these inspectors to come out and write up violations and complaints, the district courts responsible for handling them were so clogged with more serious criminal cases that they never got around to hearing the housing complaints.[12]

For years, tenants and tenant groups had been advocating for creation of a special housing court that would do nothing but handle those complaints. In October 1971, they were finally able to persuade the Massachusetts legislature to create one. It was the first of its kind in the state, and when it was proposed the city's housing inspection commissioner estimated it might hear as many as 800 cases a year. Tenant advocates thought the number would be twice that. But both predictions proved to be way off. In its first year, the Boston Housing Court heard 3,400 cases.[13] By its second year, it was on a pace to hear five times that number, a clear indication that the court was much needed and long overdue.

Paul Garrity was the first judge to preside over the Boston Housing Court. Young, energetic, and unconventional, Garrity held regular daytime sessions in downtown Boston at the Suffolk County Court House, but frequent evening sessions in the neighborhoods, in places like the Roxbury Multi-Service Center and Dorchester's St. Ambrose Church Parish Hall. He ran the court, according to tenant organizer Felix Vasquez, so that "you don't have to be afraid to file a complaint." In one case, in which a landlord's lawyer claimed a tenant organizer had no right to bring suit on behalf of a group of tenants, Garrity declared the organizer "a private attorney general" with the power "to enforce social legislation." In another case, in which a Jamaica Plain landlord refused to make the court-ordered repairs to his properties, Garrity sentenced him to spend every night until he complied with the order at the Deer Island House of Correction.[14]

But even the new, innovative housing court couldn't address the biggest problem facing tenants—the ever-rising rents in the New Boston. To do that, tenants embarked on a campaign to bring rent control back to Boston, something the city had been without since the severe housing crisis in the Old Boston during and just after World War II.

Much of the pressure to bring back rent control came from tenants in Allston and Brighton. There, block after block of apartment buildings that had once been home to families and elderly residents were now being filled by groups of college students, who could afford to pay much higher rents. In 1968, a survey by the Brighton–Allston Area Planning Action Council found that 85 percent of the tenants in the neighborhood had recently received rent increases of more than 20 percent, and that some elderly residents were being forced pay as much as 60 percent of their fixed incomes on rent.[15]

Anita Bromberg emerged as an unlikely leader of the tenants' movement in Allston–Brighton. Prior to her divorce, her best friend Mary Honan recalled that Bromberg had so little interest in politics "that I had to tell her who the state rep was. But afterward she got involved because she had to keep a roof over the heads of her daughter and her parents, and she knew she had to do it herself." [16]

Another tenant leader in the neighborhood was Frank Manning, by this time president of the Massachusetts Legislative Council for Older Americans. But Manning was a former textile union official, who was described by a friend as "a labor organizer who just happened to get old." Unlike many of those in the tenants' movement, Manning didn't blame local college students for forcing families and the elderly from their apartments. Instead, he maintained, they were just being "used as pawns by greedy landlords." [17]

In July 1968, the push to bring back rent control heated up quite literally when more than a 150 elderly tenants from Allston–Brighton packed a State House hearing on a rent control bill. The hearing was being held in a small, un-air-conditioned room, but the presence of so many senior citizens prompted the chairman to move it to a larger, air-conditioned room because he feared that some of them might pass out due to the heat. A few days later, tenants turned the heat up themselves, when "one of the largest crowds of the year" descended on the City Hall to demand that the city council enact a rent control ordinance for Boston. [18]

Since the city couldn't act until the Massachusetts legislature passed a bill enabling Boston and other municipalities to enact their own rent control ordinances, tenants in Allston–Brighton persuaded their state representative, Norman Weinberg, to file such a bill. In fall 1968, while they waited for the bill to make its way through the legislature, tenants were able to pressure the city to set up an interim Rent Review Board. Although the board lacked any real power and could only hear complaints of "excessive" rent increases, in its first sixteen months it received more than 1,500 of them. That prompted the board chairman Joe Smith to predict that, unless a rent control law was passed, "This city will be seeing rent strikes, marches and demonstrations." The director of the Boston Redevelopment Authority, Hale Champion, made an even bleaker prediction. If the shortage of decent, affordable rental housing wasn't addressed, he said, it would "doom Boston to the ranks of those cities which keep as residents only the rich and the hapless poor." [19]

In the summer of 1969, the legislature passed a bill that enabled Massachusetts cities and towns to enact local rent control ordinances and gave them the choice between passing their own rent control laws and adopting a strong state rent control law that was also passed at the time. That fall, the city council held a series of marathon public hearings to decide which option Boston would choose. Some of the sessions began in midafternoon and lasted past midnight. During the hearings, tenants and their advocates lined up to tell stories of families and the elderly being forced to leave apartments in which they had lived most of their lives, and to cite statistics showing Boston had the highest rents of any city in the country. They urged the city council to adopt the strong state law. But representatives of the real estate industry lined up to testify, too, arguing that adopting any sort of rent control at all would discourage construction of new rental housing in the city and make the problem even worse.

On November 1, 1969, after what was described as an "extended debate, unparalleled in recent council history," the city council came down squarely in the middle on the issue—deciding against adoption of the strong state law and instead passing what was described as a "moderate" rent control ordinance for Boston.[20]

The law covered 60,000 units, about one-fourth of the city's rental stock. But it exempted buildings with three or fewer units, which meant that three-deckers, the most plentiful building type in Boston, were not covered. It also exempted newly built or newly renovated luxury apartment buildings. The law did, however, establish a five-person Rent Appeals Board, and require landlords to register all of their units with the board and get its approval for any major rent increases.

On March 16, 1970, the Rent Appeals Board convened for the first time. The city hall hearing room was packed with a crowd made up of "middle-class residents of the area, elderly persons, student tenants and community action activists."[21] Appropriately, the first case the board heard involved the tenant leader Anita Bromberg, who was being threatened with eviction for refusing to pay an almost 40 percent rent increase for the apartment she shared with her daughter and parents on Chiswick Road.

Bromberg told the board that until recently her eight-unit building had been filled with families, but that now hers was the only one left. When she denounced landlords demanding the kind of huge rent increase she was facing as "gougers," the crowd cheered. When the lawyer for Bromberg's landlord got up and defended his client, the crowd responded with "groans, hisses and loud asides."[22] After deliberating briefly, the board rejected the proposed rent increase and ordered that Bromberg and her family be allowed to remain in their apartment at the current rent. The crowd cheered again, even more loudly.

Despite Boston's new, moderate, rent control law, tenants continued to lose ground. Statistics showed rents in Boston had risen twice as much

Tenant demonstration in Boston City Hall lobby in April 1976. Photo by William Ryerson/Globe Staff.

as those in cities in the rest of the country and that a third of Boston tenants were paying 30 percent or more of their income for rent.[23] So in 1970, after the legislature adopted an even stronger state rent control law, tenants mounted another campaign to get the city council to replace Boston's ordinance with the state law.

Once again, the council held marathon hearings. Once again, tenants and their advocates argued for the stronger state law and the Boston real estate industry argued against any rent control law at all. Once again, the city council tried to split the difference on the issue, although this time it tilted more to the real estate industry's side.

In November 1970, instead of adopting the stronger state law, the city council passed a new rent control ordinance that extended coverage to 120,000 units by including absentee-owned three-deckers. But the new law no longer required landlords to register all of their units with the Rent Appeals Board, and it allowed rent increases to go into effect automatically unless tenants appealed them within thirty days.

Tenants and tenant groups were furious and redoubled their efforts to get the city to adopt the stronger state law. Fortunately for them, 1971 was a mayoral election year and tenants made up the largest voting block in Boston. Kevin White, running for reelection against Louise Day Hicks, showed he understood the math. Although he had not taken a stand on the issue previously, the mayor suddenly became a champion for stronger tenant protections and put up campaign billboards all over the city that read, "When Landlords Raise Rents, Mayor White Raises Hell." Thanks to a strong turnout by tenants, not only was White reelected, but three rent control supporters were newly elected to the city council as well.

In November 1972, the hard work and electoral clout of tenants seemed to have finally paid off. After holding what were described as a series of "tumultuous" hearings, the city council voted by just a 5 to 4 margin to adopt the stronger state rent control law. Mayor White signed the new ordinance into law on December 2, 1972, but for some reason made the cryptic comment, "The tenants wanted the state bill, now they got it." [24]

The new law extended coverage to 140,000 units, almost 60 percent of the rental units in the city, and once more required landlords to register all of their units with the Rent Appeals Board and get permission for all major rent increases. Tenants were ecstatic. After years of hard work, it appeared that they had finally succeeded in insulating themselves from the ever-rising temperatures of the New Boston's hot rental housing market. As things turned out, though, their relief was only temporary.

People Before Highways

URBAN RENEWAL WASN'T THE ONLY BIG, FEDERAL PROGRAM
the city employed to try to build the New Boston—the interstate highway
program was another. But if the highways built in the 1950s had helped to
drain the life out the city, a proposal to build two more in the 1960s threatened to strangle it just as it was starting to breathe again. The best account
of the fight to stop these highways from being built is contained in *Rites of
Way: The Politics of Boston and the U.S. City* by Alan Lupo, Frank Colcord,
and Edmund P. Fowler.

In 1948, the Massachusetts Highway Department produced a "Master
Highway Plan for the Boston Metropolitan Area" that included proposals
for construction of a number of highways in and around Boston. A major
reason for building these highways wasn't to *alleviate* automobile traffic
so much as to *encourage* it and promote the economic growth that came
with it. But in 1956, when Congress passed the Defense Interstate Highway
Act, the state had another reason to build these highways—"free" money.
The new highway law guaranteed that the federal government would reim-
burse states for 90 percent of the millions of dollars that it would cost to
build these highways, and the Commonwealth of Massachusetts was eager
to take advantage of the offer.

In 1951, even before this offer of federal largesse was put on the table,
the first section of the state-built Route 128 opened. The impact of the cir-
cumferential highway, completed in 1958, was a mixed bag for Boston. By
promoting development of the high-tech industry in the suburbs, it continued to drain population and jobs from the city. But it did eventually

help spur the development of the professional services industry in downtown Boston. In 1956, the John F. Fitzgerald Expressway was completed. This elevated highway, more commonly called the Central Artery, had a much more one-sided and negative effect, since it cut the city's waterfront and the North End neighborhood off from the rest of downtown Boston.

Boston residents had reason to be wary, then, in the 1960s, when a proposal to build two more highways came along. One was called the Inner Belt, a ten-mile-long, mostly elevated, eight-lane "ring road" around downtown Boston. It was to run from Charlestown, through the neighboring municipalities of Somerville, Cambridge, and Brookline, then back into Boston through the Fenway, Roxbury, and the South End. The other was the Southwest Expressway, an eight-mile-long, mostly elevated, eight-lane, mostly straight highway. It was to run from the end of the already-constructed I-95 in Canton, through the Boston neighborhoods of Hyde Park, Jamaica Plain, and Roxbury to the South End, sprout a highway spur called the South End Bypass, and then connect to the existing Southeast Expressway.

The plan to build these two highways, like the plans for all of the big construction projects proposed at the time, had the backing of Boston's "city fathers." John Hynes got behind it when he was mayor. His successor, John Collins, was described as its "strongest supporter." Ed Logue, director of the Boston Redevelopment Authority at the time, said if the highways weren't built, the city's "core business district will be hollow." The Boston Chamber of Commerce, the rest of the business community, and organized labor were all in favor. So were Boston's newspapers, which backed the highway plans in the same boosterish prose they had used to promote urban renewal. "You can't build an enormous eight-lane superroad through four crowded communities without hurting someone," wrote the *Boston Globe*'s transportation reporter A. S. Plotkin, "but modern road builders have developed ingenious ways of landscaping, for the muffling of sound and softening the aesthetic impact otherwise."[1]

But those "someones" who would be hurt by construction of the highways didn't have that same confidence in the ingenuity of modern road builders. They included the 7,500 families who stood to lose their homes, the hundreds of businesses that would be forced to move, and the residents of the towns and neighborhoods that would be split by construction of these high-rise rivers of asphalt.[2] So in 1960, when the Massachusetts Department of Public Works (DPW) began to hold public hearings on the plan to build the highways, large numbers of those people turned out to say they didn't think it was such a good idea.

Much of the early opposition to the Inner Belt came from residents of the city of Cambridge, just across the Charles River from Boston. Also founded in 1630, Cambridge soon lost out to Boston in the competition to be the capital of the Massachusetts Bay Colony, and, as a sort of consolation prize, was chosen instead to be the site for the first "schoale or colledge" in the colonies in 1634. It has been a contentious university town ever since.

On May 10, 1960, some 2,500 of those contentious Cambridge residents squeezed into the Cambridge High and Latin School auditorium and hissed and booed as the Massachusetts DPW commissioner Anthony DiNitale tried to make a case for the Inner Belt. The meeting ended with the crowd chanting, "We don't want a road. We want our homes." Two nights later, 1,100 Boston residents packed the smaller Boston Latin School auditorium for a similar presentation. "Although the audience was only half as large," said one newspaper account, "it booed [*sic*], hissed, applauded and stomped almost as vigorously."[3]

The strongest early opposition to the Inner Belt in Boston didn't come from residents but from the cultural and educational institutions located in the Fenway. That was where the highway was somehow supposed to thread its way *between* the Museum of Fine Arts and the Gardner Museum. On May 4, 1960, Perry Rathbone, the Museum of Fine Arts director-turned-anti-highway-activist, hosted a luncheon for the city's cultural and business leaders. In return for the free lunch, Rathbone felt free to lobby his guests to oppose the Inner Belt. If it were to be built, he warned, it would not only damage "rare and precious statuary, friezes and bas reliefs" in his museum, but "turn Boston, with its charm and beauty, into a precinct of no more distinction than downtown Tulsa or Wichita."[4] Soon after, the state revised the plan and announced that particularly stretch of the highway would be built underground.

Early opposition to the proposed Southwest Expressway in Boston was led by residents of a neighborhood that had most recently joined the city.

HYDE PARK *is the southernmost neighborhood of Boston. Parts of it were originally parts of the separate towns of Dorchester, Dedham, and Milton until it became an independent municipality. Hyde Park was originally the site of early paper, textile, and shoe mills. In the mid-nineteenth century, it was developed as a residential area by a group of businessmen, who named it after "the beautiful and aristocratic suburb of London." In 1912, it became the last town that allowed itself to be annexed to Boston.*

By 1960, Hyde Park was an overwhelmingly white, working-class community of 33,000 people. Its rows and rows of streets spread out from its business and industrial districts and were flanked by small, single-family bungalows in a stable, self-contained neighborhood as far as possible from downtown Boston while still within the city limits.

On September 24, 1962, however, more than 2,000 residents filled the auditorium of Hyde Park High School to show how upset they were that their location would provide no protection from the threat of the proposed highway. They were treated that evening to a particularly inept presentation by a state DPW official, whose best argument for the Southwest Expressway seemed to be that it would displace fewer people than the Inner Belt.[5] Residents were not persuaded, and, soon after, many signed a petition to secede from Boston. They sent it to the Massachusetts legislature fifty years to the day after Hyde Park had allowed itself to be annexed.

Opposition to both highways soon spread to other neighborhoods. In Roxbury, the Inner Belt was supposed to intersect with the Southwest Expressway in a massive, five-story-high interchange of loops and ramps. On October 22, 1962, 2,000 Roxbury residents packed the Joseph Timilty School auditorium, which was described as being "rocked with shouts of opposition." The residents were forced to endure a similarly inept pitch for the highway by a DPW official. Val Hyman, who was there that night, recalled, "He told this big audience of homeowners—black and white—that the state was going to tear down all their houses to build this highway. Then somebody asked him, 'Why can't you put this thing underground?' And the guy actually said, 'You know, people that drive deserve sunshine, too.' The people in the neighborhood were easy to organize after that."[6]

Even though people did get organized, most of them assumed that the highways were going to be built. So they concentrated their efforts on trying to get the state to either alter the highways' routes or change their design to do less damage to the communities in their path. In 1965, after two more years of hearings and studies and reports by the Massachusetts Department of Public Works, the state did agree to change the path of the Southwest Expressway so that, instead of costing more than 2,000 families their homes, the number would be "only" half that.[7] Soon after, Governor John Volpe predicted that Massachusetts would have "the most modern and mobile highway system in the nation."[8]

But the governor may have spoken too soon. Opposition to the highways continued to grow, not only among residents in the threatened neighborhoods and communities, but also among their local elected officials.

On February 26, 1966, hundreds of Cambridge residents marched through Central Square to protest the Inner Belt. Two days later, the Cambridge City Council voted to oppose all of the various routes proposed for the highway through their community.

Two days after that, Milton selectmen voted to oppose all of the proposed routes for the Southwest Expressway through their town. Milton residents were particularly alarmed because the highway was to run through the Fowl Meadows Wildlife Reservation, a wetlands area that experienced frequent fog. Residents claimed this would create a "death trap" for motorists, and they later stormed the State House and passed out "grimly dramatic photographs of smashed vehicles" to legislators.[9]

In 1966, advocacy planners at Harvard and MIT formed Urban Planning Aid (UPA) to help Cambridge residents fight the Inner Belt. Ever since they had been proposed, the state had acknowledged *how many* families would lose their homes to the highways. But not until UPA released a report in October 1966 did it become clear just *who* those families were. Almost all were either poor or working class, and half had incomes of less than $4,800 a year. The state had also claimed that construction of the highways would create jobs, but UPA put out another report that showed businesses employing a total of 4,000 people would have to close or move just to make way for the Inner Belt alone.[10]

On October 15, 1966, the anti-highway movement showed how much it was growing when more than 1,000 people from Boston and surrounding cities and towns turned out on Boston Common for a "Beat the Belt Rally." The crowd was made up primarily of families, and a newspaper account noted that "the usual beards and long, pressed tresses associated with Common demonstrations were absent." Speaker after speaker—elected officials as well as residents—took turns denouncing the planned highways. A Boston police officer called it "the best demonstration I've ever seen, without hesitation."[11]

As opposition to both highways grew, opposition to the Southwest Expressway spread to the next neighborhood along its route.

JAMAICA PLAIN *had begun as an area of summer estates owned by Yankee merchants—including those involved in the Jamaican rum trade, which may explain the neighborhood's name. First a part of the separate towns of Roxbury and then West Roxbury, it had long been home to residents known for supporting liberal causes—among them John Eliot ("the Apostle to the Indians"), the transcendentalist Ralph Waldo Emerson, and the feminist Margaret Fuller.*

By 1960, Jamaica Plain had a population of 53,000. While 95 percent of the residents were white, it was an economically diverse neighborhood. Most of the middle-class residents lived in single- and two-family homes west of Centre Street. Most of the poor and working-class residents lived in two-family homes, three-deckers, and public housing on the east side. Not surprisingly, that was the side of the neighborhood through which the proposed Southwest Expressway was to run.

It wasn't until fall 1967 that a small group of Jamaica Plain residents began to organize against the highway. The group, which included the Reverends Tom Corrigan and Donald Campbell and a seminary graduate named Ron Hafer, met first in the Germania Street apartment of John Bassett, who had recently moved there from Cambridge. "My contribution," he recalled, "was to alert the group to the highway and connect them with UPA. But Tom Corrigan's contribution was much more important. He connected us with the little old ladies in his parish and all of the other people who had grown up in the neighborhood, and he showed we weren't just a few carpetbaggers trying to stir things up."[12]

Corrigan had grown up in Quincy, graduated from Boston College and St. John's Seminary, and been ordained a Catholic priest two years before. He was also a member of the Association of Boston Urban Priests, which had been formed a few months earlier in the wake of the riot that followed the Mothers for Adequate Welfare occupation of the Grove Hall Welfare Office. In a letter to fellow priests, ABUP explained its reason for being. "Boston is part of a second American Revolution: the urban revolution.... Our desire is to make the Church constantly aware of the critical needs of the city—whether it be in housing, welfare, politics or any concern—secular or religious." ABUP's goal was "to prod the Church and the city to heed the cry of the minorities and the voiceless."[13]

"Some of the guys in ABUP got involved in urban renewal and building affordable housing," reflected Corrigan years later, after he had left the priesthood. "I was the one doing the street stuff." At the time, the area around his parish was suffering from the effects of absentee landlords and abandoned cars, so Corrigan and Don Campbell, the minister at St. Andrew Methodist Church, formed the Ecumenical Social Action Committee to try to put pressure on the city to do something about it.[14]

ESAC got a grant that allowed the organization to hire Ron Hafer, who had grown up in Illinois and had previously worked at the Blue Hill Christian Center in Dorchester. "In Jamaica Plain, I was supposed to work on issues that brought residents from different racial and ethnic groups together around issues of common concern," he recalled, "and the highway issue was a perfect mechanism to do that."[15]

The small group from Jamaica Plain got in touch with UPA, which suggested it meet with Fred Salvucci, by now a planner with the BRA. Salvucci had become what was referred to back then as a "guerilla in the bureaucracy," an activist who went *into* government to help people being wronged *by* government. He knew about such wrongs from personal experience.

A few years before, Salvucci's grandmother had lost her Brighton home to another highway. It was taken to make way for construction of the Massachusetts Turnpike Extension. "This was a seventy-year-old widow, who didn't speak English, had eighteen known pregnancies, gave birth to twelve children, six of whom survived. They gave her a dollar, said they would get an appraisal later, and told her to go," Salvucci recalled. "An 'eye-opener' would be the wrong term for it. I already had a concern for social justice. This was more like a warning, because here I was at MIT, studying to be one of the guys who do this very thing."[16]

Salvucci told the Jamaica Plain group that, at the very least, it should push to have the highway built below grade level. "At that time," recalled Ron Hafer, "it was still a foregone conclusion that the highway was going to be built, since it was being backed by the establishment and the local elected officials, so just pushing for that was a big step."[17] With help from UPA and Salvucci, the group put together a report and a slide show showing the damage that the elevated highway would do in Jamaica Plain. In January 1971, it released the report and presented the slide show at a series of meetings attended by hundreds of residents. That prompted formation of the neighborhood-wide Jamaica Plain Expressway Committee, and that led to the Boston City Council holding a public hearing at the Mary E. Curley School on May 23, 1968. More than 700 people packed the school's auditorium that night, and, after it was over, residents finally began to feel that they might at least be able to change how the highway was going to be built.

Opposition to both highways continued to grow in and around Boston for the rest of the year. In December 1968, the Greater Boston Committee on the Transportation Crisis (GBC) was formed to try to coordinate that opposition. "Depending on one's point of view," Alan Lupo later wrote, "GBC was a bizarre collection of unlikely allies engaged in obstruction, or it was the personification of the Great American Melting Pot idealistically engaged in citizens' action." Its members ranged from militants to moderates, and included whites, blacks and Hispanics, "ordinary people," neighborhood leaders, and professional organizers. Salvucci later credited GBC for creating a "new reality in the city and region, a new view of people's right to a say in major projects which affect them."[18]

GBC also created the idea that, if people united, construction of the highways might be stopped altogether, not just altered. On January 25, 1969, the organization held a "People Before Highways" rally on Boston Common that attracted more than 2,000 people from all over Boston and its adjacent cities and towns. The crowd was described as including "city councilors, uniformed police and firemen, working-class whites and blacks, mothers with kids, church parishioners, [and] students." Ron Hafer remembered the event being "very heartening for us in Jamaica Plain, because we had started by organizing block organizations. Then we moved up to neighborhood organizations. Now, here we were, joining with organizations from all over the city and with other cities and towns, and getting everyone's attention."[19]

The demonstration definitely got the attention of the state's new governor, Frank Sargent. The former lieutenant governor had assumed the job a few weeks earlier after John Volpe resigned to become U.S. secretary of transportation. Sargent watched it from a window in his office, then went out on the steps of the State House and addressed the crowd. He promised he wouldn't "make decisions that place people below concrete,"[20] then invited more than 40 representatives from the various groups to come inside to discuss the proposed highways with him.[21]

The event and the movement's new slogan were memorialized a few weeks later, when, under cover of darkness, Hafer, Bassett, and Charlie Cloherty painted "STOP I-95 PEOPLE BEFORE HIGHWAYS" in 10-foot-high letters with green pastel paint on the granite railroad embankment in Jackson Square. At one point, these early graffiti activists were interrupted by a pair of Boston police officers, who happened on the scene of what they could have considered a crime. "But they just smiled and left," recalled Bassett. "I think they liked what we were doing. I know all the people in the neighborhood loved it."[22] The billboard-sized slogan would remain the wall for almost twenty years, a lasting reminder of the ethos of the era.

On May 20, 1969, Governor Sargent took a major step toward making good on his promise not to put people below concrete by announcing creation of a task force, which included a number of anti-highway activists, to review all of the state's highway and transportation plans. It was chaired by MIT professor Alan Altshuler, who had once written "the very heart of modern democracy . . . lies in its mechanisms for enabling aroused 'amateurs' to constrain" it.[23]

People Before Highways rally on Boston Common on January 25, 1969. Photo by
Ollie Noonan Jr./Globe Staff.

To Sargent and Altshuler's credit, they allowed some of the anti-highway
amateurs, led by Chuck Turner, to do just that. "Chuck did a brilliant job,"
recalled Ann Hershfang, who was also a member of the task force. "He
took a group of mostly white, suburban women, created a broad coalition,
held it together, and led it. One of the ways he did that was to refuse to
make any decisions that favored one group over another and to only ask
for things that were good for all of the groups."[24]

But the state DPW kept on clearing a path for the highways. Some 300
homes had already been taken in Cambridge and Somerville to make way
for the Inner Belt. More than 1,200 had already been taken in Boston to
make way for the Southwest Expressway. "It was an amazing thing, really,"
Hafer said years later. "On the one hand, you had Governor Sargent saying he wanted to take another look at the issue and the momentum for
stopping highway was growing. But on the other, you had the DPW still
taking every bit of land they could get their hands on. It was as if the DPW
bureaucrats thought that the only people they really had to fight were the
ones whose homes they were taking—and if they took enough homes fast
enough, they'd win."[25]

Many of the homes that had been taken were in Lower Roxbury, and
they were immediately demolished. On July 15, 1969, Turner and a small

group of activists gathered, on what had been turned into a rubble-strewn swath of vacant land along Columbus Avenue, to protest the demolition by going out into the street and stopping traffic. "We didn't have a lot of residents who got involved. It was more like the 'usual suspects,'" Turner recalled. Then he admitted, "It was more smoke and mirrors, that made it seem you have more community support than you have." [26]

Many homes were also taken in Jamaica Plain and Hyde Park, but they were left standing and became targets for arsonists. "I remember a house on Lamartine Street, in which an older couple lived," said Hafer. "They didn't want to leave their home because they were afraid it wouldn't be there when they came back. Eventually, though, the woman got sick, and her husband had to take her to the hospital. He stayed with her there overnight, and when he came home the next day he found their house had been burned down." [27]

By the end of the summer of 1969, the anti-highway movement had grown to such a degree, according to Alan Lupo, that its members were "everywhere," and included "middle-class and button-down folks in Milton, community activists in the South End and Roxbury and teachers and priests in East Boston . . . planners, architects, lawyers and other professionals to work with community groups." The movement also included elected officials in the cities and towns around Boston. "Fifteen of the 16 communities affected by the highways had come out against them," recalled Fred Salvucci, "every one but Dedham—which supported the Southwest Expressway as long as it went through Milton." [28]

In Boston, however, highway opponents were still trying to get Mayor White to write a letter taking a similar stand. "We worked our butts off, and we couldn't even get him to come out against the South End By-Pass," recalled Ann Hershfang. That changed once White announced his candidacy for governor. "He wanted the support of our three delegates to the state Democratic convention," Hershfang said, "so we made it one of our demands, and presto—the letter came." [29] Pressure on Governor Sargent increased on September 26, 1969, when a group of more than 20 state legislators, led by state representative Mike Dukakis of Brookline, declared their opposition to construction of the two highways and their support for a halt to construction of all highways in and around Boston.

That pressure increased even more on January 8, 1970, when Sargent's own task force released its long-awaited report. The report admitted what most people had long suspected—that the state had pushed so hard for construction of the highways, as Alan Lupo later wrote, "not because they are the best public investment . . . [but] because they involved ten cent dollars from the state standpoint." A month later, on February 11, 1970, Governor Sargent announced a halt to work on the Inner Belt and Southwest Expressway and a moratorium all highway construction in Greater Boston, except for the completion of a segment of I-93 north of the city. In a speech televised across the state, he admitted, "Nearly everyone was sure highways were the only answer to transportation problems for years to come. But we were wrong."[30]

Frank Sargent received a lot of credit both for stopping construction of those highways and then for making Massachusetts the first state in the country to utilize what came to called the "Boston Provision" in the Federal-Aid Highway Act of 1973 and use highway funds for mass transit instead. But John Bassett isn't sure all that credit was deserved. "As far as I'm concerned he just did what a good politician and a good poker player would do—he saw he didn't have the cards and he folded gracefully."[31]

Another anti-highway activist, Mary Ellen Welch of East Boston, had a different view. "Forging that alliance around the highway issue not only taught citizens a lesson, but also politicians—that they had to be a new kind of politician and listen to the people. It's the people who lead, and the politicians who follow them. It's a good combination. We set things up so politicians can take photo ops."[32]

◄○►

The Mothers of Maverick Street

During the time Mary Ellen Welch was involved in the coalition to stop those highways from being built, she and her neighbors had another transportation fight on their hands, one best captured in Dorothy Nelkin's *Jetport: The Boston Airport Controversy*.

East Boston *originally was a cluster of islands in Boston Harbor, one of them owned by John Winthrop and said to be the site of the first apple and pear orchards in New England. In the 1830s, William H. Sumner and his partners filled in some of the salt marshes between the islands, enabling the residential development of the new area; soon after, it became home to the shipyards that made Boston's Yankee merchants rich from the China Trade. In the mid-nineteenth century, East Boston became the point of entry for the immigrants flooding into Boston, first from Ireland and then from other countries in Europe.*

By 1960, East Boston was an almost all-white and largely Italian American, working-class community of 44,000 residents. They lived in small one- and two-family homes. Since the neighborhood was connected to the rest of the city only by a subway line and an automobile tunnel, residents might have escaped any of negative impacts of the building of the New Boston, except that it was home to the city's airport.

Logan Airport (originally called Boston Airport) opened in 1923 on one of the islands that had not yet been connected to the rest of the East Boston mainland. It was operated first by the U.S. Army Air Corps and then by the city. After being was taken over by the state in 1941, the airport was expanded dramatically by filling in more of the harbor wetlands and connecting the remaining islands to the East Boston mainland. In 1959, the airport was turned over to a new quasi-public agency, the Massachusetts Port Authority (Massport). According to a study that recommended the move, it was done so that the airport could be run more professionally and without the "formalities" of government and politics.[1]

But the removal of those formalities made it much easier for Massport to ignore the impact that the growing airport had on its East Boston neighbors, and particularly easy for Ed King, who was named Massport's executive director in 1961. King, a former offensive lineman for Boston College and the Baltimore Colts, saw it as his job to build a bigger and busier airport, and he seemed to view those trying to stop him as would-be tacklers to be cleared out of the way.

By 1960, Logan Airport already occupied two-thirds of the land in East Boston and served 1.4 million passengers a year. But King and Massport claimed it needed to grow six times larger over the next twenty years to meet the expected increase in demand in passenger and cargo service.[2] East Boston residents were told that this was the price of progress. But some of them felt they'd already paid enough and decided to fight against having to pay any more.

One of the first fights took place in 1963, when Massport announced it was going to extend a runway on the north side of the airport and take over Wood Island Park to do it. The 70-acre waterfront park, designed by Frederick Law Olmsted, was cherished by residents. Mary Ellen Welch described it as "a green jewel" that meant "there was no reason to go away in the summer."[3] In an effort to save Wood Island, residents formed the Logan Civic League and got the Massachusetts legislature to pass a bill prohibiting Massport from using its eminent domain powers to extend runways. But it turned out that the law couldn't be applied to Wood Island because the state had already given Massport title to it.

"The taking of the park was 'the Alamo,'" wrote Dorothy Nelkin. Its loss prompted residents to form another group, the East Boston Neighborhood Council, that mounted "a more forceful strategy" to keep airport expansion in check.[4] But in June 1968, the new group wasn't able to stop Massport from evicting eight families and closing off a long stretch of Neptune Road, which ran along the edge of the park. Some 200 residents made their way across the harbor to pack a city hall hearing on August 20, 1968, and protest the land taking, but to no avail.

Massport next tried to expand on the south side of the airport by filling an area called the Bird Island Flats. To do that, it sent huge dump trucks through the narrow streets of the Jeffries Point area. They rumbled through full of gravel and returned empty as many as six hundred times a day. Residents responded by forming yet another group, the First Section Civic Association, which called on Massport to build a separate road on airport property and keep its trucks off the residential streets. But the agency refused to even consider the idea.

Fed up and afraid it was only a matter of time until one of Massport's trucks ran over one of their children, a group of women who lived in Jeffries Point took matters into their own hands. They formed their own group, which, although it didn't have a formal name, came to be called "The Mothers of Maverick Street."

Anna DeFronzo was the group's leader. A short, stocky widow and mother of five, she was described by the journalist Caryl Rivers as having "the face of Anna Magnani, the great Italian film actress," and by Rivers's husband, Alan Lupo, as having a voice that "could spit gravel." "We were tired of begging the Port Authority to keep the trucks off Maverick Street," DeFronzo later explained, "so one evening we had a meeting in here, and we decided this was it, and that someday I would give them a call and we would go out in the streets."[5]

The call came on Saturday morning, September 28, 1968. The day began with state representative George DiLorenzo, described as "a colorful and vocal politician of the old school," playing the role of a modern-day Paul Revere by driving through the streets of Jeffries Point with a portable loudspeaker attached to the roof of his car and calling out "The dump trucks are coming." That led DeFronzo to make her calls. And that led scores of "housewives in print dresses, women who had borne babies and prepared meals and cleaned house and swept sidewalks" to pour out of their houses and into the street.[6] Some of the women carried their children and their strollers, and they ended up forming what was later called a "baby carriage blockade" that forced the column of dump trucks to a halt.

Traffic backed up. Truck and car horns blared. But the women refused to move. The police arrived. So did Massport and city officials. But the women still refused to move. After what amounted to a long staring match, Massport blinked first. Its drivers were told to turn around and call it quits for the day. "It was all very colorful and community theater," recalled Welch, who was among the women who refused to move. But then she admitted, "There was no plan. Nobody sat in a room and planned strategy.

The Mothers of Maverick Street blocking trucks in East Boston on October 2, 1968.
Photo by Edison Farrand / Globe Staff.

After the confrontation, then we sat down together and said, 'Where do we go from here?'"[7]

The next day was Sunday, so the mothers didn't have to go anywhere. But the days after that produced a roller coaster of events. On Monday, Fred Salvucci, by this time the manager of the East Boston Little City Hall, persuaded Mayor White to order a temporary ban on truck traffic on Maverick Street. Residents poured into the street again, this time to celebrate. But that afternoon, Massport persuaded a judge to overturn the city's ban. On Tuesday, the mothers went into the street again and resumed their blockade. But this time, the state police were brought in, and, according to the neighborhood newspaper, the officers resorted to "pushing and shoving and unnecessary force [and] cleared the way for the trucks."[8]

"Headlines this morning, we won. Headlines this evening, we lost," De-Fronzo said later. "I don't give a damn. Let them arrest me. People have taken too much. They're fed up to here. The riot won't be in Roxbury, but here. Wait, they tell us, wait. So we wait for years, and nothing happens."[9]

On Wednesday, more than 150 residents gathered—men as well as women, teenagers as well as children. They lined the sidewalks of Maverick Street and watched glumly as the trucks rolled through. One of those teenagers, Thomas Russo, told a reporter, "The only time I thought of demonstrating before this was when the Red Sox won the pennant." Then he added, "I've read about the French and the American Revolutions, and the people then were paying taxes and they couldn't get anything done, and the way I see it the case is almost parallel. Americans have fought for their rights since the Revolution and there seems to be another revolution coming unless something is done." [10]

Something was done on Thursday. The city declared a temporary state of emergency and closed the street to truck traffic again. On Friday, Governor Sargent convened a meeting in his State House office with Mayor White and Massport's director, Ed King. Although the meeting was described as a "closed session," Alan Lupo later wrote, "every time they took a vote, Eddie King was outvoted." Afterward, King announced that Massport would, after all, build a special road for the trucks on airport property. [11] The Mothers of Maverick Street had won the battle. But it proved to be just one in a much longer war.

The next battle took place back on the north side of the airport on April 23, 1969, when a Massport crew began cutting down some of the three-dozen trees lining Neptune Road. Fifty residents poured out of nearby homes to try to stop them, and, in the melee that followed, a dozen of them were arrested. That night, some 250 residents turned out for a meeting at Holy Redeemer Church, and cheered when the church's pastor, Monsignor Mimie Pitaro, vowed, "We will not remain inactive. We will participate in legal demonstrations and forms of harassment, to harass our enemies, to make them know our needs and rights." [12]

The demonstrations and harassment took place over the next several weeks and involved a series of "drive-ins." All of these demonstrations, the automotive equivalent of sit-ins, were publicized from the pulpits of East Boston churches. The first took place on Sunday, April 27, 1969, when approximately 200 men, women, and children piled into about 50 cars in the Central Square Shopping Plaza parking lot and drove over to the airport ring road. Once there, the cars slowed to a crawl, to create what was described as "one of the biggest traffic jams" in airport history. [13]

The police were called. They pulled over one of the drivers and asked him what he thought he was doing. "Just going out for a Sunday's drive," replied Reverend Albert Sallese. "You can really catch the beauty of the airport when you go slowly." After the demonstration, Mary Ellen Welch said, "The people feel good. They feel good inside." "In Italian, we have a word for it," Reverend Pitaro told her. "*Sfogare*—to get it out of your system." [14]

The next drive-in took place a week later, not at the airport but on the Massport-operated Tobin Bridge. Approximately 70 cars, driven three abreast, slowed down to about five miles an hour, forcing traffic to back up behind them. As the cars proceeded slowly across the bridge, their drivers honked their horns to protest airport expansion. The drivers of the hundreds of cars behind them honked their horns, too, but for a different reason.[15]

The third and last of the drive-ins was the smallest. But it may have been the most significant, because it also included residents of other neighborhoods who were part of the Greater Boston Committee on the Transportation Crisis, the coalition opposing construction of the proposed highways. On Friday evening, May 16, 1969, when some 70 demonstrators in about 20 cars gathered, one East Boston resident questioned why they needed help from "outside agitators" who belonged to groups such as the CAUSE and the Black United Front. But another resident told him, "We should be thankful they're here." Then the demonstrators piled into their cars—including the one driven by Chuck Turner, which sported "a poster of Malcolm X"—and headed over to the airport to slow down traffic, and, they hoped, the airport's expansion.[16]

East Boston residents ended up losing the battle for Neptune Road, but they ended up winning some new friends in the process. In the summer of 1969, they were joined by residents from South Boston, across the harbor from the airport, and by residents of the neighboring communities of Chelsea, Revere, and Winthrop, and they formed the Massachusetts Air Pollution and Noise Abatement Committee (MAPNAC), whose first director was John Vitagliano. A Winthrop native and Air Force veteran who had since graduated from Northeastern University, Vitagliano later admitted to being "completely apolitical" until he took the job. "I didn't even know what a 'coalition' was until Anna DeFronzo explained it to me."[17]

Vitagliano learned quickly, though, and he later credited the media with helping to build the anti-airport coalition. "The *Winthrop Transcript* gave us great coverage, and the *East Boston Times,* and the *East Boston Community News.* But it was Alan Lupo putting us on *The Reporters* on Channel 2 that was the turning point. It was hard for us to get the *Globe,* the *Herald,* and the other local TV stations to cover us until we were on *The Reporters.*"[18]

The increased media attention helped the coalition make another new friend in Governor Sargent, who went out to East Boston and criticized Massport for its "bulldozer techniques" and for "saying the hell with people."[19] Sargent promised he would change things through the appointments he made to the agency's board, and in April 1970 showed he meant it by making his first board appointee the Reverend Albert Sallese, the demonstrator who had remarked how beautiful the airport was—when you drove around it slowly.

It took almost five years for Sargent's appointments to make up the majority of the board. In 1974, when they did, the board fired executive director Ed King, and replaced him with David Davis, who embarked on a campaign to make the airport a much better neighbor. One of Davis's first moves, as reported in the *Christian Science Monitor*, was to meet with "many of the same individuals who organized picket lines and sit-ins." One of his next moves was to ask some of those activists to serve on a committee to create a master plan for future airport expansion.[20] Massport went on to shift many of its flights to over-the-water approaches, to soundproof all of the schools and many of the homes in East Boston, and to implement what were later described as the "the most aggressive noise abatement rules in the country."[21]

Replacing a tone-deaf Massport director with one who was a better listener didn't end the conflict between East Boston residents and Logan Airport. But it went a long way toward turning down the volume on what would prove to be a long-running debate and provided East Boston residents a little more peace and quiet in the process.

CHAPTER 16

Shadow Boxing in the
Public Garden

Most of the people swept up into the activism and
protest of the New Boston lived in neighborhoods that were home to the
city's many "have-nots." Residents of the two downtown neighborhoods
that were home to the city's few "haves" had less reason to become involved.
"We were an insular community over here," recalled Bernie Borman, president of one of the local civic associations. "Everything else that was going
on in the city had no effect on us."[1] But that changed when a proposed massive development threatened to leave those neighborhoods, quite literally,
in the dark.

Beacon Hill *and the* Back Bay *have long been seen as Boston's quintessential neighborhoods, and the home to what Oliver Wendell Holmes called
the city's "sifted few." But both neighborhoods had extremely inglorious beginnings. The former served as the town's "red light district" until, at the end of
the eighteenth century, it was "redeveloped" to attract Boston's first families. The
latter was an actual bay, until a misguided attempt to create a dam and harness
the tidal power turned it into "a great cesspool." Only after the whole area was
filled during the second half of the nineteenth century was it able to accommodate those Proper Bostonians who couldn't all fit on or had grown tired of
Beacon Hill.*

*By 1970, the Back Bay and Beacon Hill had a combined population of some
27,000 residents, 96 percent of them white, and many at least upper middle class.*

If those residents engaged in any sort of activism, it was likely to be in the so-cial, charitable, or civic spheres, and not the rough-and-tumble of Boston politics. Beacon Hill's last brush with anything resembling actual protest had probably occurred in 1945, when a group of matrons, described as, "maintaining their poise and dignity" by the Boston Post, *staged a successful demonstration to stop Mayor Curley from replacing their cherished brick sidewalks with plebian concrete.*

Beginning on May 30, 1970, however, residents of those neighborhoods were given a reason to belatedly join the era of activism and protest. That was when the Boston Redevelopment Authority issued a Request for Pro-posals (RFP) for what was described as a "privately funded urban renewal plan" for the Park Square area. A commercial district across Boylston Street from Beacon Hill and the Back Bay, Park Square had become somewhat down-at-the-heels and was beginning to attract the "adult entertainment" establishments that the city was trying to confine to the "Combat Zone" on Lower Washington Street. Since federally funded urban renewal was winding down at the time, the city and BRA were hoping that they could interest the private sector to take its place.

The RFP for Park Square didn't arouse that much attention, but the plan that it subsequently attracted and the developer chosen to implement the plan did. Called Park Plaza, it was described as "a city within a city." The plan called for clearing 35 acres and building a 6-million-square-foot wall of mid-rise and high-rise luxury apartment and commercial buildings along the south side of Boylston Street, with the tallest building a 650-foot hotel at the corner of Arlington Street.[2] The developer chosen to build Park Plaza was Boston Urban Associates, led by Mort Zuckerman, who was a good friend of and generous campaign contributor to Mayor White.

The Park Plaza plan won the immediate support of the "pro-growth co-alition" of government officials, the business community, organized labor, and the city's newspapers. Unlike the West End, Park Square wasn't a resi-dential neighborhood, so the only opposition to its demolition came ini-tially from owners of the buildings that would be taken and torn down, and from their commercial tenants who would be forced to move. The Beacon Hill Civic Association did register a mild objection on aesthetic grounds. But at the time, according to Borman, who would later serve as its president, the group consisted of only of "eight or ten people … who only cared about architectural preservation."[3]

Eventually, however, a more grassroots coalition began to form in oppo-sition of the Park Plaza plan. When it did, one of its most effective mem-bers was a small group made up of people who weren't so much interested in preserving nondescript commercial buildings, but in saving the grass, flowers, and the trees in one of the city's most revered parks.

The Boston Public Garden was founded in 1837 by Horace Gray and a few other wealthy, amateur horticulturists, originally as a private botanical garden. After Gray went bankrupt, the city took it over and began to make the charming additions—the lagoon, faux suspension bridge, and beloved Swan Boats—that turned the park into the crown jewel of Boston's so-called Emerald Necklace.

By 1970, however, that jewel had lost much of its luster, so Back Bay resident Stella Trafford and some her neighbors decided to try to polish it back up. They formed a group called the Friends of the Public Garden and prevailed upon one of the their neighbors, Henry Lee, to become its volunteer executive director. Lee, a member of one of Boston's first families, was a Harvard College graduate who, after a stint with the State Department, began a career as a private school teacher and administrator. He was also a perceptive, humorous, and self-deprecating student of the city and its politics.

"The 'New Boston' might have started under Mayor Hynes," according to Lee, "but the parks lagged a decade behind everything else." He attributed the deterioration of the Public Garden to "lack of maintenance, the enormous numbers of hippies who camped there in the late 1960s, and the motorcycle police who drove across the grass trying to grab every long-haired kid with a guitar sitting under a tree."[4]

Concerned that Park Plaza would only further that deterioration, Lee and the Friends joined the new coalition that included the Park Square building owners and businesses, the Beacon Hill Civic Association, the Back Bay Civic Association, the Neighborhood Association of the Back Bay, and other groups. They then formed what they called the Park Square Civic Advisory Committee (CAC), hired one of the city's top real estate lawyers to represent it, and compiled and released a report that criticized the plan for being too big and monolithic in design and for generating more pedestrian and automobile traffic than the area could bear.

The CAC wasn't out to stop the project from being built. It just wanted to scale it down, modify its design, and lesson its impact. But when the committee asked the developer to make some changes to the plan in order to do that, Zuckerman flatly refused. When the CAC appealed to Mayor White, it met with the same result. As Robert Kenney, the BRA director at the time, later explained, "Mort played to Kevin's ego. He wouldn't negotiate at all."[5]

In October 1971, when the city council held hearings on the Park Plaza plan, Henry Lee suspected that most of the councilors saw the Public Garden as just a neighborhood park for the very well-off, and he tried to counter that in his testimony by explaining it was a treasure used and enjoyed by people from the entire city. To prove his point, he introduced a newspaper photo of two kids returning to the North End after a day of skating on the frozen lagoon—since councilor Fred Langone, a North End resident, was chairing the hearing. Lee recalled that "Freddie had to admit that when he was a kid, he used to skate there, too."[6]

The evidence the Friends introduced next, however, proved to be the most powerful argument against the Park Plaza plan. In a move rare up until this time, the Friends had commissioned two studies to assess the environmental impact of the project on the Public Garden. The first study showed that the shadows from the proposed wall of tall buildings along Boylston Street would keep most of the park in the shade during most the day for much of the year. The second showed that those buildings would create a "sail effect" that could generate winds of as much as 60 miles an hour. "In terms of impact," Lee said later, "it was the same as putting Mount Monadnock next to Central Park."[7]

This environmental argument attracted a lot of media attention and swung public sentiment against the project. It also got Zuckerman to budge, slightly, and agree to lower the height of the hotel to 550 feet. But it took a chance meeting with Mayor White in the Public Garden to convince Lee that the opposition was on the right track. "The mayor said to me, 'You're doing good work,' then he added, 'but I'm going to fight you on this Park Plaza thing.' Well, I went home elated. The mayor of Boston said he was going to *fight* us. He didn't say he was going to *squash* us. He thinks we're *somebody*!"[8]

That the Friends and the other opponents of Park Plaza were "somebodies" was further confirmed on June 9, 1972, when the Massachusetts Department of Community Affairs rejected the plan. DCA's commissioner, Miles Mahoney, said his ruling was based on a number of factors, including that the developers had failed "to safeguard effectively the Public Garden and Boston Common."[9]

Now all of the opponents of the plan were elated. But supporters—especially Mayor White—didn't take the rejection well. The mayor called the decision "personal, arbitrary, and strictly political," and a few weeks later allegedly had a hand in organizing the biggest "pro-growth" demonstration held yet in the New Boston.[10]

On June 28, 1972, some 20,000 angry construction workers marched from Boston Common to the State House to protest the state's rejection of Park Plaza. As they marched, they chanted, "We want jobs! We want jobs!" Governor Sargent, who was already in hot water with the unions for halting construction of those two proposed highways, gamely went out on the steps of the State House to face the hard hats. "You want jobs, I want jobs," Sargent told them. "You want Park Plaza, I want Park Plaza; but the plans have to be right." The next day, the governor reportedly told DCA commissioner Mahoney to "see if there isn't some way for us to work this out."[11]

But Mahoney couldn't find a way. Although a second Park Plaza plan was subsequently submitted, it differed little from the first. So on February 26, 1973, Mahoney rejected that one, too. He also felt compelled to submit his resignation to the governor. Mahoney's courage as a public servant won him a lot of praise, attracted a lot of publicity, and generated even more sentiment against Park Plaza. The city council rescinded its approval for the plan.[12] A few months later, the *Boston Globe*'s development reporter Ian Menzies questioned Mayor White's continued support for it—as well as the mayor's memory—when he wrote, "Has White forgotten how Mayor Hynes was saddled with the rap of the West End, or how Edward Logue, architect of the 'New Boston,' could run no better than fourth in the primary run-off for mayor in 1967?"[13]

In 1974, after Zuckerman agreed to lower the height of the hotel to 450 feet and the BRA agreed to recognize the Civic Advisory Committee as the project's "official" neighborhood review organization, the Massachusetts Department of Community Affairs finally approved the Park Plaza plan. But a year later, the state's new Office of Environmental Affairs found that the "shadows from the proposed towers were far worse than the BRA and developers had indicated," and demanded further changes before it would give its OK.[14]

The plan was further revised. The now-official CAC suggested 29 changes and the BRA agreed to 28 of them.[15] On October 21, 1976, the Park Plaza plan finally received the necessary approvals from the state. By this time, the size of the project had been reduced from 6 million to 2.3 million square feet and the height of the hotel from 650 to 350 feet.[16] The Friends of the Public Garden and their friends in the opposition could live with this plan. But it turned out the developer couldn't. Zuckerman and his Boston Urban Associates pulled out of the project, apparently deciding that if they couldn't build it the way they wanted to, they wouldn't build it at all.[17]

Park Square was eventually redeveloped, but by various developers, in stages, and at a scale and in a manner that reflected the recommendations made by the Civic Advisory Committee. The battle over Park Plaza showed that even well-heeled residents were prepared to resort to activism when the quality of life in their neighborhoods was threatened. It also showed, once again that, in building the New Boston, the people of Boston didn't have to go along with every plan that was put in front of them.

The battle also left the Friends of the Public Garden with a reputation as something of a giant killer. Some years later, Henry Lee got a phone call from someone in New York who was a member of a group trying to stop a massive project that Zuckerman, who had since moved to New York, was trying to build in midtown Manhattan. " 'We have Robert Redford and Mrs. Onassis with us,' the man said," Lee recalled. "Then he asked me, 'Who did you have?' I told him, 'Oh, just a few tulip lovers.' "[18]

CHAPTER 17

◄◦►

Boston Jobs for
Boston Residents

THE STRONGEST ARGUMENT FOR BUILDING ANY OF THESE proposed projects in the New Boston was always that they created jobs, particularly constructions jobs. Eventually, the people of Boston began to ask just who was getting those jobs—and demand a greater share for themselves. The best source for much of the story of their campaign to gain that greater share is Mel King's *Chain of Change: Struggles for Black Community Development.*

As far back as the early 1960s, activists in the black community had raised the jobs issue. On June 26, 1963, one of the STOP Campaign–sponsored demonstrations was held in the front of the still-under-construction Prudential Center. It led to an agreement with the building trades unions to set up apprenticeship programs for minority workers. But not until four years later, during the implementation of the ill-fated Boston Urban Rehabilitation Program (BURP), did the jobs movement really began to heat up.

On November 8, 1967, a contractor working for one of the BURP developers, Sidney Insoft, fired more than fifty local, black construction workers—some with as many forty years experience and some Vietnam veterans—and replaced them with workers brought in from Canada. The laid-off workers complained to the New Urban League. The next day, the workers and activists set up picket lines that shut down more than a dozen job sites in Roxbury and threatened to keep them shut until the workers were rehired. With Otto Snowden at Freedom House serving as a moderator, all but six of the workers were rehired a few days later, and the rehired workers contributed to a job fund to support the remaining workers until they found other jobs.[1]

In February 1968, some other black construction workers and members of the Black United Front stormed into the downtown office of another BURP developer, Maurice Simon, and presented him with a copy of a complaint from the Massachusetts Commission Against Discrimination and a list of demands that he hire more minority workers on his projects. When Simon threw the papers on the floor, a scuffle ensued and several file cabinets were overturned. The Boston police were called and they ejected the demonstrators. But on their way out, some of them threatened to damage Simon's BURP properties. As the BURP projects proceeded, almost all of the properties suffered from unusually high rates of vandalism and theft, but Simon's most of all.[2]

As time went on, jobs activists began to demand that more minorities be hired, not just as part of BURP but on construction projects throughout the city. On May 27, 1968, a picket line was set up in front of a site that was part of the Government Center urban renewal project. Some of the protesters carried signs that read "Jobs for Our Black Brothers, Now, Now, Now."[3] Ironically, the building under construction was the new headquarters for the Massachusetts Division of Employment Security.

Initially, the minority jobs movement was led by the more militant activists in the black community, such as Chuck Turner and Mel King, and the more militant organizations such as the Black United Front and New Urban League. Gradually, moderates and more moderate organizations signed on, and the Boston Branch NAACP was calling on the city to implement "a nondiscriminatory action clause to be incorporated in all city contracts."[4]

The increased pressure eventually got the attention of the federal government. On June 7, 1968, officials at the regional office of the Department of Housing and Urban Development convened a meeting with all of the BURP contractors and ordered them to step up their minority hiring. According to the HUD official Edward Sidman, the contractors were told that "the government means business and that they've got to get on the ball."[5]

At the time, contractors and labor unions across the state were not only not on the ball, but unlikely to get on it any time soon. Only 58 of the more than 3,000 apprentices in the building trades union in Massachusetts were African American, only 8 of the 661 apprentice electricians, and only 7 of the 300 apprentice plumbers. Overall, African Americans made up less than 2 percent of the apprentices registered in the state's building trades unions.[6]

To keep the pressure on, workers and activists formed the United Community Construction Workers Association, (UCCWA), which threatened — if minority hiring didn't improve soon — to seek stop-work injunctions in federal court. "We're going to count noses," said Marty Gopen of the New Urban League, "and the nearer to the ghetto they get, the more black workers they're going to have to have. We want black people to rebuild their own neighborhoods."[7]

The campaign continued on both the protest and legal fronts. On October 25, 1968, some 60 black construction workers left their jobs on other projects to set up a picket line on Seaver Street in Roxbury and halted a project being built by the Perini Construction Company. After two more days of demonstrations, Perini, one of the largest contractors in the state, agreed to hire more minority workers. Not long after that, a group of labor unions agreed to hire and train 200 local African American workers for projects that were part of Boston's Model Cities program.[8]

In the spring of 1969, UCCWA did start filing those injunctions and restraining orders against contractors who had failed to hire more minority workers. That fall, local college students joined the jobs campaign, picketing building projects on their campuses and demanding their schools tell contractors to hire more minority workers.

Progress was slow, however, so slow that the federal government stepped in again. On November 9, 1970, the U.S. Department of Labor named Boston one of six "high priority cities" that were told to either develop a more effective minority-hiring program or have one imposed on them. A "Boston Plan" was subsequently drawn up that called on contractors and unions to "make every effort" to hire or enroll nonwhites "proportional to their percentage" in the Boston area. But unlike the "Philadelphia Plan" it was patterned after, it didn't set a specific figure that contractors and unions were expected to reach.[9]

Contractors and unions signed onto the Boston Plan, and the UCCWA did too, albeit reluctantly. But the New Urban League, the Black United Front, and even the Boston Branch NAACP refused to endorse it. The then-NAACP president Leon Nelson called it "vague" and lacking "strict enforcement provisions."[10] A year, the Boston Plan was moving at a "snail's pace," and by October 1971 it was pronounced "dead."[11]

The jobs movement in Boston languished for the next several years. During that time, Latino and Asian groups began to lobby for more jobs for their members. At one point, Mel King recalled, Chuck Turner called a meeting of the various minority jobs groups and "told them it was foolish to let them play us off against one another."[12]

In 1975, Turner and others formed the Third World Jobs Clearinghouse to recruit and train minorities for construction jobs. In the spring of 1976, the organization's political arm, the Third World Construction Association (TWCA), held a series of demonstrations to demand that half of all of the constructions jobs in what it called Boston's "third world communities" — which it defined, according to Mel King, as including Dorchester, the South End, Jamaica Plain, Roxbury, Mattapan, and Chinatown — go to minorities. At one demonstration on April 12, 1976, two dozen TWCA members shut down construction of a branch library in Dorchester's Codman Square.[13] At another, on May 2, 1976, 100 members halted work on a pumping station on Malden Street in the South End. The shutdowns angered contractors and labor unions so much that they decided to hold their own demonstration — one that would play a crucial role in the Boston jobs movement.

On May 7, 1976, 2,000 white construction workers marched from Boston Common to City Hall Plaza to protest what they called the "harassment" at their work sites. Asked why he was there, one of the marchers explained, "It's my job. I need a job. You been workin' ten-twelve years, somebody comes along from this Third World and grabs your job. What the hell?" When the burly protesters got to city hall, they pushed past the police who were guarding the entrance and made their way inside. "The cavernous City Hall lobby was swamped with hostile hard hats [who] repeatedly jeered and denounced Mayor White," according to one newspaper account. The hard hats left only after the mayor promised to provide police protection and keep their job sites open in the future.[14]

But the demonstration by the hard hats didn't just get the attention of the mayor. It happened that Chuck Turner was in City Hall at the time, and he recalled experiencing something of an epiphany as he looked down from a window at the thousands of angry white construction workers on the plaza below. "I realized we were both fighting for the same thing — jobs — and that all we had to do was unite the two groups under the employment umbrella of residency to break the power of the suburbs."[15]

For the next two years, Turner, King, and other activists did just that. "We had started out trying to build an organization to serve construction workers in the minority community," Turner recalled. "But the reality was that workers in the white community were also being discriminated

Hard-hat demonstration against job stoppages in Boston City Hall lobby on May 7, 1976. Photo by Philip Preston / Globe Staff.

against for not being related to people who were already in the unions. . . . So we thought, 'Why not merge affirmative action for minorities and women with residents?' You also had cases where community development corporations were putting up housing in their neighborhoods, but they couldn't get jobs on the construction projects for people that lived in their neighborhood. The politics were perfect." [16]

Perfect or not, it took some persuading to get some local union leaders on board. "I told them, 'You think you're protecting white jobs,'" Mel King recalled. "'But what if I went and told your neighbors that the jobs you're protecting are all going to people who live in the suburbs, or who live in New Hampshire, or even in Canada?'" [17] Bowing to either King's logic or to the threat of being embarrassed in front of their neighbors, the local, white labor leaders joined the effort.

The new, improved, and expanded movement called itself the Boston Jobs Coalition and adopted the slogan "Boston Jobs for Boston People." In July 1978, the coalition announced what came to be known as the Boston Residents Jobs Policy. It called for contractors on all government-assisted projects in the city to make their best efforts to see that 50 percent of their workers were Boston residents, 25 percent were minorities, and 10 percent were women. It also called for construction unions to set similar goals for apprenticeship and job training programs. It was not only the right thing to do, the coalition argued, but it would generate 80,000 construction jobs a year for residents and $1.6 billion in wages they could spend in the city.[18]

The Boston Residents Jobs Policy might have been just a good idea whose time had not come, except for one thing—1979 was a mayoral election year, and one of those running was Mel King, the first African American candidate for the job in Boston history. King made adoption of the jobs policy the centerpiece of his campaign. But Kevin White was also a candidate, running for reelection to a fourth term, and he knew a good issue when he saw one. White snatched it away from King, and on September 11, 1979, less than two weeks before the preliminary election, signed an executive order making the Boston Residents Jobs Policy official city policy.[19] Just as with welfare reform ten years earlier, it was a case where good politics helped make good policy.

Contractors and labor unions subsequently challenged the jobs ordinance, and it was struck down by the Massachusetts Supreme Judicial Court. But that decision was overturned by the U.S. Supreme Court, and eventually the Boston Residents Jobs Policy became law. Before it was implemented, 80 percent of the workers on construction jobs in Boston came from outside the city, and the percentages of those who were minorities and women were negligible. After being in effect for only one year, the percentage of jobs held by Boston residents doubled to 40 percent, and the percentages held by minorities and women increased dramatically.[20] A movement that began by dividing residents eventually united them, and the people of the city got a lot more jobs building the New Boston as a result.

CHAPTER 18

◄◦►

The Battle over Busing

T HE SUCCESSFUL COALITIONS FORMED TO STOP CONSTRUCTION of the two proposed highways and to obtain a greater share of Boston jobs for Boston residents showed what the people of the New Boston could do if they worked together. "For a while there, it seemed like there was going to be an attempt to forge a city-wide activism movement," Alan Lupo said wistfully many years later, "but then busing came along and eliminated the possibility." [1]

"Except for the violence and the bigotry—which is a very big *except*"—recalled the journalist Renée Loth, "the antibusing movement was very much like the other community movements of the time. It was a grassroots, neighborhood-based movement made up of people who were against an indifferent institution—in this case the court—telling them how to live their lives. A lot of their tactics and a lot of their inspiration came from what the Left was supporting. We didn't happen to agree with their position, but a lot of us agreed with the impulse completely." [2]

The violence was obvious and inexcusable. But how much of the opposition to busing was based on bigotry and how much on resentment by people at being told how to live their lives was then—and continues to be—a subject of debate.

Unlike some of the other protest movements that took place during this era in Boston, busing has been the subject of many books. The best are Ronald Formisano's *Boston against Busing*, Anthony Lukas's *Common Ground*, Alan Lupo's *Liberty's Chosen Home*, and Ione Malloy's *Southie Won't Go: A Teacher's Diary of the Desegregation of South Boston High School*.

Yet despite all that has been written, the story of the battle over busing remains a difficult one to retell. Unlike those other protest movements, this one wasn't a case of a good, grassroots "us" and against a bad, monolithic "them." And unlike those others, it didn't unite the people of Boston. Instead, it divided them as nothing in the city's history—with the possible exceptions of the Revolution and abolition—had done before.

The battle over busing began in August 1965, where the fight for school desegregation left off, with the signing of the Massachusetts Racial Imbalance Law. Although the law's ends—to reverse segregation in the state's schools—couldn't be faulted, the means it used certainly could be, and they were.

The biggest fault in the law was that it defined racial imbalance as occurring when more than 50 percent of a school's enrollment was made up of minority students. By doing that, the law focused on *which* students were in a school rather than *how* they came to be there. By doing that, the law failed to respect the traditional practice of assigning students to the schools nearest their homes, something that parents had come to count on and around which neighborhoods were built. It was also a practice that the U.S. District Court of Appeals—in a case involving Springfield, Massachusetts, handed down five weeks *before* the law was signed—ruled as not necessarily constituting segregation.

Defining racial imbalance this way also meant that the law would only apply to Boston and the two or three other cities in Massachusetts that had a significant number of minorities among their predominantly poor and working-class populations. Ronald Formisano likened the Racial Imbalance Law to the Pentagon's draft policies, in which "once again poor blacks and lower-class whites were the foot soldiers for a war initiated and pursued by liberal elites, and most of the affluent and college-educated were exempt." As Hillel Levine and Lawrence Harmon wrote, "Rarely had a piece of legislation so nakedly betrayed its class bias." They likened its effect to that of the similarly flawed Boston Banks Urban Renewal Group minority loan program, which they described as "a tragedy of good intentions."[3]

Another fault in the law was that it required those few urban school districts to which it did apply to develop mandatory student assignment plans to address the so-called imbalance, and rewarded those that did with additional state funds, and punished those that didn't by withholding aid.[4] This enforcement mechanism not only proved ineffective at getting adults to comply with the law, but it also punished children in those districts when the adults did not.

A final fault in the law—in Boston at least—was that by the time it went into effect, complying with it would mean a massive disruption of the school system, of neighborhoods, and of families. In 1963, when the much more modest Atkins Plan was proposed, there were only 16 segregated schools in Boston and they could have been desegregated by redrawing a few school district boundaries and without resorting to any busing at all. But by 1965, the state classified 45 schools in Boston as being "racially imbalanced," and compliance meant that thousands of students would have to be bused. That prospect didn't appeal to many parents, white or black. A few years after busing began, Ellen Jackson, one of the founders of Operation Exodus, admitted, "If the schools in Roxbury were better, I have a feeling the parents would want their children back here."[5]

While the antibusing movement might have been similar to other protest movements in Boston at the time, it differed in one important respect—its leadership didn't come from the bottom up, but the top down. From the start, elected officials rushed to it, like the one in the French proverb, who ran alongside the crowd explaining, "I'm a politician. I must get in front to lead them."

Louise Day Hicks, a Boston School Committee member at the time, got there first, and in doing so attempted to revive the politics of division that had been practiced for so long in the Old Boston. But instead of attempting to divide the people over ethnicity and class, as James Michael Curley and others had done, she tried to divide them based on race. "The NAACP had given her a platform," Tom Atkins noted years later. "She became a symbol. We had created a monster."[6] Hicks used that platform to launch a number of attempts—most of them unsuccessful—at higher office—and in the process prevented the New Boston from continuing to move to a higher plane.

From the day the Racial Imbalance Law was signed, Hicks and the other elected officials who got in line just behind her did everything possible to keep it from succeeding. Every year, Hicks and the school committee submitted imbalance plans they knew wouldn't satisfy the requirements of the law. And every year, the state Board of Education rejected those plans, and eventually began withholding millions of dollars in education aid from Boston's already financially struggling public school system.

Not until 1970, when Hicks was no longer on the committee—having parlayed her "leadership" of the antibusing movement into a seat in the U.S. Congress—did the school committee finally seem ready to comply with the law by accepting state funds to build a new Lee School in a racially diverse part of Dorchester, with the understanding that the school would be racially balanced. By the time the school was ready to open in 1971, however, the area had become a predominantly minority neighborhood. So in August 1971, the school committee voted to bus some 400 white students from the nearby Fifield and O'Hearn Schools so that it could meet the requirement for those state funds.

The decision touched off a firestorm of protests, both from white parents who didn't want their children bused this short distance and from black parents who wanted their children to attend this long-overdue new school close to their homes. On the very warm night of September 21, 1971, more than 500 parents—most of them white—filled the auditorium of the O'Hearn School for a special school committee meeting in which the board was to discuss reconsidering its vote. "The place was packed and it was a rip-roaring crowd," recalled Jim Hennigan, a committee member at the time.[7] The size and the mood of the crowd had a particularly strong effect on school committee member John Craven, who had already announced his intention to try to advance his political career by running for the city council in the next election.

When Craven switched his vote that night, it caused the Lee School to become racially imbalanced and the Massachusetts Board of Education to withhold $14 million in state aid due Boston schools that year and freeze some $200 million that had been set aside for the construction of new schools in the city.[8] The change also prompted the state board to stop waiting for the Boston School Committee to come up with an acceptable racial imbalance plan and announce it would develop one of its own and impose it on Boston instead.

"People said there was no leadership," complained Hennigan at a spirited discussion of busing held at the Old State House in Boston more than thirty years later. "But when we tried to show leadership, the people didn't want it." He later added, "the vote that night did more damage to this city than anything else."[9]

While the school committee was doing all it could to avoid complying with the Racial Imbalance Law, many of the members of the Boston delegation in the state legislature were doing all they could do to repeal it. Every spring since its passage in 1965, repeal bills were filed on Beacon Hill. In the first few years, those repeal bills were defeated by wide margins in both the Massachusetts House of Representatives and in the state Senate. However, as the years went by and as more people turned out at the annual hearings to testify and demonstrate against the law, support for its repeal grew.

In 1972, after 1,000 people demonstrated outside the State House, the repeal bill first passed in the House of Representatives, but was again defeated in the Senate. In 1973, more than 1,000 people turned out every day during the two weeks of hearings on the repeal bill. On one of those days, Hicks led 5,000 people in a march that circled the State House. As they marched, the demonstrators chanted, "They won't go, they won't take the bus. They're our kids, they belong to us." That year, both houses of the legislature voted for the repeal bill. Only Governor Sargent's veto preserved the Racial Imbalance Law for another year.[10]

But the antibusing movement continued to grow. In February 1974, a group calling itself Massachusetts Citizens Against Forced Busing was formed. MCAFB claimed to include more than 3,000 parents "from South Boston to Springfield." One of its founders was Fran Johnnene, a Hyde Park mother of three. "I was raised in a tightknit community and I wanted the same for my kids. . . . They walked to school with other children, often accompanied by a parent of a little one just starting school. The kids played together after school and had the opportunity to make friendships that could last a lifetime. Sometimes the kids were even able to come home for lunch. I was a working single parent and when my kids got sick at school, I could call a neighbor to pick them up. It was working out just as I had prayed it would."[11]

Johnnene got involved in the antibusing movement, she said at the time, because "I feel my rights are being taken away. People need things they can be involved with, and what makes a community worth living in is local churches, stores people can trust, Little League teams, and most importantly, neighborhood schools."[12]

MCAFB came to be seen as a group that attracted the moderates in the antibusing movement. But it was soon eclipsed by another group that attracted the militants—and the majority—of the movement. Originally called the Save Boston Committee, it soon renamed itself Restore Our Alienated Rights to create a more menacing acronym. Although ROAR claimed it had no "official" leaders, the fact that it held its weekly meetings in the chambers of the Boston City Council, on which Hicks was now a member, suggested otherwise.

Hicks and her fellow councilor Albert "Dapper" O'Neil later took advantage of their positions by pasting big white letters to the inside of their City Hall office windows that spelled "ROAR" so that anyone looking up from the plaza below could read them. The location of this message was in marked contrast to some of the other iconic protest signs of the times, like the "To Hell with Urban Renewal" sign in the front yard of a soon-to-be-demolished home in Allston or the "People Before Highways" message painted on the railroad embankment in Jamaica Plain.

On April 3, 1974, the first day of the annual hearings to repeal the Racial Imbalance Law, the antibusing movement showed just how much it had grown, when more than 25,000 people marched on the State House. The marchers were led by a phalanx of elected officials that included the entire Boston School Committee and all but one member of the Boston City Council. The crowd was described as primarily mothers in their thirties with young, elementary school–age children.[13] It included residents from all over the city, who wore colored armbands to identify their neighborhoods (green for South Boston; brown for Charlestown; purple for Hyde Park; red for Dorchester; etc.). Many carried banners that read, "Ban Busing in Boston."

That year, the hearings and demonstrations lasted for almost a month. On April 30, 1974, both houses of the legislature again voted to repeal the Racial Imbalance Law, this time by overwhelming margins. Governor Sargent again vetoed the repeal bill. But, knowing his veto would be over-ridden, he filed his own bill to dramatically amend the Racial Imbalance Law, and it was quickly approved by the legislature.

The new Racial Imbalance Law continued to use the 50 percent figure to define imbalance. But it no longer required school districts to submit imbalance plans or withheld funds from districts that didn't. Instead, it rewarded school districts that voluntarily submitted plans with additional state funds. Tom Atkins, even though he had by now become a member of Sargent's cabinet as Secretary of Communities and Development, de-nounced the new law as "inequitable, unclear, illegal, and not feasible." But Sargent's top aide, Al Kramer, defended it and called busing "an idea whose time has come and gone."[14]

Boston voters seemed to confirm that view. On May 21, 1974, a special election was held in which only a single, nonbinding referendum question appeared on the ballot. It asked, "Shall any Boston public school children be assigned to a particular Boston public school on the basis of race, sex, or creed without the consent of their parents or legal guardian?" Turnout for the election was only 12 percent, but more than 31,000 people voted "no" on the question, while just over 2,000 voted "yes."[15]

Support for busing seemed to be fading even within the black community, where some activists and elected officials had begun to look at other alternatives. One of those alternatives was called "Community Control of

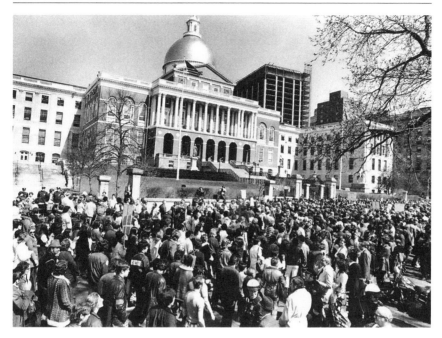

Demonstration for repeal of the Racial Imbalance Law in front of State House on April 3, 1974. Photo by Joseph Dennehy/Globe Staff.

Schools," an experiment that had been tried with very mixed results in Brooklyn, New York, a few years earlier. It involved allowing local residents to decide how the schools in their neighborhood should be run, what they should teach, and how the resources allocated to them should be spent.

On June 13, 1974, the activist-turned-state representative Mel King and other members of the Massachusetts Black Legislative Caucus invited their white colleagues in the legislature from Boston to a meeting in the State House to discuss the idea. The session "broke up with real possibilities for a plan in the air," wrote King. "But when Ray Flynn [then a state representative from South Boston] went to talk to the teachers union they wouldn't buy it." According to King, that was because "the issue was not busing kids from school to school. The issue was economic control." [16]

The question of who would control the Boston schools was settled a week later in U.S. District Court. Nine years earlier, the Boston Branch NAACP had reluctantly filed the class action suit in federal court that charged the Boston School Committee with creating and perpetuating a racially segregated school system. Although that suit didn't ultimately go forward, a subsequent one did. Filed in 1972, it came to be called *Morgan v.*

Hennigan, after one of the plaintiffs, Tallulah Morgan, a twenty-four-year-old Mattapan mother of three, and the then Boston School Committee chairman Jim Hennigan. The case was heard by the U.S. District Court judge W. Arthur Garrity, the former U.S. attorney whose office had been picketed by protesters demanding federal protection for civil rights marchers in 1965.

On June 21, 1974, after two years of hearings that had produced thousands of pages of testimony, Judge Garrity ruled in favor of the plaintiffs. In his decision, he found that the Boston School Committee "had intentionally brought about or maintained a dual school system [that was] unconstitutionally segregated." He found that it had done this not by assigning children to the schools closest to their homes, but by implementing a "neighborhood school policy ... so selective as hardly to have amounted to a policy at all"—one that included "busing, open enrollment, multischool districts, magnet schools, citywide schools and feeder patterns, [that] were antithetical to a neighborhood schools system." [17]

Garrity also found that the schools in the black community "were the most crowded, the oldest, the least well-maintained, and the most poorly staffed that the School Committee could offer." In doing so, he confirmed the complaints that Ruth Batson, the Boston Branch NAACP, Citizens for Boston Public Schools, and others had been making for years.

A close look at the evidence in the case makes it impossible to criticize Garrity's *decision.* It shows that all the while the committee was denying the existence of de facto segregation, it had actually been practicing de jure segregation, even resorting to busing students—black and white—to schools other than those closest to their homes.

But a close look at what the court did next makes it hard not to criticize Garrity's *remedy.* On June 27, 1974, just six days after his ruling, the judge ordered the School Department to implement the plan drawn up by the state Board of Education three months earlier to satisfy the original Racial Imbalance Law—even though the law was in the process of being substantially amended, even though Garrity admitted he had not fully read the plan, and even though Boston's schools were scheduled to open in just ten weeks. [18]

The Board of Education plan was described as a temporary plan and came to be called Phase I. It covered a third of the city, and called for busing between 17,000 and 19,000 high school and junior high students to schools a half hour or more from their homes. Phase I also "paired" for cross-busing the neighborhoods of South Boston and Roxbury, the two poorest in the city and the two with the highest concentrations of white and African American students, respectively.

Many people tried to tell Judge Garrity that the plan was deeply flawed, and suggested he either consider other plans that had been offered or else hold off and spend the next year developing one of his own. "But he wouldn't listen. He just wouldn't listen," recalled Herb Gleason, who was then city corporation counsel. "It was a tragedy. But there was no talking to him. There was just no talking to him." [19]

Phase I was everything those in the antibusing movement had been fighting against, and once Garrity announced that it would be implemented when the school year began, they fought even harder. In doing so, they borrowed tactics from other movements of the era, but employed them at a larger scale and with greater intensity.

They demonstrated—but, from the first, their demonstrations were larger and angrier. On September 9, 1974, for example, some 10,000 people marched from Boston Common to Government Center. A stage had been set up on Cambridge Street so speakers could address the crowd. But when Senator Edward Kennedy, a busing supporter who had been invited to speak, tried to do so, he was pelted with eggs and tomatoes, and had to flee across the street into the federal office building named for his brother, the slain president.

They held motorcades—but unlike the coy "drive-ins" used in East Boston by opponents to airport expansion, these were intimidating convoys that brought their protests out to the suburban homes of those people they felt were trying to tell them how to live their lives. On October 4, 1974, for example, 350 cars descended on Judge Garrity's home in Wellesley, and demonstrators got out of their cars and picketed out front for several hours. A 500-car motorcade went out to the home of the state education commissioner in Needham, and 1,000 cars went out to the home of the president of the *Boston Globe* in Natick.

Like other local protest movements, they pointed out the parallels between their protest and the one in Boston during the American Revolution. At a reenactment of the Battle of Bunker Hill in Charlestown, they carried a banner that read, "We're Right Back Where We Began Two Hundred Years Ago." At a reenactment of the Boston Tea Party, they threw "GarriTEA" bags into Boston Harbor, along with their children's school assignment slips. They held their own version of the March on Washington, when some 2,000 people followed the route of the original march in the nation's capital despite a pouring rain. One of the marchers was nine-year-old Joseph

Yotts of South Boston, who wore a tri-corner hat and cut-down colonial-era military uniform, and told a reporter, "The weather didn't stop them in 1776, and it isn't going to stop us today."[20]

They started their own schools, akin to the "freedom schools" started ten years earlier by black parents trying to help their children escape the horrible conditions of the schools in their community. The antibusing "academies" they founded were an attempt to allow their kids to go to school within their neighborhoods, but they, too, were short-lived.

The fiercest opposition to busing came from three neighborhoods—South Boston, East Boston, and Charlestown. Back then and to this day, some people assumed this was because the residents of these neighborhoods were somehow more bigoted than those in the rest of the city. But Robert Dentler and Marvin Scott, the two Boston University professors who served as Judge Garrity's "experts" in the case, suggested a more acceptable and understandable reason. For years, Dentler and Scott wrote, the school committee had done all it could to segregate the Boston public schools, even forcing some 30,000 students to take buses, streetcars, subways, or automobiles to "out-of-neighborhood schools." So that by 1974, the two men found, these three geographically isolated "enclaves" were the only communities that still had anything resembling "vestiges of neighborhood school subsystems."[21] It was no wonder, then, that their residents fought to keep what little they had left.

It was also no wonder that, when school opened in September 1974, South Boston would be the center of the resistance to what those in the movement called "forced busing," since it was the only one of those three neighborhoods that was included under the Phase I plan.

South Boston wasn't particularly welcoming to "outsiders." But the same thing could have been said of most Boston neighborhoods back then. Robert Guen, who would later become the second Asian American on the Boston School Committee, grew up in Brighton during this time. "Oak Square was the next neighborhood over and I never went there," he said. "I knew the Italian kids lived in East Boston, the Jewish kids in Mattapan and Franklin Field, the blacks in Roxbury, the Irish in Southie. But we never ventured out into those places."[22]

Paul Johnson, one of the first African Americans on the command staff of the Boston Police Department and someone who grew up in the Sugar Hill area of Roxbury, expressed similar sentiments. "I looked down on the people that lived down below," he recalled. "I was just as apt to get beaten up there as I was in South Boston." Leonard Alkins, later president of the

Boston Branch NAACP, remembered, "We used to go to City Point, Castle Island [in South Boston], and never had a problem—until busing."[23]

Busing came to South Boston on the morning of September 12, 1974. Only 68 of the almost 750 white students assigned to South Boston High School showed up on the first day, trudging into the in the sprawling, yellow brick building perched on the hill from which the colonists had driven the British out of Boston in March 1776.[24] The parents of the other white students had kept their children home in response to ROAR's call for a school boycott.[25] Across the city, the parents of 25,000 students, more than one-fourth of the system's enrollment, followed suit.

Outside South Boston High, a crowd of several hundred students and adults gathered. Only 56 black students of the almost 800 assigned to the school were intrepid enough to make the trip. When the buses arrived, the crowd booed and taunted the students with racial epithets as they got off and entered the school.[26]

During the day the crowd dispersed, but it reassembled just before school let out. Once again, those in the crowd taunted the black students as they got on the buses that took them home. A few blocks away, at the nearby Gavin Junior High School, the buses carrying black students there were pelted with eggs, rocks, and bottles. Eight of the students and an adult bus monitor were injured in what was the first—but wouldn't be the last—busing-related violence.[27]

That evening, a group of black community leaders and activists met in the suburban home of Judge Joseph Mitchell to discuss what they should advise black parents to do. The group included Paul Parks, Otto and Muriel Snowden, Ellen Jackson, Betty Johnson, and Ruth Batson, who a week before had admitted, "My main feeling now is, what did I start? Ten years ago, I had no doubts." As the historian Robert Hayden recalled, "We debated until almost midnight, and when a vote was finally taken, everyone voted to recommend that the students should keep going to school."[28]

ROAR, on the other hand, called on white parents to continue the boycott. There was a certain irony to this because, ten years earlier, Louise Day Hicks had called the tactic "illegal" when black parents held their "School Stayouts for Freedom." The call for this boycott forced parents into making the difficult decision of whether to keep their children home and jeopardize their education for a protest that might not work, or to send their children to school and risk being called "collaborators"—or worse.

Parents in East Boston, for example, were pressured to go along with the boycott, even though the neighborhood was not and never would be included in the busing order. But Evelyn Morash, who lived there, refused to go along with the boycott. The daughter of Italian immigrants and the mother of five, she'd been involved with the schools for years, starting when she found out that the milk delivered to her son's school went bad because there was no refrigerator to keep it in. "From warm milk, it led to wondering 'What are they teaching our kids?'"[29]

Morash's refusal to keep her children home caused her to become something of an outcast in her own neighborhood. "I had my windows broken. I had paint smeared on the house. And the thing is, I knew all these people. I had grown up with the mothers who were my age, and I knew the younger ones from having them in Girls Scouts."[30]

Many parents in many neighborhoods did go along with the boycott, however, and for several weeks, school attendance was less than half of total enrollment. Some parents tried to transfer their children into local parochial schools, but since Cardinal Humberto Medeiros declared the archdiocese wouldn't allow its schools to be used as a refuge from busing, not many succeeded. As the weeks went by, with no other alternative available, most parents began sending their children to school. Within two months, attendance climbed to between 60 and 70 percent.

Although the boycott ended, the demonstrations continued, not only in South Boston, but also in the other neighborhoods included under Phase I. The ugly name calling and violence continued as well. Because it was taking place in Boston, the "Cradle of Liberty," it attracted the attention of the national media. Almost every night, the network news featured footage of jeering crowds, attacks on school buses, and police clashing with demonstrators, and busing in Boston was frequently a front-page story in newspapers across the country. "It must be one of the greatest ironies of our time," wrote a reporter for the *Dallas Times Herald*, "when black children quietly and peacefully board buses to desegregate schools in Selma, Atlanta, Richmond and Dallas, but are stoned in Boston."[31]

The media coverage even caught the attention of President Gerald Ford, who had only recently assumed the office after the resignation of Richard Nixon. On October 9, 1974, Ford issued a statement in which he said, "I deplore the violence that I have read about and seen on television." But then he added, "The court decision in that case, in my judgment, was not the best solution to quality education in Boston. I have consistently opposed forced busing to achieve racial balance as a solution to quality education and, therefore, I respectfully disagree with the judge's order."[32]

Six years earlier, President's Johnson announcement that he was stopping the bombing of North Vietnam and wouldn't run for reelection had buoyed the spirits of those in the Boston antiwar movement—until they watched the war continue. Ford's statement similarly buoyed those in Boston's antibusing movement—until it became clear the court order would continue as well.

The violence also continued. Inside school buildings, fights between white and black students were common and sometimes serious. On October 15, 1974, a black student stabbed a white student inside Hyde Park High School, prompting all of the white students to walk out of the building in protest. On October 27, 1974, black students refused to get off buses outside Charlestown High School, claiming they weren't safe inside the school. On December 11, 1974, when another black student stabbed another white student inside South Boston High School, all of the white students walked out of the building that day, and the next day "sympathy walkouts" were held by white students at Brighton, East Boston, Hyde Park, and Roslindale high schools. That night, the mother of the most recent stabbing victim appeared at a school committee meeting and pleaded with the board to close all of the schools "before someone is killed."[33]

The schools were not closed and the "temporary" Phase I plan continued. In February 1975, Judge Garrity appointed four "masters" to hold hearings, review proposals from school, parent, and community groups, and develop what he called a "permanent" plan for the next school year.[34] On March 21, 1975, the masters released what came to be called the "McCormack Plan," named for one of them, former Massachusetts attorney general Edward McCormack.

The McCormack Plan covered the whole city, except for hard-to-reach East Boston, whereas Phase I had covered only a third. But it actually *reduced* the number of children to be bused from between 17,000 and 19,000 to about 15,000, and it assigned them to schools closer to their homes. The plan was able to do that by dividing the city into nine pie-slice-shaped school zones and assigning students to schools within those zones in such a way that each school's enrollment reflected the overall racial makeup of the zone it was in.[35]

The racial makeup of each zone under the plan did vary, however, depending on the residential population in each. But the masters thought this would be acceptable to the black community. In fact, the Freedom House Institute for Education had recently issued a report that stated,

"We support efforts to rid the Boston schools of discriminatory pupil place-ment, but we do not seek racial balance or any rigid formula for fixing the racial proportions in school buildings."[36]

The McCormack Plan received wide if not deep support from residents and groups across the city. It was seen as the best that could be hoped for under the circumstances. "We pretty much had reached a consensus," McCormack said later, noting that ROAR "wouldn't support the plan, but they wouldn't vote to oppose it." But the Boston Branch NAACP did vote to oppose it, according to McCormack, because the group's "national pol-icy" stipulated that the enrollment of every school in a city implementing a desegregation plan reflect a single, city-wide racial "percentage formula."[37]

Tom Atkins, by this time president of the Boston Branch NAACP, called the McCormack Plan "a massive capitulation to violence or the threat of violence." McCormack disagreed, arguing, "To be married to a numbers game—where every school in every section of the city has to have a fixed percentage—gives no credence to quality education."[38] The decision be-longed to Judge Garrity—and in a classic case of "the perfect being the enemy of the good," Garrity rejected the McCormack Plan and instructed his two "experts," Dentler and Scott, to come up with yet another plan, one that turned out to be far from perfect.

The "experts plan," which came to be called Phase II, was released on May 10, 1975. It, too, covered the entire city except for East Boston and di-vided the system into nine school districts. But Phase II *increased* the num-ber of students to be bused to at least 25,000 according to some sources and to as many as 28,000 according to others. It also assigned students to schools much farther from their homes, even though elementary students would be forced to participate for the first time. Phase II had to do both these things if every school in every district were to reflect what came to be called the "ideal racial percentages" of the entire system, which by now was 52 percent white, 36 percent black, and 12 percent other minorities.[39]

Phase II was full of absurdities. It allowed children who lived on the odd-numbered side of a street to stay in their local schools and bused those who lived on the even-numbered side to other neighborhoods—or vice versa. It assigned siblings—even twins—to different schools in different parts of the city. It sent children who lived in racially diverse neighbor-hoods to schools in neighborhoods that were not.

In the South End, the two daughters of Herb and Ann Hershfang, white, middle-class newcomers who had moved there precisely because it was so diverse, were assigned to different schools in different white neighborhoods because someone at School Department headquarters assumed from their address that the girls must be black. "One of my daughters was very optimistic, at first," Herb recalled. "She told us 'Well, at least I'll get a chance to make new friends.' But not long after she started, she came to us and said 'It's hard to go from a school where you're one of the leaders to one where nobody will talk to you.'"[40]

To achieve the ideal racial percentages in every school, Phase II also closed some 20 schools—most of them in the black community—leaving parents who had complained about the quality and conditions of the schools in their neighborhood with no schools at all.[41] In a final absurdity, Phase II assigned students who had been taken out of one school and sent to another under Phase I to their third different school in three years.

The plan provoked outrage all over and at every level of the city. Mayor White said he was "bitterly disappointed that Judge Garrity saw fit to set aside the work of his own masters . . . [and by doing so] virtually guaranteed a continuation of the present level of tension and hostility throughout the city." The *Boston Globe* called Phase II a plan "that almost no one now defends and most of the city detests." "My children were to be separated and sent to three different schools in three different geo-codes, one over eight miles away in Dorchester," recalled Fran Johnnene. "I did not own a car. What if my kids got sick or hurt, missed a bus, or simply forgot their lunch? Three different schools, three different areas of Boston, and me with no car, no choice, no exception, and no appeal!"[42]

Thanks to Phase II, parents throughout the city, including those in two of Boston's most suburban neighborhoods, began to wonder whether to continue to send their children to the Boston public schools—or whether to even stay in the city at all.

WEST ROXBURY *and* ROSLINDALE *had originally been part of the Town of Roxbury, but with Jamaica Plain formed their own town when Roxbury allowed itself to be annexed to Boston. By 1874, however, they followed suit, drawn by the promise of better services, particularly of what was called back then "pure water," and became part of Boston as well.*

By 1970, West Roxbury had a population of almost 35,000 and Roslindale a population of almost 40,000. Both neighborhoods were almost all white and largely middle class. The majority of their residents lived in single-family homes. Many of those residents worked for the city as teachers, firefighters, and cops, even though they lived in what felt like self-contained suburbs. In a way, they had the best of both worlds—until their schools, too, came under the Phase II plan.

On April 24, 1975, some 50 West Roxbury mothers showed their dissatisfaction with Phase II by picketing in front of the new West Roxbury High School, still under construction. The mothers were upset at reports that, after waiting for a high school of their own for years, only 20 percent of the students assigned to it would come from within the neighborhood. But according to Janet Palmariello, a West Roxbury parent, the biggest problem with Phase II didn't have to do with the high school, but with the fact that half of the students to be bused would be children in grades 1 through 5. "If he [Garrity] thinks these parents are going to put their little kids on a bus, they're just not going to do it."[43]

Some parents tried to do it, even though they were worried as they did. In Jamaica Plain, John Bassett told his six-year-old daughter to be careful on the school bus, only to have her reply, "Don't worry, Daddy. When we go down Harrison Avenue, all the white kids duck down. And when we go along Dorchester Avenue, all the black kids duck down."[44] This wasn't the way parents wanted their children to learn their way around the city, and in spring 1975, after Phase II was announced, they took 10,000 of their children out of the Boston public schools.

Phase II was so bad, Ronald Formisano later wrote, that it "actually succeeded in reviving the militant antibusing movement," which had been losing momentum and suffering from a growing "factionalism." One of the first instances of that factionalism had already occurred in September 1974, when Ray Flynn, a state representative from South Boston, broke with Hicks and the others in ROAR and refused to sign a "Declaration of Clarification" stating that they opposed busing because they didn't want to send children into "crime-infested Roxbury."[45]

"My opposition was never over what kids were going where," Flynn said later, "but that all of them and their parents were being forced to take part in a social experiment by bureaucrats who didn't understand families or neighborhoods."[46] Flynn joined other moderates in the Massachusetts Citizens Against Forced Busing. But hard feelings between the groups continued and ROAR militants would occasionally disrupt MCAFB's meetings.

On September 7, 1975, the day before Phase II and the school year started, ROAR sponsored an antibusing rally that drew 10,000 people from neighborhoods throughout Boston and even from the suburbs to City Hall Plaza. Speakers included parents, union leaders, radio talk show hosts, and elected officials, including Hicks, who warned, "We're watching the demise of this great city."[47]

When schools opened the next day, the center for much of the opposition to busing shifted to Charlestown, which was for the first time included under the busing order. "We took a different approach," recalled resident Moe Gillen, whose wife Helen was one of the founders of Powder Keg, Charlestown's chapter of ROAR. "Unlike in South Boston, where the antibusing movement was led by elected officials, in Charlestown the 'establishment' left it up to ordinary people, who just had strong views on how to educate their children."[48]

Many of the demonstrations in Charlestown were "Mothers' Marches." The first took place on September 9, 1975, when more than 400 women and children marched from school to school throughout the neighborhood, singing songs and reciting the "Hail Mary" along the way. The marchers were turned back by police when they tried to enter the schoolyard at Charlestown High School, and, in the confrontation that followed, five of them were arrested. More Mothers' Marches followed over the next several weeks. Soon they spread to South Boston, Hyde Park, and West Roxbury, and gave rise to "Men's Marches" and "Children's Marches" as well.

Charlestown's antibusing movement was also different, according to Gillen, "because we allowed parents the right to decide whether to put their kids on a bus or not. It was up to them."[49] He recalled that he and his wife felt particularly betrayed by busing, because ten years earlier "we had taken a lot of heat for supporting urban renewal in Charlestown. We did it because we were going to get two new elementary schools out of it and a new high school. But then busing came along and they told us our kids couldn't go to those schools. Now you ask yourself 'How would any parent feel?'"[50]

Phase II and the school year continued. So did the demonstrations and occasional violence. And so did the factionalism in the antibusing movement. In March 1976, some ROAR members got wind of what was described as a "secret meeting" between Louise Day Hicks and Mayor White, at which she supposedly agreed to tone down her criticism of the mayor in return for political favors. Members who saw this as a betrayal responded by forming a new group called United ROAR, which they claimed represented "the ordinary people,"[51] even though its leaders were the city councilor John Kerrigan and the antibusing activist-turned-school committee member Elvira "Pixie" Palladino, who by this time had replaced Hicks as the most strident voices against busing.

In spring 1976, the violence associated with the movement reached a horrible climax. On April 5, 1976, after a demonstration on City Hall Plaza, a South Boston teenager, using a staff holding an American flag, attacked Ted Landsmark, an African American lawyer on his way to a meeting in City Hall. Although he was left bruised and bloody, Landsmark refused to "indict" whites in general for his beating. Instead, he pointed to "community leaders who manipulate and use the community for their own selfish gains." Then he added, "Racism diverts people from the real issues, which are more economic than racial."[52]

In choosing his words carefully, Landsmark was able to capture some of the complexity of the busing controversy—which was something the *Boston Herald American* photographer Stanley Forman's now well-known Pulitzer Prize–winning photograph of the attack failed to do. The photograph was picked up by the news media all over the country and even around the world. But the crude power and obvious irony of the image of a black man attacked by a white man wielding an American flag steps from Faneuil Hall, "the Cradle of Liberty," only reinforced the too-simple notion that the battle over busing in Boston was only about race and not also about class and community.

In an apparent reaction to the attack on Landsmark, the violence increased over the next several weeks. The worst incident took place nine days later, when Richard Poleet, a white auto mechanic, was pulled from his car at a traffic light in Roxbury and beaten by a group of young black men. The beating left Poleet in a coma, from which he never recovered. "The beating at City Hall did not justify or explain the random stoning of cars in Roxbury, which did not justify the beating of black bus drivers in South Boston," Mel King said a few days later, "which does not justify the beating of Mr. Poleet and other misguided expressions of frustration and rage occurring throughout the city."[53]

Eventually the violence abated. But the frustration and anger didn't. Parents showed theirs that spring by taking another 10,000 children out of the city's schools.[54] In the two years since busing started, the system had lost 20,000 students, including approximately one-third of its white students.[55]

By fall 1976, as the permanent Phase II continued to be implemented, the battle over busing was essentially over. The demonstrations and violence faded away, but so did more parents and their children. During the next three years, another 10,000 students left the system.[56]

Except for the violence, the racial division, the loss of those 30,000 students, many of whose families left the city, and the fact that the schools had not improved—all very big *excepts*—Judge Garrity's intervention in the Boston public schools did produce some positive results. The lack of equity among schools and neighborhoods was ended, as each school was now allotted comparable resources. School buildings across the city were renovated, many more minority teachers were hired, and minority administrators and principals were appointed for the first time.

But in 1972, when Garrity began hearing the *Morgan* case, the enrollment of the Boston public school system was approximately 96,000, and 61 percent of those students were white and 39 percent minorities, according to Hubie Jones. By 1994, enrollment had dropped to under 60,000, 20 percent of the students were white, 80 percent minority, and many of them, according to a *Boston Globe* editorial, "receive a substandard education."[57]

In marking the twentieth anniversary of Garrity's decision in the *Morgan* case, a *Globe* editorial admitted, "Busing has been a failure in Boston. It achieved neither integration nor better schooling." The editors went on to say, "In the quest for equality, an important requirement for community — a sense of control over governing forces — was tossed aside like so much dross."[58]

The battle over busing revealed the dark side of populism. It showed what could happen when people are needlessly pitted against one another by flawed plans imposed by institutions impervious to political pressure. The battle over busing not only damaged the reputation of the New Boston and defined the city for decades, but it divided the people of the city just when they had begun to build successful coalitions to make the city so much better.

"Garrity's decision to order forced busing changed Boston and the lives of its people," Fran Johnnene said many years later. "We cried and fought. Husbands and wives divorced from the strain. Friendships were forged and others destroyed. Families crumbled and neighborhoods changed forever as close-knit, multi-generational, ethnic enclaves were torn apart when younger members moved away to other towns so that their kids could still walk to school. Was it worth it? Was the havoc wrought on Boston's schools, Boston's neighborhoods and families, and an entire generation of students even necessary?"[59]

CHAPTER 19

◦

Fighting for a Fair Share

IN THE MID-1970S, EVEN AS BUSING WAS DIVIDING THE PEOPLE of Boston, a new organization—Massachusetts Fair Share—was launched whose express purpose was to bring people from different neighborhoods and communities together around issues of common concern. For a while, anyway it was spectacularly successful.

In 1973, the first Fair Share chapter was founded in the small, predominately working-class city of Chelsea, across the Chelsea River from East Boston. It was created by Lee Staples, Mark Splain, and Barbara Bowen, All three had worked for the National Welfare Rights Organization during its short-lived bid to compete with the Mothers for Adequate Welfare five years earlier. Based on that unpleasant experience, Staples said later, "We were looking for a new model. We wanted to build a statewide organization that would bring a multiracial and multiethnic group of low- and moderate-income people together across the state over a range of issues."[1]

Working from a storefront office on Broadway, the young organizers offered free help in preparing income tax returns to residents and at the same time tried to get them to join this new organization. Within a year, Chelsea Fair Share had 400 members and had launched campaigns that succeeded in getting hot lunches served in the public schools, crossing guards posted at busy intersections, and which had tried unsuccessfully to get residents reduced tolls on the Tobin Bridge.[2] The young organization's most dramatic victory had come, when, after holding demonstrations against a local slum landlord and putting up "WANTED" posters with his picture on them all over town, they got police to arrest the landlord for failing to respond to a court order and then haul him away in handcuffs.

The success of Chelsea Fair Share prompted an invitation to its organizers to form a chapter in East Boston that helped in the fight against airport expansion, and one in Waltham that helped organize a drive for rent control. The three Fair Share chapters worked separately on narrower issues and together on broader ones, like a campaign to roll back the big increases in car insurance premiums the state's drivers faced after the Massachusetts legislature deregulated the state's auto insurance industry. On December 13, 1974, members from all three chapters turned out at a hearing of the Massachusetts Insurance Commission and presented the lawyer for the auto insurance industry with a slab of bologna to show what they thought of his arguments for the higher premiums. After a three-year fight, Fair Share helped 600,000 drivers across the state get more than $55 million in insurance rebates.[3]

By 1975, Fair Share's staff had doubled to six. But while there was no shortage of work for them, there was a shortage of funds with which to pay them. The grant money that had helped to start the organization had run out, and the minimal membership dues the organization charged didn't generate nearly enough to pay the young men and women anything close to a living wage. For a while, they took turns getting laid off and collecting unemployment so they could continue their organizing. But then Staples and Splain heard about an organization like theirs in California that supported itself by hiring a company that sent canvassers door-to-door to ask for donations to support its work. "We signed a contract with a former encyclopedia salesman," Staples explained. "At the time, I was in charge of bookkeeping and kept the books and all the paperwork in a cardboard box in the trunk of my car. Our annual budget was something like $40,000. Within about two months, the canvassing was bringing in something like $20,000 a week."[4]

Flush from this new revenue source, Fair Share expanded dramatically, adding a dozen new chapters, including Boston chapters in Allston–Brighton, Hyde Park/Roslindale, and Roxbury/North Dorchester/Mattapan. Soon after that, Fair Share grew even larger by merging with two organizations doing similar work in Boston's largest neighborhood.

Like many other neighborhoods, DORCHESTER *started as a separate town. Founded a few months before Boston in 1630, it might have become the capital of the Massachusetts Bay Colony but for an accident of geography. "Had not the waters of Dorchester Bay been more shallow than those of the other side of Dorchester Heights," a nineteenth-century historian wrote, "we should probably have had to record the annexation of Boston to Dorchester instead of the reverse."⁵ That annexation occurred in 1870, and Dorchester soon developed into a classic "streetcar suburb," with rows of streets lined by three-deckers that were quickly thrown up and just as quickly filled by families escaping the crowded confines of Boston's inner city neighborhoods.*

By 1970, Dorchester was home to more than 107,000 residents, one-sixth of the city's population. Most were working or lower middle class. More than 75 percent were white, but more and more African Americans were beginning to move in from neighboring Roxbury and some Hispanic Americans were moving there from the South End.

Except for construction of the Southeast Expressway in the late 1950s, which sliced its bay and beaches off from the rest of the neighborhood, Dorchester had escaped most of the big projects and programs that had threatened other neighborhoods in the New Boston. But by the 1970s, it faced smaller, more insidious threats. One came from landlords, who weren't maintaining their properties but were increasing rents. The other came from the city itself, which was providing low-level services but assessing homes at much higher levels than they were worth. Longtime residents responded by becoming more active, reviving some long-dormant neighborhood organizations, and joining with some newcomers who started new ones.

One of those new organizations was the Dorchester Community Action Council (DCAC). Founded in 1968 by Reverend Bob Stuhlmann, an Episcopal minister, it included longtime residents like Joseph Dunn as well as newcomers like Lew Finfer. The former Harvard student whose sentiments about the unfairness of the draft had not been shared by his dormitory mates had since moved to Dorchester to become a tenant organizer. "DCAC had originally been called the Dorchester Tenants Action Council," Finfer recalled, "but it had changed its name and broadened its focus to include neighborhood improvement issues because only about 20 percent of Dorchester residents were tenants of big landlords at the time, and the other 80 percent were homeowners or the tenants of homeowners."⁶

DCAC continued to work with tenants, but also took on homeowner-related issues, such as challenging the city's assessment practices. It also got involved in issues that were of concern to all residents, such as improving the delivery of city services and supporting the formation of local crime watches. By October 1975, DCAC had grown to approximately 500 members, but it decided it could be even more effective by merging with this even more broadly based up-and-coming organization called Fair Share.

Another new organization was started by Michael Ansara and other former SDS members, who had moved to Dorchester to organize "across class lines." The group began by opening a thrift store and food co-op, and then started a short-lived community newspaper called *The People First.* Years later, Ansara admitted, "We brought with us all the baggage of the college antiwar movement. A few people liked us. But a lot of people disliked us, and a few even hated us. It was pretty clear that we did not know what were doing." Kit Clark, a Dorchester native and activist, agreed. "They moved so quickly. I think their background was of concern to all of us. Remember, we had just come out of an era when there was unrest in the schools, and that didn't sit very well with most of us. It was a very frightening name to me, the SDS. It scared a lot of us." [7]

Faced with this less-than-warm welcome, the young radicals retrenched and formed Citizens Action Program on Energy, an organization with a much less ideologically driven goal. CAP Energy aimed to help residents fight the huge increases they were seeing in their electric and gas bills as a result of the Massachusetts legislature's decision to deregulate the utility industry. At one point, CAP Energy found itself competing with Fair Share for a grant from the Archdiocese of Boston's Campaign for Human Development Fund. "CHD said, 'We won't give either of you a $120,000 one-year grant,'" recalled Ansara, "'but if you merge, we'll give you a $250,000 grant every year for years.'" As a result of this "shotgun marriage," CAP merged with the larger group. [8]

On November 18, 1975, Massachusetts Fair Share celebrated what it called its "official" founding with a press conference at the Statler Hilton Hotel in downtown Boston. [9] The event attracted clergy, labor leaders, and community activists from all over the city, and "both sides of the busing issue." [10] One of the activists who was there was Anna DeFronzo of East Boston. She told the crowd, "Ten years ago, thirty mothers set out to save our neighborhood from the airport. They told us you can't fight power. They were wrong. Just imagine if all the neighborhoods get together, there isn't anything we can't win." [11]

The new, improved, and much-expanded Fair Share moved its headquarters to downtown Boston, established a Boston Fair Share to coordinate chapters within the city, and a Metro Fair Share to coordinate and organize new chapters in the suburbs. It started new chapters in Worcester, Springfield, the Merrimack Valley, and Fall River, and began to publish a monthly newsletter, *The Fair Fighter.* Mark Splain, one of the founders of the original Chelsea chapter, was its first executive director, but he was soon succeeded by the more dynamic Ansara.

"The idea behind Fair Share was that all the institutions that supported blue collar residents were declining," Ansara recalled. "Reformers had destroyed the political machines and ward politics that helped people get jobs. All the power growth was in the suburbs. Inflation was robbing people of a lot of what they had. We felt it was possible to build a suburban-urban coalition to replace what had been lost." But he later admitted to a reporter, "To be truthful, I didn't think we would make it. We tried to impress on public consciousness that we were here to stay—but we did it with smoke and mirrors." [12]

However they did it, Fair Share quickly made a strong impression on the public consciousness across the state. The organization and its various chapters proceeded to launch a dizzying number of campaigns—too many to describe here. A sample of Dorchester Fair Share's activities is enough to give some idea of their range and effectiveness.

Dorchester Fair Share got 600 minority homeowners, who'd all been victimized by the notorious Boston Banks Urban Renewal Group program, thousands of dollars each in rebates for home repairs from the Federal Housing Administration. It got the city to release a list of all the major tax delinquents, got the *Boston Globe* to print it, and got some of these scofflaws—including one who owed more than $50,000 in back taxes—to pay up. [13]

The Dorchester chapter organized a meeting for 600 homeowners at the Grover Cleveland School to discuss property tax abatements with Mayor White—and when the mayor didn't show up, it rented buses and brought 300 of those homeowners to picket in front of the mayor's Beacon Hill home in what was described as a "taxpayer pilgrimage." Later, Reverend Tom Corrigan, who by this time had been assigned by the archdiocese to work full-time with Fair Share, commented, "I have to say that we've given the mayor a very clear message. Residents are very angry in this city, and they are willing to come out in the cold to show it." The mayor and the city apparently got the message. Eventually, more than 2,400 homeowners received abatements. [14]

Fair Share and its various chapters would rack up numerous victories. But its biggest success may have been in getting so many people to become

Massachusetts Fair Share demonstration against branch bank closing outside First National Bank in April 1978. Photo by Edward Jenner/Globe Staff.

activists and giving them the confidence to be effective. "When I used to call city officials and say I was from Fair Share, they'd say, 'So what?' and put me on hold," said Diane Roberts of Dorchester. "Now it's, 'What can I do for you, ma'am?'" Mike Regan of Charlestown reflected, "All my life, I was working two jobs, raising a family, and feeling angry, but with no way to express that. Now I have a way of getting up in front of 500 people and expressing myself, a way of talking to politicians face to face. My whole life has changed."[15]

Carolyn Lucas of Hyde Park said, "I never thought I'd ever march on a picket line. And when I did for the first time, I said to myself, 'What are you doing here?' If the other people there had had long hair and beards, I never would have stayed. But they didn't. They were people like me and Mike Regan." Her sister, Evelyn Hannigan, recalled that before joining Fair Share she was "just an average housewife, never questioning anything, just believing that we didn't have enough money in the family because my father didn't work hard enough—which, of course, he did. Now I have a whole different perspective on the connections between politics and people's lives."[16]

Fair Share was most effective when it focused on small, local issues. It had a much harder time when it took on big, statewide campaigns—like the one against the Massachusetts electric industry. At the time, electric companies charged residents, who used less energy, much higher rates than big commercial users, who used much more. In 1976, Fair Share pushed for what it called a "Flat Rate" system under which all users would be charged at the same rate, and it collected more than the 80,000 signatures in order to get its Flat Rate question on the statewide election ballot.[17]

Fair Share mounted a spirited campaign from Boston to the Berkshires to try to get voters to support the Flat Rate. It argued that not only would the Flat Rate system be fairer, but it also would promote energy conservation, save families 10–20 percent on their energy bills, and save small businesses 30 percent on theirs.[18] But the utility companies and the business community responded with their own much more well-funded campaign, which included billboards and television commercials claiming the measure would hurt the economy and produce massive layoffs. They even got employers to attach campaign literature containing this message to the paychecks of their employees. On November 2, 1976—whether it was due to the advertising or the arguments—the Flat Rate question was defeated by a 4 to 1 margin.

After losing the Flat Rate campaign, even some Fair Share staff members questioned whether the organization should have taken on the fight in the first place. "I thought we were moving too fast," recalled Renée Loth, who handled communications and jokingly referred to herself the "minister of propaganda." "We bit off more than we could chew, we went into debt, and the organization never recovered." [19]

Despite its debt, Fair Share continued to add members and spend money. By 1980, according to *The Real Paper*, it claimed a membership of 50,000, and had a full-time paid staff of 55 and an operating budget of $1.3 million. But the organization seemed to have undergone an identity change. A city official in Boston complained that Fair Share had become more interested in "consciousness raising" than in getting results. One of its founders, Lee Staples, said it had become "too slick. It was one thing to use the media to get credit for the base. But it was another thing when it was all smoke and mirrors." As Staples told Lew Finfer, "Some of us felt it had become too much of a white, middle-class organization, and was no longer about wealth redistribution." [20]

Ansara disputed that charge. "We were large enough to do both urban and suburban," he maintained. "The biggest problem with Fair Share wasn't the split between the suburbs and the city, it was the split over race.

We weren't allowed to go into South Boston. The South Boston Improvement Association wanted us there, but [antibusing leader] Jimmy Kelly and [organized-crime boss] "Whitey" Bulger said no. Mel King and the black community were off and on with us. Sometimes they'd be our friends and sometimes they wouldn't." Tom Corrigan later reflected, "I wish we had done more to encourage inter-racial cooperation. But the busing issue was just too big for us to bridge the divide between the two sides."[21]

Fair Share also found itself in conflict with city hall and in competition with another group. The conflict arose when Mayor White refused to approve a federal grant for the organization so that it could develop an arson prevention program for Boston, which would soon be called "the arson capital of the world." Ansara said at the time, "I don't understand it; here the federal government is willing to give us $250,000 and the mayor doesn't want it to happen." His only explanation was, "White's political machine wants to control every penny that comes into Boston."[22]

The competition came from the National Association of Community Organizations for Reform Now. Despite Fair Share's efforts to dissuade it, ACORN decided to open a Boston chapter. It did focus on wealth redistribution and urban neighborhoods, and it also got involved in local electoral politics, something Fair Share couldn't do unless it changed its nonprofit status, which it subsequently did.[23]

But it was Fair Share's refusal to face its financial problems that finally did the organization in. In the summer of 1983, a long overdue audit revealed the organization owed more than $1 million in federal and state withholding taxes, health insurance premiums, and bills to creditors. Ansara was forced to resign as executive director. The organization was forced to lay off most of its staff and close down many of its chapters. Fair Share limped along for a few years at a much-reduced level, but it eventually had to declare bankruptcy and shut down.

Despite its inglorious end, Fair Share had a remarkable run while it lasted. It not only fanned the flame of activism that was flickering at this time, but it gave many more people in Boston and across the state the skills and the confidence to engage in activism and to continue it long after Fair Share was forced to close its doors.

CHAPTER 20

——◄○►——

A Downturn in Activism

BY THE MID-1970S—WITH THE NOTABLE EXCEPTIONS OF THE antibusing movement and Fair Share—the flame of activism *was* flickering in the New Boston. One reason had to do with policy changes in Washington. For the last decade, federal spending for domestic programs— particularly those for cities—had been cut to pay for the Vietnam War. But for some reason, even though the war had ended, the promised "peace dividend" failed to materialize.

The Nixon administration, as part of its "New Federalism" policy, also changed how it funneled existing funds to cities, replacing urban renewal with the Community Development Block Grant program. For all its faults, urban renewal invested large amounts of federal money in cities like Boston, required local government to work with residents to decide how the money was spent, and encouraged residents in different neighborhoods to work together. The CDBG program provided much less funding, left decisions on how to spend it up to local officials, and forced residents and neighborhoods to compete with one another to get any of it.

As far back as 1967, at the urging of mayors and other local officials, Congress had passed the Green Amendment, which reigned in community action programs promoting the "maximum feasible participation" of residents. The Nixon administration went even further and set out to dismantle entirely the Office for Economic Opportunity (OEO).

"Except for that brief period in the 1960s, community organizing has always been considered a fringe activity," reflected Val Hyman, who by the mid-1970s was working for the Madison Park Community Development

Corporation. "There's no identifiable product, and so there's no funding for it. That was the thing about OEO—they funded it. But times change, and so do administrations. OEO started under Sargent Shriver. It ended under Donald Rumsfeld."[1]

Other reasons that the flame of activism was flickering in Boston had to do with what was going on in the city itself. In terms of neighborhood redevelopment, urban renewal might have been over, but community development corporations were still going strong. "But now they were being run by a different cast of characters than the ones who started them," Hyman pointed out. "And they had to be. Most activists don't plan for the future. They live for the moment and so they're not very good at being managers. Now that they'd gotten stuff built, CDCs needed managers, not community organizers."[2]

In terms of civil rights, "I think we thought: 'We're done, we've opened those doors,'" said Sarah-Ann Shaw years later. "And we thought those doors would stay open and others would open, and that we just didn't have any more work to do."[3]

In terms of the Boston public schools, many white activists had ended their involvement after busing, taken their children out of the system, and themselves out of the city. Many black activists were content to let the federal court do their work, and many black parents pursued other routes to try to get a better education for their children, including the Metropolitan Council for Educational Opportunity program. "People don't want to talk about it," recalled Gail Snowden, "but kids who went to school through METCO—their parents became more focused on what was happening in the suburbs than in their own neighborhood. They were more concerned with Lincoln-Sudbury than Roxbury."[4]

With the war in Vietnam over, many of the young people who had been involved in the antiwar movement got on with their lives. Although quite a few of them continued their activism in Boston neighborhoods, they did it in a much more subdued way.

Changes in the local media also contributed to the downturn in local activism. The city was down to two daily newspapers, and, when the *Herald* was bought by the Hearst Corporation, it became more concerned with scandal than civics. At the *Globe*, all those young reporters brought in ten years before were now ten years older. Many had married, moved to the suburbs, and lost touch with Boston's neighborhoods. "We were always getting criticized for not covering the city anymore," recalled Renée Loth, by this time a *Globe* reporter. "Billy Bulger [the state senator from South

Boston] used to joke that if you wanted to call somebody on the Urban Team now, you had to dial 'I' first and then the number," Loth said, referring to the procedure that had to be used back then to call someone outside of the city. Sarah-Ann Shaw, who was still reporting for WBZ-TV, later called the Boston media "fickle. Its interest had gone from civil rights to antiwar to ecology. But there was never a consistent plan that was put in place to ensure ongoing coverage of the neighborhoods."[5]

Welfare had receded as an issue after the state assumed the responsibility for operating it. Construction of the two superhighways had been stopped. The MBTA was in the process of relocating the Orange Line to the route along which the never-built Southwest Expressway was to have run, and residents were engaged in trying to figure out what should be built on all of the vacant land that had been cleared. But this was long, slow but steady work that called more for patience than protest.

In 1978, East Boston residents did get a scare when former Massport director Ed King surprisingly was elected governor. But, fortunately for them, King was defeated when he ran for reelection and before he could use his appointments to the Massport board to reassert control over the agency.

Many of Boston's leading activists, including Reverend James Breeden, Noel Day, and Ted Parrish, had left Boston. Many of those who remained had moved on with their careers. Bob Coard was still running Action for Boston Community Development, but it was now the largest social service provider in the city and its days of fomenting unrest were over. Ruth Batson and Jean McGuire were running METCO, and McGuire would soon be elected to the Boston School Committee. Julian Houston and Herb Hershfang were practicing law and would soon be appointed judges. Byron Rushing had become president of the Museum of Afro-American History. Hubie Jones was dean of Boston University's School of Social Work. Herb Gleason was the city's corporation counsel. Reverend Michael Haynes, Mel King, Doris Bunte, and Monsignor Mimie Pitaro had all been elected state representatives (Pitaro was the first Catholic priest ever to serve in the Massachusetts legislature). Tom Atkins, Paul Parks, and Fred Salvucci all held cabinet positions in state government. Dan Richardson had been named regional director of the U.S. Department of Housing and Urban Development. Anne Hershfang and Evelyn Morash were serving on the boards of the Massachusetts Transportation Department and Education Department, respectively.

The fact that so many activists had attained such prominent positions was unquestionably a great benefit to the people and the neighborhoods of Boston. But the fact that they were no longer out in the streets providing that day-to-day leadership at the grassroots level was also something of a loss.

But perhaps one of the biggest reasons for the downturn in activism and protest in Boston, had to do with Kevin White, the city's longtime mayor. When he was first elected, White had paid long-overdue attention to the city's neighborhoods. Since then, though, he seemed to have spent most of his time running for higher office, running for reelection when no other opportunities presented themselves, or focusing his attention elsewhere.

After losing a bid for governor in 1970, White was reelected mayor in 1971. But rather than concentrating on the job he had, he kept looking for another. He was nearly chosen as the Democratic Party's nominee for vice president in 1972, an experience that those close to him admitted had left the reluctant mayor with a lingering case of "Potomac fever." For the next few years, White appeared to be pursuing another route to Washington by wining and dining visiting dignitaries at the Parkman House, a restored, city-owned mansion on Beacon Hill. The result, wrote Alan Lupo, was that "two terms after his election, on a platform of turning government to the needs of the neighborhoods, Boston's neighborhoods were still in dire need."[6]

In 1975, with no better option available, White was forced to run for re-election again. This time he found himself in a surprisingly close race with Joe Timilty, an ex-Marine, former city councilor, and now the state senator from Mattapan. The two men engaged in a campaign that was more like something from the Old Boston. It was later described as a "mud fight reminiscent of when Curley blackmailed Fitzgerald out of the race in 1914."[7] On November 4, 1975, White barely escaped becoming the first incumbent mayor to lose a bid for reelection since Curley in 1949, beating Timilty by just 81,000 votes to 73,000.

Rather than see this as a signal that he should go back out into the neighborhoods, White withdrew even more. "When he won that election narrowly, he said 'O.K., I'm going to go with the political machine and I will never face *that* again,'" recalled Barney Frank. The political machine that White subsequently created was the closest thing to a Chicago/Richard Daley–style operation that Boston had ever seen. "Every department head, no matter how high or mighty, no matter how professionally renowned or apolitical, would now have political responsibilities as well as his normal official duties," explained the *Boston Globe* columnist Ken Hartnett.[8]

Funded primarily by campaign contributions from downtown real estate interests, that machine was so effective at extracting every vote from city workers, their families, and friends, that it relieved White of the responsibility of having to address the dire needs of the neighborhoods. "He stopped going out there," recalled Paul Grogan, then an aide to White. "It was as if he wanted to be mayor, but he didn't want to go to the meetings."[9]

Tenants in Boston were among the first to feel the effects of White's withdrawal. On December 24, 1975, the mayor, who had once promised to "raise hell" if landlords "raise rents," signed a new rent control ordinance that gutted tenant protections. It cut the number of rental units covered by more than half, to 60,000, and it exempted "luxury apartments," like the ones at Charles River Park owned by Jerome Rappaport, who had insinuated himself back into city politics to such an extent that he was being called "Boston's Tenth City Councilor." As far as tenants were concerned, however, the worst part of the new law was its "vacancy decontrol" provision, which removed apartments from regulation once they became vacant, as one-third of them did every year in Boston.

Shortly after signing the new law, White further revealed his change of heart on the issue by declaring, "Rent control stinks," and then firing Bill Edgerton, the city's rent control administrator, who had come under "criticism from the city's landlords" for being too sympathetic to tenants. Edgerton noted that the new law resulted in "the visible melting away of the tenant groups." Jim Creamer, then a tenant organizer, later agreed. "A lot of tenants and tenant organizers felt like what they'd gained had now been lost. Landlords took advantage of vacancy decontrol to harass a lot of tenants, especially the more active ones, into leaving apartments. Those who were left figured that it was just college students who were moving into the vacancy decontrolled units now, and they didn't really feel like fighting for them."[10]

Tenants in one neighborhood, however, did feel like they had to fight—but not so much against higher rents that threatened to force them from their homes, as against a wave of arson that threatened their lives.

The FENWAY–KENMORE *neighborhood was created as an extension of the filling of the Back Bay in the late nineteenth century. Despite the fact that a Brahmin named Jack Gardner described it back then as a "barren waste land," he encouraged his New York–born wife Isabella to build a museum there, and a number of the city's premier cultural and then health care institutions soon followed. Long rows of apartment buildings were subsequently put up in the neighborhood as well, initially as homes to middle-class Bostonians.*[11]

By 1970, however, the population of almost 33,000 residents, 90 percent of whom were white, had changed dramatically. It was now made up mostly of college students and recent graduates, elderly residents on fixed incomes, and an increasing number of transients and low-income families.

In 1973, residents of one small part of the neighborhood began to fear for their lives, when a series of suspicious fires broke out along Symphony Road, a block-long street lined with four-story brick buildings behind Symphony Hall and just a few blocks from the Prudential Center. More than twenty fires took place over the next few years, and on September 12, 1976, one of those fires killed a four-year-old girl.

A few years earlier, a group of about 30 residents, including a number of college-educated activists, had formed the Symphony Tenants Organizing Project to try to do something about the deteriorating housing conditions in the area. This STOP group (not to be confused with the civil rights STOP Campaign of the 1960s) turned its attention to trying to stop what the group was convinced was an arson-for-profit campaign being carried out by property owners.[12]

David Scondras was one of the leaders of STOP. Born and raised in Lowell, he was a Harvard graduate and Northeastern University mathematics instructor, who had done his master's thesis in economics on property ownership patterns on Symphony Road. Scondras's data showed that "it could be more profitable for landlords to burn their buildings than to rent or manage them" if they took out insurance policies that placed a value on those buildings that was much more than they were actually worth.[13]

The group used Scondras's data to persuade the city council to hold a rare Sunday hearing on the fires in November 1976. It even got Mayor White to make what was becoming an increasingly rare neighborhood appearance a few months later. Unfortunately, Scondras complained at the time, "We couldn't get anywhere with the city." The *Boston Globe* reporter Ken Hartnett wrote that there were three reasons for this. One was a "bureaucratic inflexibility" on the part of the city. Another was a "conservative unease at dealing with community organizers who neither dress, talk, or behave in the middle-class manner." The third reason was a "history of antagonism" with STOP because Scondras had "contributed to Joseph Timilty's position paper on the city's economic condition in the 1975 campaign."[14]

Stonewalled by the city, STOP turned to the state and got much better results. On March 30, 1977, Governor Mike Dukakis came out and toured Symphony Road. A week later, he returned and announced that he would support a bill STOP had filed in the legislature that would take the profit out of arson by prohibiting owners from insuring their buildings at inflated values and insurers from paying claims on properties with code violations. The bill would also require that, before any claims were paid to owners, tenants would first be paid for their relocation costs.[15]

As the bill was making its way through the legislature, however, another fire broke out on a street adjacent to Symphony Road that killed four more people. The STOP group responded by launching a "media blitz" that led to stories in the local papers, prompted appearances by members of the group on television and radio talk shows, and got the attention of the Massachusetts attorney general's office. "We were amazed by the tenants' work in establishing patterns of ownership," said Assistant Attorney General Stephen Delinsky, who had been named to lead the state's new arson task force. "They organized and fought their way into recognition."[16]

On October 17, 1977, that recognition translated into the first of a series of pre-dawn raids by the state police in which 33 people were arrested for engaging in what was called "a huge conspiracy to burn Suffolk County for profit." Those arrested were landlords, lawyers, insurance agents, contractors, and public officials—including the chief investigator in the state fire marshal's office and the former head of the Boston arson squad.[17] After 29 buildings had been burned, some 400 families had lost their homes, and five people had lost their lives, the fires on Symphony Road were finally stopped.[18]

But STOP didn't stop there. In the spring of 1978, it received a $200,000 federal grant to operate an anti-arson program described as "the first of its kind in the nation and [which] is intended to be used as a model for other American cities." On July 15, 1978, Governor Dukakis went out to the neighborhood again, this time to sign the bill that was "designed to take the profit out of arson." He did it in front of a crowd of 150 residents who had gathered in the Edgerly Road playground, and told them, "All of us owe a debt of gratitude to you."[19]

At the risk of spoiling the celebratory mood of the event, Scondras, who five years later became the first openly gay member elected to the Boston City Council, reminded the crowd of something. Everyone, he said, "had been telling us that the fires were set by Puerto Ricans, by newly moved-in blacks, by the tenants themselves. [But] when the indictments came down, there was not one black or Puerto Rican among them. It was the suburbanites who did not even live in Boston and who wanted to burn us out of our homes, out of our community, for profit, for a buck."[20]

While Boston neighborhoods were experiencing these and other challenges, Mayor White was turning his attention to the city's downtown. The mayor micromanaged the tail end of another development boom and even overruled the Boston Redevelopment Authority's choices for the developers to renovate the Quincy Market buildings and build a new hotel on Long Wharf. "He seemed to go through a different BRA director every six months," recalled Langley Keyes.[21] White also spent a lot of time promoting the city's lavish 1976 Bicentennial celebration and traveling to Boston's new "Sister Cities" around the world. Everywhere he went, the mayor extolled Boston as a "livable" and "world-class" city, and pointed to its booming downtown and revitalized waterfront to prove his case.

But the neighborhoods were becoming less livable and there was nothing classy about the level of services that residents were receiving. "All the city's big service institutions were being taken over by the courts," recalled Bob Turner, then a *Boston Globe* reporter and later an editor. "The schools, the Boston Housing Authority [after a suit by tenants over housing, health, and building code violations], the jail [after a suit by inmates over living conditions], the harbor [after a suit over pollution], the police and fire departments [after a suit over hiring discrimination]. I couldn't figure out why a city that is supposed to be so sophisticated would let that happen. But then Barney Frank explained it to me. He said it was *because* White's campaign operation was so sophisticated that they could get away with it. They knew how many votes they needed, knew they could deliver those votes, and so they knew there would be no political price for screwing up."[22] The people of Boston seemed to understand this prevailing political calculus, as well, and it seemed to undercut their ability to press for any better treatment from City Hall.

By 1979, when White ran for reelection to a fourth term, he was being criticized in terms almost identical to those that he and others had used to criticize his predecessor, John Collins. Joe Timilty, making another run for the office, claimed White's last two terms had been "all bricks and mortar." Mel King, making his first run for mayor, charged, "The neighborhoods don't have the same access to City Hall as the business community."[23]

CHAPTER 20

But White's political machine was able to perform as expected. On November 6, 1979, White again beat Timilty, this time by the somewhat wider margin of 78,000 votes to 64,000.

During his fourth term, Kevin White couldn't have paid much attention to Boston's neglected neighborhoods even if he had wanted to—because by then the city was facing its worst financial crisis since the birth of the New Boston. One reason for the crisis was the severe recession that the whole country was experiencing. Another was the city's own fault. In 1979, in a case known as *Tregor v. Board of Assessors of Boston*, the Massachusetts Supreme Judicial Court found that the city had over-assessed major commercial property owners by a whopping $143 million. Paying the money back put a severe strain on the city's pocketbook.

But the third and biggest reason for the city's financial woes was that Massachusetts voters, like California voters two years earlier, staged a taxpayers revolt against what they felt was the too-high cost of state and local government. On November 4, 1980, they passed a ballot measure called Proposition 2 1/2 that drastically reduced the amount of revenue that cities and towns could raise through property taxes. Prop 2 1/2 hit Boston particularly hard, forcing the city to cut its budget by one-fourth, lay off 3,000 employees, and close neighborhood police and fire stations.[24]

The budget cuts forced the city to phase out a number of programs, including two that White had had introduced with such fanfare. "The official line at City Hall is that these programs were the victims of Boston's fiscal plight," wrote the *Boston Globe* columnist Carol Surkin at the time, "but behind the scenes, White has wanted to dispose of Little City Halls and Community Schools since his 1975 re-election campaign . . . not satisfied with the[ir] re-election value . . . and irked that the program served many who did not work or vote for him."[25] Residents weren't sorry to lose the Little City Halls, which by now were seen as patronage havens that handed out political favors. But they did fight against the closing of the community schools and were able to keep them open.

By the beginning of the 1980s, the New Boston was being described in terms eerily similar to those that had been used for the Old Boston. The *Washington Post* said the city was "suffering from financial anemia, serious racial problems, ongoing political corruption and a disintegration of city services in the poorer neighborhoods." The *New York Times* noted, "As skyscrapers spring up, schools and public housing become so dilapidated that the courts take them over. As new restaurants and hotels open,

204

neighborhood stores close." *Time* wrote, "While some high-profile parts of the city are burgeoning, a lot of the rest is coming apart at the seams." [26]

The Brookings Institution ranked Boston as one of the four "most distressed cities" in the country, despite all the talk about its world-class downtown. One of the authors of the report noted, "New buildings can improve the tax base or economy of the city without improving the situation of all its residents." [27]

The New Boston needed a major course correction. Fortunately for the people of Boston, they had the chance to make one in the next mayoral campaign.

Back to the Neighborhoods

"NINETEEN EIGHTY-THREE WAS THE YEAR OF THE NEIGHBOR-hoods in Boston politics. It was the year in which the old Boston struck back against the 'New Boston,'" wrote Jack Beatty, the biographer of James Michael Curley, the quintessential mayor of the "Old Boston." Beatty went on to describe the city in 1983 as one with a downtown transformed "into a parody of midtown Manhattan"—neighborhoods that had "deteriorated dramatically," residents feeling "left behind in Boston's giddy rise to the status of a 'world-class city,'" and a "psychology of exclusion [that] kindled Boston's urban populism."[1]

This kindled—or rekindled—urban populism had begun to manifest itself two years earlier. That was when voters approved a change in the city charter that replaced the nine-member Boston City Council, to which members were elected at-large, with a thirteen-member body to which four members were elected at-large and nine by district. It was an attempt to undo the over-correction made in the charter in 1949 to a completely at-large council and to once more guarantee that every neighborhood would have a representative on the city's legislative body.

But since Boston's charter invests most of the power in the city in the mayor's office, the people of Boston knew that if they really wanted any of it back they'd have to change mayors, something that is a particularly difficult thing to do in Boston. On May 26, 1983, however, Kevin White made it easy for them by announcing that he would not run for what would have been at the time an unprecedented fifth term—he was stepping down after sixteen years in office.

In a newspaper article the next day, White defended his legacy and explained why he had shifted his focus away from the neighborhoods during his long tenure. "As a new mayor, my first task was to prove that city government could work—for everybody. To do this, it meant physically spending most of my first years in office out in the streets, in the neighborhoods," he wrote. But "bringing life to the neighborhoods would mean nothing if the downtown were to die. Without rebuilding the city's economy the neighborhoods would wither, like branches on a dead tree. So I began to invest and develop and to create a process that would guarantee our future, but at the same time preserve our past."[2]

Kevin White "worked vigorously and creatively to establish Boston's reputation as a world-class city," wrote the historian Thomas O'Connor, a city that was "a far cry from the depressed and run-down backwater it had been less than twenty years earlier." But the *Boston Herald* columnist Wayne Woodlief called White "a political Jekyll and Hyde" who left "two distinct legacies. . . . One is as sparkling as the new skyline White shaped, generating investor excitement, and a construction boom which, his supporters proclaim, leaves Boston with a solid tax base for years to come. The other is as dingy as the unswept streets and boarded-up commercial buildings in the neighborhoods which, White's detractors insist, he built up and then allowed to deteriorate."[3]

In the spring of 1983, however, the people of Boston were less concerned about what their current mayor had done than what their next one would do. A large number of candidates stepped forward to be considered for the job, including five that the *Boston Globe* declared had "demonstrated the experience and intelligence to lead this city capably."[4]

The three front-runners among the handful singled out by the *Globe* were David Finnegan, a lawyer, former chairman of the Boston School Committee, and now a radio talk show host; Larry DiCara, who twelve years earlier, at age twenty-two, had been the youngest person ever elected to the Boston City Council and was now practicing law; and Dennis Kearney, a former state representative from East Boston, who was now Suffolk Country Sheriff.

When it was still assumed that White would run for reelection, Finnegan had been seen as the strongest challenger among the three, a point he emphasized with the campaign slogan, "Finnegan or Him Again." When White dropped out, Finnegan became the heavy favorite and inherited many of White's former campaign workers and contributors—which led detractors to tweak the slogan and suggest, "Finnegan *Is* Him Again."

There was a larger truth to that rewritten slogan, since Finnegan, DiCara, and Kearney all presented themselves as traditional candidates, unlikely to rock the boat or shake up the status quo. It soon became clear that if voters really wanted a change, they would have to look at the other two candidates among those five—Mel King and Ray Flynn—who were described as "duking it out for the vote of the dispossessed, the little guy, the renter or three-decker owner who's felt lost in the Kevin White shuffle."[5]

In many ways, King and Flynn were remarkably similar. Both were the sons of union dockworkers. Both had had grown up in families that had been forced to go on welfare when times were tough. Both had been top-notch high school athletes. King won a scholarship to play football at Claflin College in South Carolina. Flynn was an Academic All-American basketball player at Providence College in Rhode Island and had even gotten a try-out with the Boston Celtics. Both had come back to Boston and settled down in the neighborhoods in which they had grown up—King in the South End and Flynn in South Boston. Both had married and were the fathers of six children. King began his career as youth worker and Flynn as a probation officer. Both had served in the Massachusetts House of Representatives. By 1983, King was an associate professor in urban studies at MIT and Flynn was a Boston city councilor.

But in other ways, the two could not have been more different. King, nine years older, was an African American and activist-turned-politician. He was known for his fierce demeanor, fiery rhetoric, and radical leftist ideology. "Mel emerges as the head chef" of this era of activism, recalled the University of Massachusetts Boston professor and labor historian James Green. "There was something in his political thinking that went far beyond community organizing. It was anticapitalist, even socialist. He gave the activist movements an identity when he ran."[6]

Flynn, an Irish American, seemed to be more of a traditional Boston politician. He was seen as a "regular guy," not known for his oratory, and was difficult to categorize ideologically. As a state representative, he was very much involved in the right-to-life and antibusing movements, which indicated that he was a social conservative. But after his election to the city council in 1977, it was hard to find anyone more liberal on economic issues. "Flynn was a populist, not an activist," contended Tunney Lee, an urban studies professor at MIT.[7]

Flynn later explained how he'd come to take those liberal positions on housing, development, and consumer issues. "I didn't know any left-wing radicals at the time, but I listened in the House chamber and on the council to the arguments for putting in some kind of rent control ... and I heard all these stories about landlords and how badly they were treating their tenants. And the issues they brought to my mind were of the injustices that had happened in the West End because of urban renewal and in Mattapan because of block-busting."[8]

Flynn had also been involved in the fight to control the expansion of Logan Airport when South Boston joined the Massachusetts Air Pollution and Noise Abatement Committee coalition, and he eventually joined forces with Massachusetts Fair Share, albeit reluctantly. "I didn't want anything to do with Fair Share originally," he recalled. "But then I saw them fighting against the utility hikes, and I knew that Boston Edison had all of a sudden started charging my mother an extra $6 a month on her bill, so I joined with them on that issue and then on other things, too."[9]

One other thing that King and Flynn had in common was their unorthodox sartorial style. On the campaign trail, King generally wore jumpsuits or dashikis. If he had to wear a tie, he would sport a colorful, oversized bow tie, as if in protest. Flynn, an avid runner, often showed up to events in his sweat clothes. Although this might appear to be a trivial detail, years later Larry DiCara ruefully remarked, "The rest of us were all wearing suits. But the people were tired of suits."[10]

The people weren't tired of issues, though, and, during the 1983 preliminary campaign the candidates had plenty of opportunity to talk about them. Seventy-eight "candidates' nights" took place in church basements, school auditoriums, veterans' posts, and living rooms all around the city. Sometimes there were two or three a night, and the pressure was on the candidates to show up at all of them.

Rent control and condominium conversion were "two of the most talked about political issues in Boston," according to the *Boston Herald,* because "tenants have made sure of it." Since being abandoned by Mayor White in 1975, the tenants' movement had built itself back up. A new statewide group, the Massachusetts Tenants Organization (MTO), had been formed, and its local chapter, the Boston Tenants Campaign Organization, was described as "a new force at the ballot box."[11]

But the real estate industry was also still a force—and the biggest source of campaign contributions to mayoral candidates. It was not surprising, then, that the three traditional candidates who took moderate positions on rent control and condo-conversion had healthy balances in their campaign accounts, or that the two with the lowest balances—King and Flynn—

were described as so pro-tenant as "to send shivers of disgust through real-estate entrepreneurs."[12]

Another major, real estate–related issue in the 1983 campaign was whether Boston should follow San Francisco's lead and become the second major city in the country to adopt a so-called linkage policy. Linkage required developers of big, downtown, commercial projects to make contributions, based on the size of their project, to support the construction of affordable housing in the neighborhoods. The Boston real estate industry was strongly opposed any sort of linkage policy, claiming it would discourage investment in the city, and Mayor White had already vetoed a linkage ordinance that had been passed by the city council. The other three top-tier candidates favored a "weak" or "moderate" linkage ordinance that wouldn't ask too much from developers. But King and Flynn supported the "strong" linkage policy that groups like MTO, Fair Share, and the Boston Affordable Housing Coalition were promoting.

These issues were very important. But, twenty-five years later, Mel King said that the most important thing about the 1983 campaign was its "focus on communities. In prior years, the campaigns were focused on downtown. It was easy to show graphically how the neighborhoods had been cleaned out, in terms of urban renewal and lack of attention. . . . Everybody could see clearly the impact of the policies that the prior administrations had put in place. And you could make the case for turning it in the other direction."[13]

As preliminary election day neared, Finnegan was seen as the clear front-runner, so it appeared that if the people of Boston wanted to set a new direction for the city, they would have to choose either King or Flynn to run against Finnegan in the final. The day before the election, a *Time* magazine reporter described the two as "both running on a promise to shift money and urban planning energies away from glamorous downtown and harbor front development toward rebuilding Boston's neglected working-class neighborhoods."[14]

On Election Day, October 11, 1983, however, voters decided not to choose between King and Flynn—and instead they chose both. Each finished with some 48,000 votes to make it into the final election, while Finnegan finished with 42,000 and was out of the running.

The next day, a *Boston Herald* editorial proclaimed that, "the City of Boston was a big winner yesterday" and praised "a campaign fought on the issues." The *Boston Globe* columnist David Nyhan wrote a few days later that "King's Rainbow Coalition and Flynn's blue collar crusade prevailed

Mel King and Ray Flynn campaigning for mayor in October 1983. Photo by John Tlumacki/Globe Staff.

over candidates who spent far more money and had equally impressive endorsements," and, he noted, "the campaign was free of race-baiting, racial incidents, and the kind of rhetoric that has made the city ashamed in the recent past." Nyhan called the election "a healing and cathartic experience" that "took Boston beyond the race question: the victors won on plain concerns of working-class voters." James Green, writing two weeks after the election in the *Globe*, noted that the two winners "have aroused democratic enthusiasm among constituencies demoralized by the domination of business interests and the Kevin White political machine [by] offering populist economic solutions to the problems that affect blacks and whites."[15]

Although Boston might have been the winner in the preliminary election, the surprising results left the people of Boston—especially those who had engaged in so much of the activism and protest over the previous decades—with a difficult choice to make in the final election. Some likened it to the one faced by opponents of the Vietnam War in the 1968 Democratic presidential primary, when "purists" backed Eugene McCarthy because he had come out against the war sooner, while "pragmatists" backed Robert Kennedy, because they thought he could do a better job.

Race, of course, would be a big factor in the final election. A King victory would make him Boston's first African American mayor, and his candidacy prompted more than 20,000 new voters to register in the black community, where voter registration rose from 48 percent the previous year to 82 percent in 1983.[16] Flynn would be just another in a long line of Irish-Catholic mayors, albeit the first to be elected from South Boston. Boston's population was still 70 percent white, though, and whites made up an even larger percentage of the electorate.

Race also became an issue in the four-week final campaign. "I talk basically and bluntly about discrimination as a serious issue in this city," said King at the time. "I don't try to cover it up by saying the problems of South Boston and Roxbury are the same." Flynn responded that he spoke out "as much as anyone in the city on the issue of discrimination." Then he added, "Parents are concerned that their children are not receiving an adequate education, that they are not getting jobs, that the adult unemployment rate is comparable. Those are the economic issues that I think will unite the city and bring those neighborhoods together."[17]

In the final election on November 15, 1983, Ray Flynn was elected mayor with 129,000 votes to Mel King's 69,000. But perhaps a more important statistic that day was the fact that nearly 200,000 came out to the polls, almost 70 percent of registered voters—the largest turnout since Hynes beat Curley to usher in the New Boston in 1949. Clearly, the people of Boston wanted a change and were excited to be able to vote for these two candidates who promised to set such a similar new direction for the city.

That night, the words "people" and "neighborhoods" peppered the remarks by both men. In his concession speech, King congratulated Flynn "for joining me in waging a decent, hard-working campaign that does honor to Boston's neighborhoods and to the people who have for too long been ignored or repressed." In his victory speech, Flynn promised, "The campaign to share the benefits of Boston's economic progress with all its people has just begun."[18]

That campaign to pay more attention to the people of the city's neighborhoods and to share the benefits of Boston's progress led to much of what residents had fought for in the 1960s and 1970s becoming city policy in the 1980s. Although somewhat recent to qualify as history, the best book on the subject to date is Pierre Clavel's *Activists in City Hall: The Progressive Response to the Reagan Era in Boston and Chicago.*

The campaign benefited greatly from the comeback made by the local economy. Fueled by the growth in financial services, it was dubbed "The Massachusetts Miracle" and not only helped Governor Mike Dukakis become the Democratic party's nominee for president but also put the city's finances back in the black.

The new mayor's personality and style also helped. Unlike the shy Hynes, the remote Collins, and the mercurial White, Flynn was a "neighborhood guy"—affable, energetic, and not averse to mixing in a little self-promotion with his populist politics. He spent little of his time in city hall and most of it in the neighborhoods—shooting baskets with kids at playgrounds, singing songs with the elderly at Golden Age parties, visiting families in time of tragedy, and riding along on snowplows during winter storms. More than once, he led people out of burning buildings. But the mayor's high-octane, up-close, personal approach to the job was all part of a very conscious strategy on his part.

"A lot of blacks in this city think whites are getting all the services because they're white," Flynn told the *New York Times* reporter Anthony Lewis. "A lot of whites think blacks are getting all the services because they're black. I walked in here with the firm belief that neither was getting much of anything." Lewis called Flynn's approach "the politics of symbolism," then added, "but symbols do matter." [19]

It also helped that Flynn brought many activists into city hall with him. Many of the older activists were veterans of the fights against urban renewal and the highways and for civil rights and rent control, whereas the younger ones were coming out CDCs, Fair Share, and the Boston Community Schools. Some of them had even supported Flynn's opponent in the recent election. "People who'd worked in my campaign, and who I'd worked with around community development stuff . . . would come to me and say, 'I have a chance to go work for the mayor,'" recalled Mel King. "I'd say, 'Just make him do the kind of things we would do.'" [20]

But the most important things the new administration did were the policies and programs it put into place that can be directly traced to the activism and protests of the previous two decades. When it came to neighborhood development, Flynn chose Steve Coyle as his BRA director. Coyle, who had grown up in public housing, embraced the same Robin Hood approach to urban policy as Flynn. According to the MIT professor Langley Keyes, "Coyle tried to out-Logue Logue, and to succeed where Logue had failed." [21] In the West End, Coyle and the BRA "de-designated" Jerome Rappaport as developer of the last remaining parcel of land there, then turned it over to the old West End CDC and Catholic Archdiocese of

Boston so it could build a mixed-income housing development in which former West Enders would be given preference for the new units.

The BRA revisited the South End by creating the South End Neighborhood Housing Initiative, which according to Keyes "amounted to completing urban renewal on the vacant land still there by using the city's own money." When the question came up—as it invariably did in the South End—as to who should get this housing, "Coyle backed up the Mel King–led wing of the community and said a third of it was going to be low income, a third moderate income, and a third would be market rate—and because the city was using linkage money to build it, he was able to make that stick." [22]

Flynn and King had been the only two candidates in the recent mayoral campaign to back a "strong" linkage policy that would extract significant contributions from downtown developers to build affordable housing in the neighborhoods. After the preliminary election, when it became clear that one would be the next mayor, Kevin White had signed what was described as a "diluted" linkage ordinance. When he took office, Flynn wasn't able to get the city council to consider a new linkage bill. But he did get the council to shorten the time period over which those contributions had to be made, effectively doubling the real dollars for affordable housing.

Over the next several years, Boston built more of that housing than any city in the country its size, much of it in collaboration with community development corporations. "Boston became the leading city for CDCs in the country," recalled Paul Grogan, who by then had moved to New York to run the Local Initiatives Support Corporation that worked with CDCs all over the U.S. [23] Of the many successful city-CDC partnerships that took place over the next decade, two in particular stand out.

One was Tent City, built on the site that Mel King and others had occupied for three days back in 1968 to protest the shortage of affordable housing in the South End, and which had remained vacant ever since. But although vacant, the site was had been the scene of more demonstrations in the intervening years—particularly after the White administration decided not to use a $20 million dollar federal Urban Development Action Grant (UDAG) to build housing there, but instead use it to help a developer build the high-end Copley Place shopping mall across the street.

In 1984, the BRA designated the Tent City CDC that residents had formed as developer of the site and persuaded the shopping mall owner to become the CDC's partner. Then the Flynn administration used another $20 million UDAG grant to make the project work. On March 8, 1986,

Mel King returned to the scene of his arrest eighteen years earlier not as a protester, but as "head chef" at a cookout/groundbreaking ceremony for a 200-unit mixed-income housing development.[24]

Another notable city-CDC partnership occurred in the Dudley Triangle, an area of weed-choked vacant lots left over from the never-completed Washington Park urban renewal project. The full story of this effort is told in *Streets of Hope: The Fall and Rise of an Urban Neighborhood,* by Peter Medoff and Holly Sklar. But its climax occurred on November 10, 1988, when the BRA board—after being called down to the mayor's fifth-floor office for a stern talking-to by Flynn—delegated its eminent domain power to the Dudley Street Neighborhood Initiative (DSNI) so the CDC could assemble enough land to finally build housing there.

It was the first time in U.S. history that a city agency had given up such power to a community group, and afterward Flynn told DSNI members why he had pushed so hard for it. "I've seen professional planners screw up more things than you could shake a stick at, and I've seen a lot of projects that have been unsuccessful because they were jammed down people's throats in the neighborhoods."[25]

The city and the BRA took other steps to keep projects from being jammed down people's throats. One of the most important was to change the zoning code so it required community advisory committees (CACs), such as the one pioneered during the Park Plaza fight, to be part of the development review process for all major projects. When the change was made, residents debated how much authority these committees should have. More militant activists pressed unsuccessfully for CACs to have veto power over all decisions. Moderates settled for them playing an advisory role. But the fact that these committees were now written into the zoning code made the twenty-five-year-old promise of "planning with people" more than just a catchy slogan.

When it came to matters of civil rights and race, Flynn's earlier opposition to busing and the fact that he'd just defeated King in the mayoral election were hurdles he had to overcome. But according to a *Bay State Banner* editorial, Flynn "made dramatic moves to bring the city together." Among those moves, the editors listed his appointment of numerous blacks to "key positions in his administration" and praised his accessibility (an accompanying cartoon depicted Flynn crossing a welcome mat into a home, as one resident said to another "Mayor Flynn's up in Roxbury more than he's in City Hall"). The *Banner* also singled out one of those symbolic moves at which Flynn excelled—hand-delivering an $850,000 check to the widow of black man slain by Boston police and thereby settle a wrongful death suit against the city that had dragged on for ten years.[26]

More important than symbolism, though, were the new policies and programs that were put into place to replace the old. The city tried to make up for the failure of the Boston Urban Rehabilitation Program by convincing the Department of Housing and Urban Development to turn over nearly 2,000 units of housing, most of them in Roxbury and Dorchester, to tenant and community organizations.[27] It tried to make up for the failure of the Boston Banks Urban Renewal Group program by creating a "linked deposit" program that required banks holding city funds to make loans to residents and businesses. Boston also became the first city in the country to sponsor a study of bank lending practices in minority neighborhoods, which led to a $1 billion mortgage loan to help residents buy homes all over the city, not just in one neighborhood.

When it came to the schools, the administration wasn't nearly as successful. In 1985, Judge Garrity returned day-to-day control of the schools to the Boston School Committee, but retained the right to approve any changes to the student assignment process. Garrity allowed the city to replace his Phase II with a "Controlled Choice" lottery-based plan, through which parents could submit a list of schools they would like their children to attend. But the judge insisted that each school's enrollment continue to reflect the citywide "ideal racial percentages," so very few parents got their choice and the plan wasn't much of an improvement after all.

The city was able to make some big improvements, however, when it got control of the Boston Housing Authority back from another court. One of the biggest took place on October 26, 1984, when Flynn named Doris Bunte to be the new BHA administrator, making her the first former tenant and first African American woman to lead a public housing authority in a major American city.

On her first day on the job, Bunte recalled, she asked which was the worst development in the city. "Then I took a chair and a stapler, and I went out there and collected complaints from the residents, and I stayed there for a couple of weeks. I was not going to let people sit downtown and make policies for a place they had never seen. I was trying to set a tone for the authority and I think it worked pretty well."[28] Under Bunte, the BHA dramatically reduced the number of vacant units awaiting renovation and finally integrated all of the public housing developments in the city.

During the 1983 mayoral campaign, Flynn promised to strengthen rent control in Boston, where the number of regulated units had fallen from

140,000 to 25,000. But his bill to do that was defeated by the newly restructured city council. The council did agree to pass a less ambitious, compromise ordinance that let tenants appeal dramatic rent hikes and prevented the elderly and handicapped from being evicted so that their apartments could be converted into condominiums.

On July 31, 1985, Flynn and Governor Mike Dukakis went to Roxbury to sign a city-state agreement to promote development on the vacant swath of land cleared along what had come to be called the Southwest Corridor, and Dukakis gave credit to residents at the event. "Had it not been for the vision and courage of so many of you, we wouldn't be standing at the Ruggles Street station today, we'd be standing at the interchange of the Southwest Expressway and the Inner Belt. And it would be jammed with traffic moving at three miles an hour." [29]

A few weeks earlier, on July 12, 1985, Flynn had signed an agreement to dramatically expand the Boston Residents Jobs Policy by extending it to cover privately funded as well as publicly funded development projects. The move fit perfectly with Flynn's oft-expressed belief that addressing class issues was the most important challenge facing the city. Flanked by the jobs activist Chuck Turner, the local Bricklayers and Laborers Union president Tom McIntyre, and the developer Don Chiofaro, the mayor signed the bill and said he could "think of no initiative that's more healing for the city than getting jobs for poor whites and poor blacks, for all the working people of Boston." [30]

Flynn and his administration weren't without their faults—even within the areas discussed here. The frenetic pace that the mayor kept, as well as his nonstop string of press releases on every local, national, and even international issue under the sun, prompted suggestions that the city might benefit more if he slowed down and focused on a few priorities. Some of the activists he brought into city hall with him turned out to be less-than-effective managers. Coyle stumbled early on, when he had the Boston Redevelopment Authority put together a "secret plan" to redevelop Dudley Square, which outraged Roxbury residents when they found out about it. Not all of the many policies and programs designed to share the benefits of the city that were put in place received the follow-through or enforcement they should have.

All the progress that had been made to heal the city's racial wounds was jeopardized in Flynn's second term, first by the Boston Police Department's implementation of a "stop and search" policy to try to combat the crack cocaine epidemic that was sweeping Boston and other American cities at the time, and then by the handling of the bizarre Stuart case, in which a white suburbanite falsely claimed his pregnant wife had been shot and killed by a black carjacker on Mission Hill. Frustrated at the lack of progress in the schools, Flynn allowed himself to be talked into mounting a campaign that led to replacement of the elected Boston School Committee with an appointed board—hardly a "populist" move and one he later admitted regretting. By Flynn's third term, the *Boston Globe* reporter Chris Black wrote, "His administration drifted, key officials left for other pursuits, and the mayor's attention shifted to national affairs." [31]

But during the 1980s, according to the Cornell professor Pierre Clavel, the Flynn administration in Boston and Harold Washington's in Chicago were the two that resisted "the norm then and later ... that cities, whatever the inequities, would be run by political machines working with business elites," and that "'growth' took precedent over 'equity' and 'social justice.'" Their "single-minded focus on redistributive policies made it easier for their successors [and] pushed the fundamental structures of economic bias and political power a bit more toward equality in a decade when the nation was moving toward an insupportable inequality." [32]

Years later, Flynn explained what he had attempted to do as mayor. "I always imagined it as an invisible bridge from the downtown to the neighborhoods. I'd visualize people walking over the bridge, like the little guy in the *Monopoly* game, carrying bags of money to pay people who got jobs and carrying those little green houses that would be built in the neighborhoods." [33]

Close observers at the time suggested that this campaign to pay more attention to the neighborhoods and share the benefits of the New Boston more equitably was largely successful. Thomas O'Connor called Flynn "The People's Mayor." George Merry, a veteran political reporter for the *Christian Science Monitor*, wrote, "No Boston mayor in the past half-century has been more neighborhood-oriented. Unlike predecessors John Hynes, John Collins, and Kevin White, who concentrated on changing the physical face of Boston with new buildings, Mayor Flynn has focused on improving municipal services and on people." [34]

In 1993, after Flynn announced that he was stepping down as mayor to become U.S. ambassador to the Vatican, the *Boston Herald*'s editorial page editor Rachelle Cohen wrote, "In the days before neighborhood people were given respect, it was still okay for entire communities to be bulldozed. Remember the West End (may it rest in peace). And it was okay to ignore the needs of certain neighborhoods because, hell, those people didn't vote much anyway. It's not okay any more." [35]

CHAPTER 22

───◄◦►───

Boston Today

"BOSTON TODAY IS MORE BEAUTIFUL THAN PARIS," SAID FORMER Massachusetts governor Mike Dukakis at a recent event celebrating the restoration of the missing link in the Emerald Necklace of parks designed by Frederick Law Olmsted.[1] Boston's economy is strong today, its budget is balanced, its tax rate is low, and its bond rating is among the highest of any city in the country. Its major service agencies are well run and court receivership is a thing of the past. Its streets—in most neighborhoods—are safe.

Since 1980, Boston has been growing again, and today its population tops 620,000. Boston is also more diverse, a "majority minority" city in which 53 percent of the residents are Hispanics or people of color. Boston continues to attract immigrants, a trend reflected in the fact that an estimated 27 percent of its residents are foreign born.[2] It's a smart city, in which almost 45 percent of its adults have college degrees, and it's a young city, home to the largest percentage of young people aged 20 to 34 of any major city in the country.[3] The city generates more jobs than it has residents and attracts more than 20 million visitors each year.

The New Boston has come a long way from the Old Boston, but all this progress didn't come about by accident. For the last sixty years, the city has benefited from having capable leaders (particularly its mayors), strong institutions, and the imagination and nerve to strike off in new directions. But it also benefited—in the 1960s and 1970s—from having residents who refused to just follow along. "Like Alan Lupo told me one time," said former West Ender Jim Campano, "'the city owes you a debt of gratitude because you didn't go quietly.'"[4]

Because the people of Boston didn't go quietly, urban renewal proceeded minus its early excesses and errors. Demolition was generally kept to a minimum, preservation was encouraged, and fewer people, at least initially, were displaced. Thanks to Boston's more than two dozen community development corporations, 25,000 units of housing were built, enabling thousands of residents to remain in their neighborhoods.[5]

Because they didn't go quietly, Boston, which had long been a socially progressive city, became a politically and economically progressive one as well. Groundbreakings and swearing-in ceremonies are no longer monopolized by well-off white men, although the boards of directors of the city's largest businesses sometimes continue to be.

Because the people of Boston didn't go quietly, Boston's public schools became—for a time, anyway—the center of the city's attention. Some Bostonians could sport bumper stickers on their cars that read "Don't Blame Me, I'm from Massachusetts," and others could display yellow ribbons. Welfare recipients and the residents of public housing began to be treated with greater dignity and respect.

Because they didn't go quietly, East Boston is still a neighborhood and not just an airport parking lot, and two highways were never built. If they had been, one activist claimed, "Boston would today not be known as a livable city."[6]

Because the people of Boston didn't go quietly, Boston's most beloved park is not shrouded in shadows for much of the year. "Every night, when I sit down to read the newspaper," revealed Bob Kenney, a former Boston Redevelopment Authority director now retired and living on Beacon Street, "I look out over the Public Garden and I thank Henry Lee and the Friends of the Public Garden for stopping Park Plaza. It never should have been built."[7]

Because they didn't go quietly, thousands of Boston residents, minorities, and women got jobs building the New Boston; thousands of homeowners got the property tax abatements they deserved; hundreds of thousands of consumers across the state got a break on their utility and insurance bills.

But despite the efforts of the city's leaders, its institutions, and its people, Boston is not better today in every way. Problems persist, work remains, and ironies abound.

In the West End, the old neighborhood may be gone but it's not forgotten. Since 1985, former residents have published and supported *The West Ender,* a neighborhood newspaper for a community that no longer exists. In 2004, some of those former residents opened a museum dedicated to keeping the neighborhood's memory—and the story of its destruction—alive. Four years later, the neighborhood even got its old name back. When the developer Jerome Rappaport finally sold his interest in Boston's most notorious urban redevelopment project, the new owners commissioned a marketing firm to come up with a new name for the Charles River Park complex. The admen and women put their heads together and selected . . . "The West End." Asked why, they said the name "reflected a sense of place that only the West End can offer."[8]

But residents of other neighborhoods who used the example of the West End to inspire them and fight to make urban renewal better wonder if they may have succeeded too well. "Charlestown is gone," said a lifelong "Townie," Moe Gillen. "It's been decimated by the 'yuppies.'"[9] Not long ago, some of the newcomers who live in the condominiums at the converted Charlestown Navy Yard showed how little they cared about the neighborhood's history by complaining about the noise from the twice-a-day firing of the cannon on the USS *Constitution*—a tradition that dates back to 1798.[10]

In the South End, Joan Wood, one of those "urban pioneers" who moved there in 1965, waxed nostalgic for the way things were. "Back then people sort of banded together. You had a basic neighborhood with a lot of people coming in who worked with them to make it better. Now you've got this fancy neighborhood where . . . people plunk down a lot of money and sort of move behind their door."[11]

But Mel King, the éminence grise of Boston's activists, disagreed. Ticking off the names of a dozen affordable housing developments within a stone's throw from Tent City, he maintained, "There's no question that without organizing, all the number of folks with low incomes would not be here today. No question."[12]

For all the progress that the New Boston has made in civil rights, racial harmony, and diversity, at least one downside has resulted. "We still have organizations, but there is less commitment from the community" and we have fewer and fewer volunteers, noted former Boston Branch NAACP president Leonard Alkins. "There is a perception that civil rights issues have all been achieved."[13]

No such perception exists when it comes to Boston's public schools. Efforts to improve the quality of education have yielded painfully slow results. Total enrollment is down from 93,000 in 1974 to 57,000 today.[14] The parents of a quarter of the city's school-age children don't use them. Parents who can afford the tuition send their children to parochial or private schools; many who can't try to get them into charter schools or the Metropolitan Council for Educational Opportunity program. Many parents leave the city when their children reach school age.

Today, South Boston's Castle Island is probably the most integrated place in the city during warm weather months. But in the Boston public schools, 13 percent of the students are white, 87 percent are minorities, and almost three-quarters come from families living in poverty.[15] In 1999, efforts to desegregate the schools were abandoned, when, on the twenty-fifth anniversary of Judge Garrity's ruling to integrate the schools, white parents sued the Boston School Committee, charging the use of racial quotas was unconstitutional, which prompted the School Committee to drop race as a factor in assigning children to schools.

In 2004, a committee appointed to review the BPS student assignment plan found that "parents in every neighborhood said they would prefer to send their children to quality schools near their homes."[16] But the now mayoral-appointed school committee refused to return to a neighborhood school system because of complaints from minority parents that there aren't enough good schools in their neighborhoods—the same complaints Ruth Batson, the Boston Branch NAACP, and Citizens for Boston Public Schools were making more than fifty years ago.

In 2011, the last vestige of local opposition to the Vietnam War disappeared, when Harvard University became the last Boston-area college to allow the ROTC program back on campus, after the Defense Department ended its "Don't Ask, Don't Tell" policy. But in praising the "greater inclusiveness within the ranks of the military," Harvard president Drew Gilpin Faust failed to note today's "all-volunteer army" is made up almost exclusively of young men and women from the ranks of the poor and working class.

The "old media" that did so much to promote activism and protest in the New Boston is in eclipse here, as everywhere. While Boston is fortunate to be one of the few "two-newspaper towns" left in the United States, all of its "alternative" and "community" newspapers have folded. The last to go was the *Boston Phoenix,* which tried unsuccessfully to rise from the ashes by merging with a glossy, consumer-oriented magazine appropriately called *Stuff.* The "new media"—web-based and social—that has been so effective in promoting activism and protest in places like Tiananmen, Tahrir, and Taksim Squares, has yet to exert a similar influence in Dudley, Codman, or Hyde Squares.

Welfare is back in the local news, but the recent calls for "reform" are really demands to restrict what recipients can buy with their newfangled Electronic Benefits Transfer (EBT) cards. In responding to those demands, Massachusetts governor Deval Patrick, who grew up in a family forced to go on welfare, used language that sounded like it was lifted from the Mothers for Adequate Welfare newsletter when he declared, "This notion of humiliating poor people has got to be separated from how we make a program work." [17]

Boston's Mattapan neighborhood is still waiting for a program promoting home ownership there to work. Wracked by the blockbusting caused by the Boston Banks Urban Renewal Group more than forty years ago, the once-Jewish, now largely black working-class community has been one of hardest hit by the 2008 subprime mortgage loan scandal that flooded the area with "low teaser rates, with high face values and weak income verification and stiff prepayment penalties." The result, according to the *Boston Globe* columnist Paul McMorrow, is that despite "a multi-billion-dollar nationwide foreclosure settlement and a tough new state foreclosure prevention law . . . the struggles in Mattapan drag on." [18]

Despite cuts in federal funding, changes in federal tax laws that have reduced private funding, and the failure of the city to raise its linkage fees to keep up with inflation, community development corporations carry on. Over the years, CDCs have met the considerable challenges of building, managing, and maintaining oases of affordable housing in the city's neighborhoods. But today they face a new challenge. "The people who live there now don't know how they were built," said Val Hyman, "and they perceive a CDC as just another landlord." At the Emergency Tenants Council, executive director Vanessa Calderon-Rosado tries to remedy that by showing a ten-minute video "re-creation" of ETC's origins at every community event. "My kids always ask me 'Do we have to watch it again?' And I tell them 'Yes, because it's important to remember.'" [19]

The Boston Housing Authority continues to be well run, and a former tenant, Bill McGonagle, serves as the administrator. But recently, after forty years of autonomy, residents at Bromley Heath handed back responsibility for running their development to the BHA, admitting that they have been unable to cope with local drug dealers and gang members, who have been described as having "morphed into sly imitations of community organizers." [20]

In 1994, tenants in Boston's perpetually hot private rental housing market lost what little leverage they had left when Massachusetts residents voted to abolish rent control—even though voters in Boston and the two other communities in which it remained voted overwhelmingly to keep it. Rents are so high that the Northeastern University economist Barry Bluestone recently warned of "more out-migration of young working families." David Mailloux, a member of one of those families, agreed. "I grew up here, but you have to move on. If rents keep going up, you're going to have to be some superstar lawyer or businessman to afford a decent place in Boston."[21]

Only now, some fifty years later, are some portions of the land cleared for construction of the never-built Inner Belt and Southwest Expressway being developed. But one positive irony left over from the highway fight involves Boston's "Big Dig," which involved putting the city's elevated Central Artery underground and building a third harbor tunnel to Logan Airport. Amid all the criticism of the massive project for not being built either on time or on budget, little attention was paid to the fact that it was completed without displacing a single resident or the loss of a single home. The fact that the project's two biggest proponents—Massachusetts governor Mike Dukakis and his transportation secretary Fred Salvucci—had been two of the biggest opponents of those highways may have had something to do with that.

In East Boston today, residents continue their never-ending vigil against unchecked airport expansion. But now they have a new complaint. "You go to community meetings and you see the same old war horses you've been seeing for 25 years," vented a longtime resident, Rose Marie Ruggiero. "It would sure be nice to see some of the newcomers get involved."[22] It would be especially nice now that the Massachusetts legislature has legalized gambling and East Boston faces a new threat—construction of a proposed billion-dollar casino and hotel complex next door that could generate as much traffic as the airport ever has.

Residents in Boston's downtown neighborhoods continue the fight that began forty years ago to save the Boston Public Garden from shadows and wind. A bill filed recently by the activist-turned-state representative Byron Rushing would expand protections to the Esplanade, Commonwealth Avenue Mall, Copley Square Park, Back Bay Fens, and Christopher Columbus Park in the North End.[23]

But an unintended consequence of establishing community advisory committees as part of the city's development process has been that sometimes they stop good—as well as bad—projects from being built. "In East Boston, there is strong opposition to building any affordable housing, and none of the opponents are more than thirty-five years old," complained

John Vitagliano. "There is that same snobbishness in other neighborhoods. I have to wonder 'Are we victims of our success?' Yes, we preserved the neighborhoods, but what about our values?"[24]

Good jobs at good wages are still very important to Boston's residents, and the Boston Residents Jobs Policy is still on the books. But between 1993 and 2008, according to the *Boston Globe*, "even as a boom in real estate development brought tens of thousands of construction jobs to the city, the proportion of jobs performed by residents dropped from 44% to 32%, by minorities from 38% to 30%, and by women from 2.8% to 2%." The chief architect of the policy, Chuck Turner, said the reason it hasn't been enforced is that "we never got the people of the neighborhoods to adopt it as their own."[25]

Turner should have been in a good position to do that, especially after his 1999 election to the Boston City Council. In 2011, however, Turner was forced to step down from the council after being convicted of accepting cash from a constituent he had been helping, who turned out to be a paid FBI informant. Turner claimed he was targeted for prosecution because of his activism, and, unrepentant, vowed not to stop. "I'm an organizer. I was born to be an organizer. If they're going to send me to jail, I'll organize in jail."[26]

For all the progress the city has made, there is one crucial thing missing today—that spirit of activism and protest that contributed so much to make the New Boston better.

Paul Grogan, now president of Boston Foundation, described his 1998 return to Boston after a decade in New York as "a kind of a Rip Van Winkle experience. What's happened during that time is kind of bewildering. The city has really changed. It's become a placid place."[27]

In 2008, Boston had become so placid a place that city councilor Maureen Feeney sponsored a one-day Summit on Civic Engagement to "combat the voter apathy ... and address a decrease in active community leaders."[28] The event was held at the glitzy new Boston Convention and Exhibition Center. Refreshments and transportation were provided. Bad enough, an elected official felt compelled to put together such an event. Worse, the sessions were criticized for not addressing the problems faced by the city, and it failed to produce any uptick in the level of community involvement.[29]

All its progress has not made Boston a city with nothing left to fix. "Sure, a lot of the big problems have been resolved," said Grogan "The old racial boundaries have softened and blurred. It's more open, compassionate, and tolerant. It's a more affluent place. But something certainly has been lost. Some monstrous injustices haven't been addressed," he continued, citing youth violence and work that still needs to be done in the schools at the top of the list. Then Grogan added, "There's a troubling acquiescence. We could benefit from new outrage."[30]

Mel King had used the same word, when he was interviewed on the thirtieth anniversary of the Tent City demonstration. "You know, there was a place for that anger. I look around today, and I don't see outrage; I should. We had outrage."[31]

One reason for the lack of outrage in today's Boston, of course, has to do with the times we live in. "People got tired of fighting and riots," said Renée Loth, who today is a *Boston Globe* columnist. "There was a turning of society away from external activism and toward paying attention to the inner self, to the 'I, me, and mine.'"[32] Beginning in the mid-1970s, there was also a turning away from more localized activism toward the generalized activism associated with the feminist, environmental, and LGBT movements that followed.

Other reasons have to do with the retreat by the federal government from efforts to help the nation's cities and the increased reliance by local government on the private sector to fund physical "betterments" and provide municipal services. It seems much harder to find a target against which to mount a protest. The nonprofit sector has tried to assume the mantle for promoting "community building," but the activism it produces seems manufactured and polite—more attuned to holding meetings than demonstrations and to applying for grants than issuing demands.

Another reason for the lack of outrage may be that state and local governments have learned how to better engage with the citizenry. "I think most of why it is different now, why some of the juice is gone, is because public officials just know how to involve others, and they are better listeners," said former governor Dukakis, now a professor of political science at Northeastern University.[33]

Former mayor Ray Flynn wondered if he and his administration might be partly responsible. "In a way, we took too much power out of the neighborhoods by bringing all these idealistic people into City Hall. It should have been a case of new people getting involved, seeing that this is how you get power, and taking their turn to get involved in their neighborhoods. But for some reason, that didn't really happen."[34]

Flynn's successor, Tom Menino, might bear some responsibility for that. A lifelong resident of Hyde Park, former aide to state senator Joe Timilty, and former district city councilor, Menino is a graduate of the University of Massachusetts Boston. He became acting mayor in July 1993, when Flynn stepped down midway through his third term, and on November 2, 1993, Menino defeated state representative Jim Brett of Dorchester by 74,000 votes to 41,000 to be elected in his own right. Since then, he was reelected four times and became the longest-serving mayor in the city's history.

A gruff, blunt-spoken man, Menino proved to be a hybrid of his recent predecessors. Like Flynn, he spent much of his time in the city's neighborhoods. Like White, he involved himself intimately in downtown development and put together a formidable political machine. In Menino's case, it was one described as running on "loyalty and fear."[35] Like Collins, he was an autocrat, and an even thinner-skinned one at that. Like Hynes, he had no ambition for higher office.

But unlike all of the city's recent mayors, Menino never tired of the job—nor did he bring anything resembling a new vision to the New Boston. As the *Boston Globe* reporter Michael Levinson wrote, "After Kevin H. White churned out urban policy experiments and sought to raise Boston's profile in the 1970s, and Raymond L. Flynn worked to heal racial wounds in the 1980s, Menino eschewed lofty goals in favor of brass tacks."[36]

Menino's major accomplishment—no small one—was to keep the city running smoothly, and for that he was dubbed "The Urban Mechanic." "He has given the people what they wanted," wrote the historian Thomas O'Connor, "and what they wanted was normalcy, was peace and quiet and ordinariness."[37] The peace and quiet suited Menino well, since he bristled at the least hint of criticism. Far more than his predecessors, he used the considerable power of his office to control even the smallest details of municipal life and to discourage any sort of dissent.

One of the few residents who dared to disturb that peace and register dissent during this period was Shirley Kressel of the Back Bay. In 1996, she founded the Alliance of Boston Neighborhoods, but her throwback, outspoken style—"I stand on the shoulders of giants," she admitted—so infuriated Menino that he refused to meet with the group, and it eventually disbanded. "People in Boston today are afraid to be seen as activists," said Kressel in a 2012 interview, "because they are afraid to be seen as against the mayor, whose capacity for retribution is legend."

On March 28, 2013, Menino announced his decision not to run for a sixth term. Shortly afterward, the *Boston Globe* columnist Lawrence Harmon wrote, "Menino has been widely praised of late for his twenty-year stewardship of Boston. But it will be a nice change if Boston ends up next year with a mayor who can make firm decisions without trying to eviscerate those who challenge him."[38]

"It is interesting that neighborhood groups have gotten weaker over time," noted Mel King some years earlier, "interesting given the fact that Boston has had supposedly more neighborhood-friendly mayors. I think that's due to people being co-opted by city hall and neighborhood groups not using the power they had."[39]

Those neighborhood groups continue to exist in Boston today. But they tend to concentrate on such "hyper local" issues as traffic and parking, liquor license transfers, and zoning variances, rather than the "big picture" social and economic justice issues that involved so many activists in the 1960s and 1970s. A few groups, such as the Boston chapter of City Life/Vida Urbana, continue to fight the good fight for affordable housing and against mortgage foreclosures. But in recent decades, with rare exceptions—a rally attended by 3,500 people sponsored by the Greater Boston Interfaith Organization in 2001 and the ten-week Occupy Boston protest on the Rose Kennedy Greenway in 2011—the city hasn't witnessed anything like the demonstrations that occurred with such regularity forty and fifty years ago.

Activism is hard to quantify, and it can't be measured merely by the size or frequency of demonstrations. But voting can be quantified, and, at least in local elections, voting too is in sharp decline.

In 1949, when John Hynes defeated James Michael Curley in the election that launched the New Boston, 300,000 people turned out at the polls, almost 75 percent of the electorate. In 1967, when Kevin White defeated Louise Day Hicks in the election that kept the politics of the Old Boston from making a comeback, and in 1983 as well, when Ray Flynn and Mel King both pledged to share the benefits of the New Boston with its people, almost 200,000 people turned out, nearly 70 percent of those registered to vote.

Since 1993, however, the number and percentage of voters in mayoral elections has been about half that—even though turnout in the 2012 presidential election was the highest in nearly fifty years. According to former mayoral candidate Larry DiCara, the local electorate has shrunk to the point where it is now mainly made up of "public employees and the captive elderly."[40]

But perhaps the main reason for the decline in activism, decrease in voting, and lack of outrage in Boston today is that the people who live here are so different from those who lived in the city fifty years ago. "Boston today is just so much more middle class," said John Vitagliano. "When I first got involved in Eastie, it was largely a blue-collar community, and when I met folks in different neighborhoods—in Roxbury, South End, South Boston, Charlestown, and everywhere—and I found out that they were really just like us. Boston was more homogenous back then, the blue-collar aspect was the common denominator. The racial thing didn't matter as much. It was kind of on the side." [41]

Statistics bear that observation out. In 1960, the proportion of Boston's population that could be described as "working class" (those in the second fifth of the income spectrum) was 10 to 20 percent higher than that of the United States as a whole. Today it is 20 percent lower. [42]

Those blue-collar residents, especially in the city's white neighborhoods, were the ones who engaged in much of that activism and protest. They were the ones who said, "To Hell with Urban Renewal" and "People Before Highways." They were the mothers who took to the streets and sat down in front of those trucks. They were the parents who chanted, "Hell No, We Won't Go," because their children and their neighborhoods were all they had.

But far fewer of those people—or people like them—live in Boston today. If they were tenants, they were forced out by the high rents. If they were homeowners, they were made offers they couldn't refuse for houses they couldn't believe were worth such prices. If they were parents, they left for places where their kids could walk to better schools. In suburban towns south of Boston, "O.F.D." (Originally from Dorchester) bumper stickers are a common sight. If former residents of other neighborhoods had adopted similar identifying decorations, "Originally from _____" bumper stickers would adorn many of the cars in suburbs all around today's Boston.

A different demographic shift has occurred in Boston's black community, where much of the activism and protest back in the 1960s and 1970s was sparked by middle-class residents—both Boston-born and from out of town. They were the ones who led the STOP Campaign, the "School Stayouts," the fight for the Racial Imbalance Law. They were the ones who brought Dr. Martin Luther King Jr. back to lead the March on Boston. Back then they lived alongside poor and working-class families because Boston's more middle-class suburbs were closed to minorities.

But thanks to the progress made in civil rights and the passage and enforcement of fair housing laws since then, people of color can live where they want to today. "The downside of all the progress since then is that there has been a dispersion to the suburbs of the black middle class, and now there is nobody left to lead the fight," said Gail Snowden, who has

followed in her parents footsteps and now serves as acting director of Freedom House in Roxbury.[43]

A third group missing from Boston today is that cadre of idealistic
young people straight out of college, who were the no-wage and low-wage
community organizers that aided and abetted many of the movements of
the 1960s and 1970s. "A very basic reason there was so much more activism
was that it was a lot cheaper to live in Boston back then," noted Renée Loth.
"Kids coming out of college could do movement work and still support
themselves. They surely can't do that now."[44]

Working-class families could not only afford to live in the New Boston
in the 1960s, they could find work. Almost half of the jobs in the city in
those days could be classified as "blue collar," while today less than one-
fifth fit that description.[45] Most of the jobs created in the city since 1960
have been "white collar"—first in high tech and professional services, then
in financial services. In recent decades, most of the jobs have been in colleges and universities, which "float in an archipelago of advanced thought
largely oblivious to the laboratory of community challenges around
them," and in health care and medical research, made up of "doctors and
research scientists on the one hand and workers (often immigrants) available and willing to do the basic but often unpleasant task that keep hospitals going."[46] In Boston today, there is little work for those in between.

Once more, the story of Boston has become a "tale of two cities." But
Boston today is not split geographically, between downtown and the neighborhoods, as it was fifty years ago, but by income and class. In 1960, the
proportions of residents who could be described as "poor" (in the lowest
fifth of the income spectrum) or "well off" (in the highest fifth) were both
20 to 40 percent lower than the national average. Today, the proportions
of both of those groups are 20 to 40 percent higher.[47]

The result is that half of today's Boston is made up of the very visible
"haves"—who are either middle class or better off—and half by the much
less visible "have-nots." Most of the "haves" are white. They live downtown
or in the city's many gentrified, safe neighborhoods, where Starbucks
proliferate and Whole Foods has replaced supermarkets named Johnnie's
Foodmaster or Hi-Lo Foods. Most of these adults have college degrees and
white-collar jobs. Most of their children do not attend public schools.
Most of these residents depend on government to do little more than keep
their streets clean. The "haves" live in Boston by choice, and they can leave
whenever better opportunities present themselves elsewhere.

Most of the "have-nots" are people of color, Hispanics, and/or immigrants. They live in the pockets of subsidized housing that remain in the gentrified neighborhoods or in the few neighborhoods plagued by gang violence, and where supermarkets have only recently replaced corner stores and bodegas. Most of these adults do not have college degrees and work in service jobs for those who do. Most of their children attend the Boston public schools, and many have no idea of what the city has to offer.

Recently, Father Richard "Doc" Conway, the well-respected "street priest" at St. Peter's Church, attended an event at the John F. Kennedy Library on Columbia Point with some young people from the Bowdoin/Geneva area of Dorchester. He later noted that, even though they had grown up only a few blocks away from it, "some of those kids had never seen the Atlantic Ocean!"[48]

Most of the have-not residents rely on government for services they can't afford to buy for themselves. They live in Boston because they have nowhere else to go or because, despite the hardships they face, the city offers more opportunities than the places from which they have come.

Boston isn't the only city experiencing this kind of split today. But in Boston, this division is especially pronounced. In 2009, the Boston Foundation published a report that showed income inequality in Boston was among the worst of any major city in the country, ranking with Miami, New Orleans, and Washington, DC—"places," Renée Loth wrote at the time, "we smugly think have far worse urban pathologies than ours."[49]

Cities—at least American cities—are supposed to be ladders that residents can climb to better lives. And if any city—by dint of its history, tradition, and the many advantages and resources it enjoys—should be able to serve as this kind of ladder, it should be Boston. In the Old Boston, the ladder was broken because it was missing its middle and top rungs—the middle class and those even more well off—and the New Boston was built to replace those rungs. In today's Boston, the ladder is broken once more because it is missing the rungs just up from the bottom—the working class—leaving those at the very bottom facing an almost impossible climb.

This tale of two cities in Boston today is particularly troubling to the community activists of the 1960s and 1970s. "You know, you feel like you tried to be a champion of the moderate-income people who used to live here, but then you watch the gentrification occur," said Ron Hafer. "I don't want to criticize the newcomers. They are just looking for a nice place to have a home. But having lived through the rebuilding of Jamaica Plain, I have mixed feelings. That's all I'm going to say."[50]

This tale of two cities is also troubling to the activists who went into government in the 1980s to try to keep it from occurring. "It may be only twenty years since they ended, but in Boston, the '80s are a distant memory," wrote Peter Canellos for the *Boston Globe*. "The revival begun by Flynn's 'Sandinistas' [the nickname for the activists in city hall, after the Nicaraguan rebels of that era] ended up serving many of the people they disdained. Those people are making Boston rich again. Now it's a city of the middle and upper classes, and no one is talking back to them."[51]

In the not too distant future, it is to be hoped, Boston will support a new generation of activists, who will rise up and begin to talk back again. "I don't claim to understand how it all works," said Alan Lupo, "but it seems like there are 'cycles of activism.' You had the muckraking of the 1890s and early 1900s. You had the New Deal in the 1930s. You had everything that went on in the 1960s. I don't know what determines when the next cycle comes along—whether it's war, the economy, or demographics. And I don't know where the next generation of activists is going to come from. Maybe they'll be immigrants. But if they are the ones, I hope they'll take on all kinds of issues and not just the things that affect them."[52]

Epilogue

W<small>HETHER OR NOT</small> B<small>OSTON SUPPORTS A NEW GENERATION</small> of activists who do rise up, those who helped build a better New Boston are glad—for the most part—that they did.

"Any story about community activism should show the personal sacrifices that were made for that activism," said Alan Lupo, shortly before his death in 2008, "and the effect it had on a person's family, on their kids, on their relationships with their neighbors. A lot of them often wondered whether it was worth it."[1]

The late Ruth Batson of Roxbury wondered. When she and other activists were asked, "What have you learned from your involvement?" she replied, "I think sometimes if I were to start my life all over again, nobody would know the name of Ruth Batson. And I would just go in my house and be my husband's wife . . . raise my children, and not get involved in all of this. I just really think that's the way I would live my life over if I had it to do all over again. It has not been easy to put yourself out there, you know; it's not easy for yourself; it's not easy for your mate; and it's not easy for your children."[2]

Evelyn Morash of East Boston, who today still volunteers at the local O'Donnell Elementary School, thanked her family "for giving me permission to be an activist. My husband could have been Joe Six Pack, but he wasn't. He helped. It was exciting, but it was tough on the family." Morash recalls her then-young son once asked her if "the Sunday People" (other activists who met at their house on that night every week) were going to be at Thanksgiving dinner. "I could tell he hoped they wouldn't be, and I told him, 'No, it's just going to be our real family.' And that made him feel much better."[3]

Michael Lerner, who moved from Mission Hill to Brookline and is now director of Rogerson House, which provides housing and health and social services to the elderly, seems somewhat bitter about his experience. "The '6os were all about communalism. But the whole sense of that is so lost from our society today. The '6os are over. We won, we built, we saved, we stopped. But now we've lost. Maybe all we did was to fight a holding pattern, so we didn't lose faster."[4]

David Parker, a self-professed neoconservative who has gone from being a carpenter to a developer in the South End, seems as if he is waiting to be thanked. "I'm still here, still doing things. But in thirty-five years, I have never had one politician come up to me and say, 'You know, you moved into this squalid slum. You know, it was great you came down here when it was really rough.'"[5]

For most of the activists of this generation, however, any regrets seem to be far outweighed by the pride they take in what they were able to accomplish. Some of that pride is personal. Dan Richardson, still active after all these years, today chairs a committee that is developing a master plan for Roxbury to "change the way urban planning is done by putting urban renewal in the neighborhood where it belongs." He said, "I can go back to Lower Roxbury today, to the place where I grew up, and say that that playing field and those houses are there because of what we did."[6]

Some of that pride is political. Lew Finfer of Dorchester, now director of the Massachusetts Communities Action Network, said, "There is an assumption today that people have a legitimate right to be included when public policy gets made. Sometimes it's window dressing and sometimes it's real. But it's always assumed. That happened because of a lot of hard work by a lot of people."[7]

Tom Lyons, who ended up becoming the city's assistant commissioner of Veteran's Affairs and then running the New England Shelter for Homeless Veterans, is proud of the example that he and his buddies set by getting the South Boston Vietnam Memorial built, which led other such memorials to be built, including the national memorial in Washington, DC. "It was the activism of Vietnam veterans to insure a place of honor for their brothers and sisters that spurred those others to do the same."[8]

For some, their pride was aesthetic. "If I were going to point to one thing in which I take the greatest pride," wrote Back Bay resident Stella Trafford, before she died, "it would be the blue sky over the south side of the Public

Garden, which, but for our determination, might be obscured by three 600-foot towers."[9]

Mel King's pride seems downright civic. Today, he volunteers at Tent City's South End Technology Center, where residents are able to learn the latest in computer skills. "Somebody asked me what did I think was good about Boston and I told him it was the advocacy, the belief in revolution, the belief that someone could alter and could change things, the number of people who believed and wanted to work for change. I think back to the times my mother and father and other people wanted to clean up backyards, and the folks and organizations, and all these struggles. I think that's the most exciting thing about being here."[10]

Acknowledgments

I want to thank all the neighborhood residents and activists, the journalists, academics and historians, and the nonprofit and public officials who were willing to speak with me. I also want to thank the readers of my manuscript—Lew Finfer, Langley Keyes, Tom Mulvoy, and Richard Tourangeau—for their suggestions to improve it; my former colleagues in the Research Division of the Boston Redevelopment Authority—John Avault, Bob Consalvo, Greg Perkins, and Eswaran Selvarajah—for sharing their knowledge of Boston; Richard Pennington, Robert Turner, and Lisa Tuite at the *Boston Globe,* Alison Barnet of the *South End News,* and Henry Scannell and Aaron Schmidt at the Boston Public Library for supporting my research; my sister Susan for her overall support; my daughter Zoe for her own activism; Lew Finfer (again), the late Alan Lupo, and Michael Patrick MacDonald for their encouragement; and Mary Bagg, Mary Bellino, Carol Betsch, Brian Halley, Bruce Wilcox, and everyone at University of Massachusetts Press for helping to bring history to the people of Boston, the commonwealth, and the region.

Notes

INTRODUCTION

1. Thomas H. O'Connor, *Boston Globe,* August 16, 1992.
2. Alan Lupo, *Liberty's Chosen Home: The Politics of Violence in Boston* (Boston: Beacon Press, 1977), 96.
3. Neil Savage, interview by author, June 26, 2012, Jamaica Plain.
4. Henry Lee, talk delivered at Beacon Hill Seminar, October 29, 2010.
5. Gerry Burke, interview by author, May 10, 2007, Jamaica Plain.
6. Moe Gillen, interview by author, September 7, 2007, Charlestown.
7. Dan Richardson, panel discussion, "We Saved a Community," October 19, 2011, Hibernian Hall; Richardson, interview by author, September 1, 2009, Roxbury.
8. Tom Corrigan, interview by author, October 29, 2008, Farmington, CT.
9. Fred Salvucci, interview by author, October 27, 2008, Cambridge, MA.

1. THE OLD BOSTON AND THE NEW BOSTON

1. Joseph P. Dineen, "Youthful Boosters Call Rally to Form Permanent Setup," *Boston Globe,* May 7, 1950.
2. John Powers, "In 1960, Timing Was Right to Begin: Collins, Planner Logue Awakened a Dying City," *Boston Globe,* September 22, 1985.
3. Barry Bluestone and Mary Huff Stevenson, *The Boston Renaissance: Race, Space, and Economic Change in an American Metropolis* (New York: Russell Sage Foundation, 2000), 56.
4. Daniel Golden and David Mehegan, "The Boston Potential: Changing the Heart of the City," *Boston Globe,* September 18, 1983.
5. Thomas H. O'Connor, *Building a New Boston: Politics and Urban Renewal 1950 to 1970* (Boston: Northeastern University Press, 1993), 108.

6. Walter McQuade, "Boston: What Can a Sick City Do?," *Fortune,* June 1964.

7. Murray B. Levin, *The Alienated Voter: Politics in Boston* (New York: Holt, Rinehart and Winston, 1960), 1–2.

8. "What's Happening to Proper Old Boston?," *Newsweek,* April 26, 1965.

9. Henry Lee, interview by author, December 3, 2008, Beacon Hill.

10. "Boston's Mayor-Elect Came Up the Hard Way," *Boston Globe,* November 9, 1949.

11. Thomas H. O'Connor, *The Hub: Boston Past and Present* (Boston: Northeastern University Press, 2001), 208.

12. Jack Beatty, *The Rascal King: The Life and Times of James Michael Curley, 1874–1958* (Reading, MA: Addison-Wesley, 1992), 489.

13. O'Connor, *Building a New Boston,* 30, citing *The Nation,* October 29, 1949, and *Boston Post,* November 4, 1949.

14. *U.S. News and World Report,* September 21, 1964.

15. Ibid.

16. Boston College Citizens Seminar, October 26, 1954.

17. John H. Mollenkopf, *The Contested City* (Princeton: Princeton University Press, 1983), 141.

2. To Hell with Urban Renewal

1. Anthony Flint, *Wrestling with Moses: How Jane Jacobs Took On New York's Master Builder and Transformed the American City* (New York: Random House, 2009), 63.

2. James O. Wilson, ed., *Urban Renewal: The Record and the Controversy* (Cambridge: MIT Press, 1996), 94; Flint, *Wrestling with Moses,* 53.

3. John H. Mollenkopf, *The Contested City* (Princeton: Princeton University Press, 1983), 144.

4. "New Spirit in Boston," Uncle Dudley editorial, *Boston Globe,* January 9, 1952.

5. Langley Keyes Jr., interview by author, November 8, 2012, North End; Mel King, quoted in Tom Henshaw, "King of the South End," *Boston Sunday Herald,* February 9, 1967; Mel King, *Chain of Change: Struggles for Black Community Development* (Boston: South End Press, 1981), 20.

6. Thomas H. O'Connor, *Building a New Boston: Politics and Urban Renewal, 1950 to 1970* (Boston: Northeastern University Press, 1993), 106–24.

7. "Preliminary Report on the New York Streets Project," Boston Redevelopment Authority, June 1952.

8. Lawrence W. Kennedy, *Planning the City Upon a Hill: Boston since 1630* (Amherst: University of Massachusetts Press, 1992), 162.

9. "Preliminary Report on the New York Streets Project," BRA, June 1952.

10. Gloria Ganno, interview by author, November 4, 2009, Hyde Park.

11. Ganno interview; "Cerel-Druker Takes Over NY Streets Area," *Boston Globe,* September 13, 1957.

12. Jim Campano, quoted in Andrew Weiner, "The Taking," *Boston Phoenix,* December 1, 2000.

13. Boston Housing Authority, Urban Redevelopment Division Pamphlet, 1951; Bruce Guarino, interview by author, March 6, 2012, West End.

14. Jim Campano, talk delivered at West End Library, March 18, 2006; Jack Thomas, "Where's the West End? Don't Ask," *Boston Globe*, January 4, 1990.

15. Herbert Gans, *The Urban Villagers: Group and Class in the Life of Italian-Americans* (New York: The Free Press of Glencoe, a Division of the Macmillan Company, 1962), 285.

16. "$20 Million Home Project for West End Revealed," *Boston Globe*, April 12, 1953.

17. Gans, *Urban Villagers*, 283.

18. Frank Lavine, interview by author, July 23, 2006, Beacon Hill.

19. Gans, *The Urban Villagers*, 296.

20. Joseph A. Keblinsky, "West End Irked by Councilors Not at Hearing," *Boston Globe*, May 15, 1953.

21. "Lee, Pickets Cry 'Land Grab' at West End Project Debate," *Boston Globe*, November 17, 1957.

22. Gans, *The Urban Villagers*, 283.

23. Jim Campano, interview by author, June 16, 2004, West End.

24. Ibid.

25. Lavine interview.

26. Jerome Rappaport, quoted in Chris Reidy, "West Enders Still Mourn: Protest 30th Birthday of Charles River Park," *Boston Globe*, September 26, 1992; Ed Martin, "Break Ground Tomorrow for Big West End Project," *Boston Herald*, March 3, 1960; Arthur Stratton, "Boston Starting $1 Billion Projects," *Boston Herald*, August 14, 1960.

27. Martin, "Break Ground Tomorrow."

28. Walter McQuade, "Boston: What Can a Sick City Do?," *Fortune*, June 1964; Peter S. Canellos, "Old Boston Grievances Die Hard," *Boston Globe*, November 25, 1997.

29. Hynes, quoted in John Harris, "Mayor Hynes Thinks It Over," *Boston Globe*, March 22, 1959.

30. Thomas P. O'Connor, "Assessing the Cost of the New Boston: Razing the West End Took a Toll," *Boston Globe*, August 16, 1992.

31. Robert B. Hanron, "Collins Continues Attack; Powers Maps New City," *Boston Globe*, October 17, 1959; Robert B. Hanron, "Business, Legislators Urged to Join Hands in Boston," *Boston Globe*, October 30, 1957.

32. Henry Scagnoli, interview by author, July 19, 2007, Jamaica Plain; Robert B. Hanron, "Powers, Collins Step Up Pace of Campaign," *Boston Globe*, October 15, 1959.

33. *Scagnoli interview, July 19, 2007.*

34. Collins, quoted in O'Connor, *Building a New Boston*, 162; Scagnoli interview, February 20, 2009.

35. Scagnoli interview, February 20, 2009.

36. Lizabeth Cohen, from a talk on Ed Logue at Harvard University, April 29, 2010.

37. Lee interview, December 3, 2008.

38. O'Connor, *Building a New Boston*, 190.

39. John Collins, quoted in *Boston City Record*, September 24, 1960.

40. Scagnoli interview, February 20, 2009; Scagnoli interview, July 19, 2007.

41. "What's Happening to Proper Old Boston?" *Newsweek,* April 20, 1965; "The Ninety Million Dollar Development Program for Boston," *City Record,* September 24, 1960.

42. Leo Baldwin, letters to *Charlestown Patriot,* April 7, 1960; Baldwin, *Charlestown Patriot,* April 28, 1960.

43. Langley Carleton Keyes Jr., *The Rehabilitation Planning Game: A Study in the Diversity of Neighborhood* (Cambridge: MIT Press, 1969), 105–6.

44. Keyes, *The Rehabilitation Planning Game,* 107.

45. Ibid., 112.

46. Moe Gillen interview by author, September 7, 2007, Charlestown.

47. Ibid.

48. Keyes, *The Rehabilitation Planning Game,* 116–17.

49. Anthony J. Yudis, "1000 Throng Charlestown Hearing, Boo Logue, $20 Million BRA Plan," *Boston Globe,* January 8, 1963.

50. Keyes, *The Rehabilitation Planning Game,* 120.

51. Anthony Lukas, *Common Ground: A Turbulent Decade in the Lives of Three American Families* (New York: Alfred A. Knopf, 1985), 356.

52. Keyes, *The Rehabilitation Planning Game,* 121.

53. Anthony J. Yudis, "1000 Throng Charlestown Hearing," *Boston Globe,* January 8, 1963.

54. Yudis, "1000 Throng Charlestown Hearing."

55. *Boston Sunday Advertiser,* January 13, 1963.

56. "Proposed Charlestown Renewal Project: Before BRA Board," cited by Keyes, *The Rehabilitation Planning Game,* 121.

57. Keyes, *The Rehabilitation Planning Game,* 129, 131.

58. Alan Lupo, "The Collins Legacy: A Changed Boston," *Boston Sunday Globe,* December 3, 1995; Anthony J. Yudis, "2500 Jam Hearing on Bunker Hill," *Boston Globe,* March 15, 1965.

59. BRA: Charlestown, "Public Hearing—Charlestown Urban Renewal Project: Rules for the Conduct of the Public Hearing," March 14, 1965, cited by Keyes, *The Rehabilitation Planning Game,* p. 135.

60. Yudis, "2500 Jam Hearing."

61. Lukas, *Common Ground,* 154.

62. BRA; Charlestown, "Analytical Summary of the Public Hearing before the Boston City Council Regarding the Charlestown Urban Renewal Project," cited by Keyes, *The Rehabilitation Planning Game,* 137.

63. BRA Fact Sheet, December 1979.

64. Keyes, *The Rehabilitation Planning Game,* 145, citing Sam Bass Warner, *Streetcar Suburbs.*

65. Richard Heath, "An Act of Faith: The Building of the Washington Park Urban Renewal Area, 1960–1975," Boston: Low Income Housing Advocacy and Research, 1990, no page numbers.

66. Keyes, *The Rehabilitation Planning Game,* 166–69.

67. Gail Snowden, interview by author, November 20, 2008, Roxbury.

68. Anthony J. Yudis, "Roxbury Folk Demand: Start Urban Renewal," *Boston Globe*, March 15, 1962.

69. Heath, "An Act of Faith."

70. Keyes, *The Rehabilitation Planning Game*, 186.

71. Anthony J. Yudis, "100 More Families Join Relocation List," *Boston Globe*, February 11, 1964.

72. Keyes, *The Rehabilitation Planning Game*, 187.

73. Anthony J. Yudis, "Renewal Project Goes Over Big with Roxbury; Logue Cheered," *Boston Globe*, January 15, 1963.

74. Dan Richardson interview by author, October 26, 2009, Roxbury.

75. Keyes, *The Rehabilitation Planning Game*, 176.

76. "Ash, Logue Clash in Public Housing Feud," *Boston Globe*, May 13, 1966.

77. Heath, "An Act of Faith."

78. Paul McMorrow, "Another Chance for Dudley Square," *Boston Globe*, March 6, 2012.

79. Peter Medoff and Holly Sklar, *Streets of Hope: The Fall and Rise of an Urban Neighborhood* (Boston: South End Press, 1994), 19, citing Ed Logue in John King, *Boston Business Journal: Monthly Real Estate Supplement*, February 1986.

80. Bob Sales, "Snowden Still Trying for Change," *Boston Globe*, May 27, 1971.

81. O'Connor, *Building a New Boston*, 219.

82. "$4.5 Million Apartments for Brighton," *Boston Globe*, June 2, 1962.

83. Bernard Redgate interview, February 16, 2008, Framingham, MA.

84. Ibid.

85. "Crowd Taunts BRA Officials in Brighton," *Boston Globe*, June 27, 1962.

86. "Storm of Protest Buries Board at Hearing on North Harvard Street," *Allston–Brighton Citizen-Item*, June 28, 1962.

87. Jim Morse, "North Harvard St. Battles the BRA," *Boston Sunday Herald*, August 15, 1965.

88. Bernard Redgate interview; Marjorie Redgate, "To Hell with Urban Renewal," unpublished manuscript, chapter 13, page 9.

89. Redgate, "To Hell with Urban Renewal," chapter 14, page 4.

90. Ibid., chapter 17, page 3.

91. Ibid., chapter 20, page 13.

92. William P. Marchione, "Barry's Corner: The Life and Death of a Neighborhood," summary of articles appearing in the *Allston–Brighton Tab* and *Boston Tab* newspapers, July 1998 to late 2001, Brighton–Allston Historical Society website, www.bahistory.org.

93. James Hammond, "Logue Vows Allston Projects Will Go On," *Boston Globe*, August 11, 1965.

94. F. B. Taylor, "BRA Evicts Student; Allston Melee Erupts," *Boston Globe*, August 4, 1965.

95. James Breagy, "Spare N. Harvard St., Planners Cry," *Boston Herald*, May 28, 1965; Stanley Eames, "Little People, Harvard Caught in Brighton Squeeze," *Boston Herald*, November 25, 1965.

96. Michael J. Bennett, "Panel Favors Owners Keep Allston Homes," *Boston Herald*, March 1, 1966.

97. David A. Ramsey, *Allston–Brighton Citizen Item*, October 30, 1969.

98. John Plunkett, "So. Boston Told; Eliminate Blight, Avoid Renewal," *Boston Herald*, October 26, 1965.

99. "Renewal Foes Protest JP Plan," *Boston Globe*, August 28, 1965.

100. Keyes interview, September 27, 2011.

3. Community Organizers and Advocacy Planners

1. Joe Slavet, interview by author, October 20, 2006, Boston; Bob Perelman, quoted in Robert C. Hayden and Ann Withorn, eds., *Changing Lives, Changing Communities: Oral Histories from Action for Boston Community Development* (Boston: ABCD and University of Massachusetts Boston, 2002), 17–19; Stephen Thernstrom, *Poverty, Planning, and Politics in the New Boston: The Origins of ABCD* (New York: Basic Books, 1969), 120–22.

2. Thernstrom, *Poverty, Planning, and Politics*, 112.

3. Hayden and Withorn, *Changing Lives*, 9.

4. Byron Rushing, panel discussion, "We Saved a Community," October 19, 2011, Hibernian Hall.

5. Hayden and Withorn, *Changing Lives*, 64.

6. Chuck Turner, interview by author, November 14, 2008, Roxbury.

7. John H. Strange, "The Impact of Citizen Participation on Public Administration," *Public Administration Review*, September, 1972, 458.

8. Slavet interview.

9. John Gardiner, quoted in Hayden and Ann Withorn, *Changing Lives*, 81.

10. Val Hyman, quoted ibid, 26.

11. Alan Lupo, interview by author, January 26, 2006, Jamaica Plain.

12. Ibid.

13. Fred Salvucci, interview by author, October 30, 2008, Cambridge, MA.

14. Anthony J. Yudis, "Logue Raps 'Academic' Planners," *Boston Globe*, November 18, 1966.

4. A Rekindled Civil Rights Movement

1. Hubie Jones, interview by author, July 6, 2006, Boston.

2. Ibid.

3. Gerald Gill, "Setting the Context," keynote address delivered at "Power and Protest: The Civil Rights Movement in Boston, 1960–1968," John F. Kennedy Library, November 3, 2006.

4. Ibid.

5. Robert Hayden, interview by author, February 12, 2009, Roxbury.

6. Fred Hapgood, "Melnea Cass—The First Lady of Roxbury," *Boston Globe Magazine*, May 13, 1973.

7. Hapgood, "Melnea Cass."

8. Henry L. Allen, "Segregation and Desegregation in Boston's Schools, 1961–1974," in James W. Fraser, Henry L. Allen, and Sam Barnes, eds., *From Common School to Magnet School* (Boston: Trustees of the Public Library, 1979), 110.

9. Gill, "Setting the Context."

10. Robert Coard, introduction to *The Negro in Boston*, by Rheable M. Edwards and Laura Morris (Boston: ABCD, 1961), 13–14.

11. Ibid., 13–14.

12. "400 College Students Picket NE Stores Linked to South," *Boston Globe*, March 27, 1960.

13. Sarah-Ann Shaw, interview by author, January 26, 2007, Roxbury.

14. Sarah-Ann Shaw, panel discussion, "We Saved a Community," Hibernian Hall, Roxbury, October 19, 2011.

15. Shaw interview.

16. Shaw, "African American Organizations, Students, and the Movement in Boston," panel discussion at "Power and Protest."

17. Alan Gartner, "Jim and Jane Crow Employment," panel discussion, "Power and Protest."

18. Julian Houston, interview by author, March 23, 2007, Brookline, MA.

19. Jones interview.

20. Ibid.

21. Robert Hayden, interview by author, September 16, 2010, Oak Bluffs, MA.

22. Reverend Michael Haynes, talk delivered January 19, 2011, at Haley House, Roxbury, MA.

23. Ibid.

24. Reverend Michael Haynes, "The Churches and the Movement," panel discussion, "Power and Protest."

25. Hubie Jones, "The Status of Institutions in Boston's Black Community," in *The Emerging Black Community of Boston*, ed. Phillip L. Clay (Boston: Institute for the Study of Black Culture, University of Massachusetts at Boston, 1985), 306.

26. Dan Richardson, interview by author, September 1, 2009, Roxbury.

5. FROM SCHOOL REFORM TO DESEGREGATION

1. Joseph Cronin, talk delivered at Boston Public Library, May 14, 2008; Alan Lupo, *Liberty's Chosen Home: The Politics of Violence in Boston* (Boston: Beacon Press, 1977), 137.

2. Peter Schrag, *Village School Downtown: Politics and Education—A Boston Report* (Boston: Beacon Press, 1967), 67; Robert L. Levey, "Everyone Joins Association, No One Participates," *Boston Globe*, November 22, 1964.

3. Dorothy Bisbee, quoted in Jane Fletcher, "Parents' Group Keeps Sharp Eye on Hub's Public School Affairs," *Boston Globe*, April 3, 1961.

4. Herb Gleason, interview by author, March 1, 2007, Boston.

5. Paul Parks, interview by author, July 20, 2006, Boston.

6. Gleason interview.

7. Ruth Batson, *The Black Educational Movement in Boston: A Sequence of Histori-cal Events: A Chronology* (Boston: Northeastern University School of Education, 2001), 3, 8–9.

8. Hubie Jones, interview by author, July 6, 2006, Boston.

9. Eva Jaynes, quoted in Batson, *Black Educational Movement*, 465.

10. "Group Charges, Haley Refuses," *Boston Globe*, May 29, 1960.

11. "Board Says Hello, Goodbye," *Boston Globe*, August 16, 1963.

12. Gleason interview.

13. Paul Parks, "Jim Crow Education in Boston: Spark of the Movement," panel dis-cussion at "Power and Protest: The Civil Rights Movement in Boston, 1960–1968," John F. Kennedy Presidential Library & Museum, November 4, 2006; Gleason interview.

14. Don Irwin, "Kennedy Warns Nation," *Boston Globe*, June 12, 1963.

15. Batson, *Black Educational Movement*, 88.

16. "Anti-Bias March on City Hall," *Boston Globe*, June 12, 1963.

17. Batson, *Black Educational Movement*, 88.

18. Anthony Lukas, *Common Ground: A Turbulent Decade in the Lives of Three Ameri-can Families* (New York: Alfred A. Knopf, 1985), 125.

19. Paul Parks, interview by author, February 16, 2006, Boston; Mel King, interview by author, January 15, 2007, South End.

20. Reverend James Breeden, keynote speaker, "Jim Crow Education in Boston: Spark of the Movement" at "Power and Protest."

21. Ruth Batson, quoted in "School Boycott on Despite Plea," *Boston Globe*, June 14, 1963.

22. Breeden, "Jim Crow Education in Boston"; Jean McGuire, "Jim Crow Education in Boston: Spark of the Movement," panel discussion at "Power and Protest."

23. Allen, "Segregation and Desegregation," 113.

24. "Hub School Boycott Planned by Negroes," *Boston Globe*, June 13, 1963; Breeden, "Power and Protest."

25. Edward G. McGrath, "Orderly March a Triumph," *Boston Globe*, August 29, 1963.

26. Hillel Levine and Lawrence Harmon, *The Death of an American Jewish Commu-nity: A Tragedy of Good Intentions* (New York: Free Press, 1992), 100.

27. Dennis Horgan, "School Board Faces All-Night Sit-In: NAACP Delegation Stages Siege at Hub Offices," *Boston Globe*, September 5, 1963.

28. Seymour R. Linscott, "School Sit-Ins Sit All Night," *Boston Globe*, September 6, 1963.

29. Gleason interview.

30. Henry L. Allen, "Segregation and Desegregation," 109.

31. "NAACP Reveals Hub School Plan," *Boston Globe*, September 13, 1963.

32. Parks interview, July 20, 2006; Dan Richardson, interview by author, October 26, 2009, Roxbury.

33. Jones interview.

34. Ian Forman, "March on Roxbury to End at 'Inferior' School," *Boston Globe*, September 21, 1963.

35. Thomas Atkins, quoted in Robert L. Levey, "6000 March for Rights in Boston: 'Don't Complain—Vote,' Atkins Urges Negroes," *Boston Globe*, September 23, 1963.

36. Robert Healy, "No One Key to the Schools," *Boston Globe*, September 27, 1963.

37. Robert L. Levey, "Mrs. Hicks Called 'Bull Connor of Boston,'" *Boston Globe*, March 1, 1965; Lupo, *Liberty's Chosen Home*, 143.

38. Reverend Vernon Carter, quoted in George McKinnon, "Negroes Urge Roxbury Secede," *Boston Globe*, November 19, 1965.

39. Jones interview.

40. Batson, *Black Educational Movement*, 185–86.

41. Ellen Jackson, quoted in Holcombe B. Noble, "Parents," *Boston Globe*, June 8, 1966; Betty Johnson quoted in Schrag, *Village School Downtown*, 123.

42. Mel King, *Chain of Change: Struggles for Black Community Development* (Boston: South End Press, 1981), 43–44.

43. Henry Allen, interview by author, August 1, 2011, Boston.

44. Holcomb B. Noble, "Operation Exodus: A Costly but Worthwhile Effort," *Boston Globe*, July 6, 1966.

45. Ken Guscott quoted in Robert L. Levey, "Negro Parents Provide Community Leadership," *Boston Globe*, December 5, 1965.

46. Robert Coles, "Busing in Boston," *Boston Globe*, October 17, 1965.

47. Robert L. Levey, "Report Maps End to School Imbalance: Racial Balance . . . 'Because It Is Right,'" *Boston Globe*, April 15, 1965.

48. "State Ready to Assist in Balancing Schools," *Boston Globe*, April 16, 1965.

49. Reverend Vernon Carter, quoted in Gloria Negri, "Clergy, Legislators Prove Contrasting Study," *Boston Globe*, June 22, 1965.

50. Ken Guscott, quoted in "Racial Imbalance Charged in Suit: School Board Named," *Boston Globe*, April 20, 1965.

51. Julian Houston, interview by author, March 23, 2007, Brookline, MA.

52. Reverend Virgil Wood, "The Churches and the Movement," panel discussion at "Power and Protest."

53. "'Vision of New Boston Must Reach Roxbury,'" *Boston Globe*, April 23, 1965.

54. Robert B. Kenney, "Demonstrators Hand Mayor 15-Point 'Bill of Particulars,'" *Boston Globe*, April 24, 1965.

6. The Conflict over the Vietnam Conflict

1. Michael S. Foley, *Confronting the War Machine: Draft Resistance during the Vietnam War* (Chapel Hill: University of North Carolina Press, 2003), 29.

2. Louis Harris, "Vast Majority of Americans Oppose U.S. Withdrawal from Viet Nam," *Boston Globe*, December 13, 1965.

3. James Miller, *Democracy Is in the Streets: From Port Huron to the Siege of Chicago* (New York: Simon and Schuster, 1987), 234.

4. Michael Ansara, interview by author, May 17, 2013, Cambridge, MA.

5. Ibid.

6. "Boston Meatpackers Jeer SDS Members Distributing Anti-Vietnam War Leaflets," *Boston Globe*, March 5, 1966.

7. Quoted in Douglas Shand-Tucci, *Built in Boston: City and Suburb, 1800–2000* (Amherst: University of Massachusetts Press, 1999), 33.

8. Tom Lyons, interview by author, August 19, 2013, Boston.

9. Ibid.

10. Foley, *Confronting the War Machine*, 79 and 62–63.

11. Lyons interview.

12. Foley, *Confronting the War Machine*, 62.

13. Howard Zinn, "History Writing Changes," *Boston Globe*, December 20, 1974.

14. Howard Zinn, quoted in Min S. Yee, "Turn In Draft Cards in Boston," *Boston Globe*, October 17, 1967.

15. Jeremiah V. Murphy, "They All Knew before the Marines Had Said a Word," *Boston Globe*, April 22, 1985.

16. Michael Kenney, interview by Sarah Boyer, Cambridge Historical Society, February 17, 2000.

17. William J. Fripp, "Vigil at B.U. Chapel Backs Sanctuary," *Boston Globe*, October 2, 1968; Ansara interview.

18. Lyons interview.

19. Ibid.

20. Michael Ansara, quoted in Frank Mahoney, "Ansara at Harvard: To Him, His Alma Mater Is 'Oppressive,'" *Boston Globe*, April 17, 1969.

21. Gloria Negri, "Harvard's Action Upsets Moderates," *Boston Globe*, April 11, 1969; Snow and Donham, "April Crisis at Harvard."

22. John Bassett, interview by author, May 12, 2012, Brookline, MA.

23. Andrew F. Blake and David B. Wilson, "A Political Woodstock on Boston Common," *Boston Globe*, October 16, 1969.

24. "The Draft," four-part series, *Boston Globe*, April 9, 1967 to April 12, 1967; William J. Eaton, "How Fair Is the Draft," *Boston Globe*, May 29, 1966; David Broder, "Draft Reform Delays has Democrats on Spot," *Boston Globe*, November 5, 1969.

25. Lyons interview.

26. Lew Finfer, interview by author, June 21, 2013, Dorchester.

27. Michael Kenney, "Thousands Pack Common for Vietnam Moratorium," *Boston Globe*, April 16, 1970.

28. John Kerry, quoted in John B. Wood, "Listless Antiwar Rally on Boston Common," *Boston Globe*, April 30, 1972.

29. Peg Canny, interview by author, August 4, 2011, Dorchester.

30. Ansara interview; Jim Canny, interview by author, August 4, 2011, Dorchester.

31. Jeremiah Murphy, "Honoring Their Pals," *Boston Globe*, September 1, 1981.

32. Ibid.

33. Lyons interview.

7. The Media and the Protest Movements

1. Bob Turner, interview by author, April 13, 2006, Dorchester.
2. Trotter's *Women's Journal* article of May 2, 1903, quoted in Mark Schneider, *Boston Confronts Jim Crow, 1890–1920* (Lebanon, NH: Northeastern University Press), 117–118.
3. Tom Mulvoy, interview by author, March 16, 2006, Jamaica Plain.
4. Ibid.
5. Anonymous interview.
6. Thomas Winship, introduction to "The Most Attractive City in America Is Our Goal, and We Will Make It," *Boston Globe*, May 21, 1967.
7. Renée Loth, interview by author, January 22, 2009, Dorchester.
8. Ken Hartnett, interview by author, February 4, 2010, New Bedford, MA.
9. Alan Lupo, "A Voice for Those Whose Feelings Are Too Rarely Heard," *Boston Globe*, December 31, 1993.
10. Alan Lupo, "Remembering a 'Fightah,'" *Boston Globe*, December 6, 1998.
11. Alan Lupo, interview by author, January 26, 2006, Jamaica Plain.
12. Alan Lupo, "Boston's Two Cities—Pride and Progress vs. Fear and Neglect," *Boston Globe*, August 17, 1967.
13. Deckle McLean, "'Say Brother,' TV and Reality," *Boston Globe Magazine*, December 14, 1969.
14. Sarah-Ann Shaw, interview by author, January 26, 2007, Roxbury.
15. Ibid.
16. Paul Solman, Ford Hall Forum panel discussion at Suffolk University, September 15, 2011.
17. Loth interview.

8. Mothers for Adequate Welfare

1. Mel King, interview by author, June 17, 2011, South End.
2. Jean Dietz, "Loopholes for Fraud; Banker's Mother Got $17,000 in Assistance," *Boston Globe*, March 25, 1965.
3. Jean Dietz, "Costs High, Progress Limited; Rehabilitation Still the Key," *Boston Sunday Globe*, March 28, 1965.
4. Ibid.
5. Val Hyman, interview by author, August 21, 2008, South End.
6. Jean Dietz, "Aims Are High—Results Low," *Boston Globe*, March 23, 1965.
7. "Mrs. Bland, Welfare Founder, 38," *Boston Globe*, January 24, 1970.
8. *Laura Morris, interview by author, January 24, 2007, Marlborough, MA.*
9. Doris Bland, quoted in "MAWs Fight Welfare Woes," *Bay State Banner*, March 14, 1968.
10. Morris interview; Marcia Butman, interview by author, April 26, 2011, Roxbury.
11. Morris interview; "Poverty in Boston: The People/The Problems/The Programs," *Boston Globe*, March 19, 1968; Doris Bland, quoted in "MAWs Fight Welfare Woes."

12. Viola Osgood, telephone interview by author, January 25, 2007; Morris interview.
13. "MAWs Fight Welfare Woes."
14. Elliot Friedman, "Welfare Mothers Cheer Volpe, Brooke," *Boston Globe*, July 1, 1966.
15. Gertrude (Nicky) Nickerson, quoted in Sara Davidson, "She Leads Marchers: Part Mata Hari, Part Robin Hood," *Boston Herald*, June 30, 1966.
16. Morris interview.
17. Davidson, "She Leads Marchers."
18. David B. Wilson, "The 'New Left' Rocks the Hill," *Boston Globe*, July 2, 1966.
19. Doris Bland, quoted in Janet Riddell, "'Our Main Concern Now . . . Is to Make Decisions,'" *Boston Globe*, June 4, 1967; Jessie Herr and colleague, quoted in Janet Riddell, "Social Workers Blame System for Roxbury Welfare Problem," *Boston Globe*, June 4, 1967.
20. "How It Began," *Boston Globe*, June 3, 1967.
21. Ibid.
22. Ibid.
23. "Timetable of Events in Roxbury," *Boston Globe*, June 4, 1967.
24. William J. Fripp, "From Quiet Vigil to Melee," *Boston Globe*, June 3, 1967.
25. "Timetable of Events in Roxbury," *Boston Globe*, June 4, 1967.
26. F. B. Taylor Jr., "Police, Mothers, Tell Different Stories on Riot's Start," *Boston Globe*, June 4, 1967.
27. Ibid.
28. "How It Began," *Boston Globe*, June 3, 1967.
29. Fripp, "From Quiet Vigil"; police officer quoted in Ken O. Botwright, "Police: 'Protestors Beat, Kicked Us,'" *Boston Globe*, June 4, 1967.
30. Hubie Jones, interview by author, July 6, 2006, Boston.
31. Ibid.; Hubie Jones, quoted in "How It Began," *Boston Globe*, June 3, 1967.
32. Doris Bland, quoted in Riddell, "'Our Main Concern Now.'"
33. *Boston Globe*, "Collins Says Welfare Can Be Improved," June 5, 1966.
34. John Collins, quoted in Elliot Friedman, "Mothers Give Hub Two Days to Act," *Boston Globe*, June 6, 1967.
35. John Collins, quoted in *Boston Globe*, "Mayor Hopes His Era Will Be Called 'Decade of Dedication,'" June 7, 1967.
36. Henry Scagnoli, interview by author, July 19, 2007, Jamaica Plain; Thomas O'Connor, interview by author, September 14, 2006, Chestnut Hill, MA.
37. Alan Lupo, "The Collins Legacy: A Changed Boston," *Boston Globe*, December 3, 1995.
38. "'The Most Attractive City in America Is Our Goal, and We Will Make It,'" supplement, *Boston Globe Magazine*, May 21, 1967.
39. Louise Day Hicks, quoted in Anthony J. Yudis, "Will Boston's Renewal Falter with Logue Gone?" *Boston Globe*, October 15, 1967, and in Min S. Yee, "Mrs. Hicks Derides Collins," *Boston Globe*, September 15, 1967.
40. Kevin White, quoted in Yudis, "Will Boston's Renewal Falter," and in Timothy Leland, "White to Stress People, Not Things," *Boston Globe*, February 16, 1967.

41. Barney Frank, talk delivered at Kennedy School of Government, May 4, 2007.
42. John Sears, talk delivered at Beacon Hill Seminar, September 25, 2008.
43. Frank, Kennedy School of Government.
44. Morris interview.
45. Lee Staples, interviews by author, March 8 and April 13, 2007, Boston.
46. Danice Bordett, "MAW Speaks on Plight of Recipients," *Bay State Banner,* September 5, 1968; Gertrude (Nicky) Nickerson, *MAWs Newsletter,* October 1968; Staples interviews.

9. THE ILLUSION OF INCLUSION AND ASSAULT BY ACRONYMS

1. Thomas O'Connor, interview by author, September 14, 2006, Chestnut Hill, MA.
2. "Hub City Hall Doors Opening 'Permanently,'" *Boston Globe,* January 29, 1968.
3. Andy Olins, interview by author, September 21, 2007, Brookline, MA.
4. Herb Gleason, interview by author, March 1, 2007, Boston.
5. Ken Hartnett, interview by author, February 4, 2010, New Bedford, MA.
6. Janet Riddell, "Black Patrols Helped to Keep a Calm City," *Boston Globe,* April 7, 1968. Alan Lupo, "Tension, but Self-Control," *Boston Globe,* April 6, 1968; "What Happened in Roxbury," *Bay State Banner,* April 11, 1968; Martin Gopen, quoted in Jo Ann Levine, "How Roxbury Handled Its Own," *Christian Science Monitor,* April 9, 1968.
7. Robert A. Jordan, "Black Police, Schools, Businesses Demanded at Rally," *Boston Globe,* April 9, 1968.
8. Kevin White, quoted in Anthony Lukas, *Common Ground: A Turbulent Decade in the Lives of Three American Families* (New York: Alfred A. Knopf, 1985), 39.
9. Hillel Levine and Lawrence Harmon, *The Death of an American Jewish Community: A Tragedy of Good Intentions* (New York: Free Press, 1992), 115–18.
10. "Rollins Attacks FHA While Weaver Turns Back," *Bay State Banner,* December 7, 1967; Anthony Yudis, "24.5M Housing Spruce-Up Launched Here by Weaver," *Boston Globe,* December 4, 1967.
11. Kay Gibbs, "Slumming It: How Millions Were Spent to Bring Drugs and Blight to Grove Hall," *Boston Observer,* March 1985.
12. Eve Curry, quoted in "Tenants Group Presents Proposals," *Bay State Banner,* June 13, 1968.
13. Andrea Coxum, "Tenants, Landlords Sign Pact," *Boston Globe,* January 24, 1969.
14. Judson B. Brown, "Rent Strikes, Involving 125 Tenants, Revealed," *Boston Globe,* July 30, 1969.
15. Judson B. Brown, "Tenants Hit FHA on Repairs," *Boston Globe,* August 2, 1969.
16. Anne Kirchheimer, "Nine Years Later, Her Dream Apartment Is Literally Falling Down," *Boston Globe,* March 12, 1977.
17. Levine and Harmon, *Death of an American Jewish Community,* 171, citing Kevin H. White press release.

18. Levine and Harmon, *Death of an American Jewish Community*, Hale Champion, interview by authors, 176–77.

19. Levine and Harmon, *Death of an American Jewish Community*, 6.

20. "Confessions of a Blockbuster," *Metropolitan Real Estate Journal*, May, 1987; David Taylor, "Black Clergyman Lauds B-BURG Efforts," *Boston Globe*, September 14, 1971.

21. Levine and Harmon, *Death of an American Jewish Community*, 325–26, citing Lawrence Shubow, interview by authors, December 21, 1987; "Crisis in Mattapan," *Boston Globe*, April 4, 1972.

22. Levine and Harmon, *Death of an American Jewish Community*, 269–70, citing Kevin White, interview by authors, December 3, 1987.

23. Levine and Harmon, *Death of an American Jewish Community*, 323, 276.

24. Willie Allen, quoted in "Crisis in Mattapan," *Boston Globe*, April 6, 1972; David Taylor, "US Senate Antitrust Panel to Probe Boston's Bank Group's Ghetto Program," *Boston Globe*, August 15, 1971.

25. Gibbs, "Slumming It."

26. Chris Wallace, "For Mayor White a 'Lost' Fourth Year," *Boston Globe*, June 6, 1971; Barney Frank, quoted in Chris Wallace, "Behind the Departure of Barney Frank," *Boston Globe*, January 3, 1971.

10. A New Threat from Newcomers — Gentrification

1. William Dean Howells, *The Rise of Silas Lapham* (Boston: Houghton Mifflin, 1885), 31; Langley Keyes Jr., *The Rehabilitation Planning Game: A Study in the Diversity of Neighborhood* (Cambridge: MIT Press, 1969), 39–42; SEPAC Special Housing Report, June 1975, 26.

2. Clare Hayes, interview by author, January 17, 2008, South End.

3. Chris Hayes, interview by author, January 17, 2008, South End.

4. Keyes, *Rehabilitation Planning Game*, 56; SEPAC Special Housing Committee Report, 28.

5. Richie Hall, interview by author, January 28, 2009, South End.

6. Boston Redevelopment Authority, South End Environmental Assessment Plan, Spring 1979.

7. Mel King, *Chain of Change: Struggles for Black Community Development* (Boston: South End Press, 1981), 65.

8. Keyes, *Rehabilitation Planning Game*, 60.

9. Val Hyman, interview by author, August 21, 2008, South End.

10. David Sprogis, discussion at South End Historical Society annual meeting, June 21, 2011, South End.

11. Anthony J. Yudis, "South End Begins to Stir II: 'We're Finding Out It's an Attractive Place to Live,'" *Boston Globe*, April 9, 1964.

12. Chris Hayes interview.

13. Herb Hershfang, interview by author, November 7, 2008, South End.

14. Ann Hershfang, interview by author, November 7, 2008, South End.

15. Keyes, *Rehabilitation Planning Game,* 81–82; Lukas, *Common Ground: A Turbulent Decade in the Lives of Three American Families* (New York: Alfred A. Knopf, 1985), 169; John H. Mollenkopf, *The Contested City* (Princeton: Princeton University Press, 1983), 178–79.

16. "South End Renewal Gets Wide Approval," *Boston Globe,* August 24, 1965; Gene Boehne, interview by author, February 1, 2008, South End.

17. Mel King, quoted in "South Enders Ask Place to Relocate," *Boston Globe,* July 5, 1967; "South End Groups Split on Renewal — 'Black Power' Blamed," *Boston Globe,* January 15, 1968.

18. Clare Hayes interview.

19. Hale Champion, quoted in "More Economy Units Set for South End," *Boston Globe,* January 28, 1968; F. B. Taylor Jr., "Protesters End South End Renewal Sit-In," *Boston Globe,* April 26, 1968.

20. "23 Arrested in Back Bay as Pickets, Police Clash," *Boston Globe,* April 26, 1968.

21. Ibid.

22. Taylor, "South End Decision Left to Lot's Owner."

23. "CAUSE Protests BRA Policies," *Bay State Banner,* May 2, 1968.

24. David Arnold, "Proud, but Still Defiant: 30 Years after Tent City, a Demonstrator Misses the Outrage," *Boston Globe,* May 2, 1998.

25. F. B. Taylor Jr., "So. End Group Quits Parking Lot," *Boston Globe,* April 30, 1968.

26. King, *Chain of Change,* 117–18.

27. SEPAC Special Housing Report, June 1975, 37.

28. BRA Fact Sheet, December, 1979; Richard Garver, interview by author, December 7, 2007, Brookline, MA.

29. SEPAC Special Housing Report, June 1975, 41.

30. David Parker, interview by author, February 20, 2008, South End.

31. Ibid.

32. Lukas, *Common Ground,* 436.

33. David Parker, interview by author, March 12, 2008, South End.

34. Peter Medoff and Holly Sklar, *Streets of Hope: The Fall and Rise of an Urban Neighborhood* (Boston: South End Press, 1994), 21, citing BRA, *South End Neighborhood Profile,* 3–6.

35. Mel King, interview by author, February 1, 2007, South End.

11. DO-IT-YOURSELF COMMUNITY DEVELOPMENT

1. Neal R. Peirce and Carol F. Steinbach, *Corrective Capitalism: The Rise of America's Community Development Corporations* (New York: Ford Foundation, 1987), 4, 20.

2. Mario Luis Small, *Villa Victoria: The Transformation of Social Capital in a Boston Barrio* (Chicago: University of Chicago Press, 2004), 23–24.

3. Rev. William Dwyer, interview by author, May 7, 2009, Springfield, MA.

4. Small, *Villa Victoria,* 36–37.

5. Jovita Fontanez, interview by author, February 12, 2007, Boston.

6. Mario Luis Small, "Urban Village: Even in a 'Model' Community, Participation Is Hard to Sustain," *CommonWealth,* Winter 2005.

7. Helen Morton, "What about My Puerto Rican Neighbors?" *South End Century Newspaper,* May 11, 1977.

8. Polly Welts Kaufman, Jean Gibran, Sylvia McDowell, and Mary Howland Smother, *Boston Women's Heritage Trail* (Boston: Boston Educational Development Foundation, 2006), 88; Reverend Richard Lampert, telephone interview by author, May 10, 2009.

9. "Statement of Hope," May 1967.

10. Lorraine Barber, "BRA Approves Grant for Emergency Tenants Council," *Bay State Banner,* December 18, 1969.

11. John Sharratt, interview by author, May 12, 2006, Beacon Hill.

12. Sharratt interview.

13. "La Comunidad: Design, Development and Self-Determination in Hispanic Communities," *National Endowment for the Arts,* 1982, and Judson B. Brown, "South End Puerto Ricans Joining in Planning of BRA's 'Parcel 19,'" *Boston Globe,* June 22, 1969.

14. Sharratt interview.

15. Christina Robb, "Nailing Down a Future," *Boston Globe Magazine,* March 31, 1985.

16. Andy Olins, quoted in "La Comunidad."

17. John Warner, quoted in Anthony J. Yudis, "Puerto Rican Community Reveals Plans to Develop S. End," *Boston Globe,* December 11, 1969.

18. "Mission Hill Residents Vote State House March," *Boston Globe,* December 10, 1964.

19. Frank Tivnan Jr., "Mission Hill March Jams State House," Boston Herald, December 18, 1964; Carl M. Cobb, "Three Thousand from Mission Hill March on Capitol in 'Revolution of Love,'" *Boston Globe,* December 18, 1964.

20. *Brigham Bulletin,* March 1969.

21. Robert J. Anglin, "ROTC Foes Seize Harvard Hall," *Boston Globe,* April 10, 1969.

22. *Doug Levinson, telephone interview by author, May 9, 2009.*

23. *Theresa Parks, interview by author, March 10, 2006, Roxbury.*

24. Christina Robb, "Saluting a Hero of Housing," *Boston Globe,* October 27, 1989.

25. Sharratt interview.

26. "Tenants View," Roxbury Tenants of Harvard Newsletter, November 6, 1969.

27. Bob Parks, Jr. "Students and Citizens Sway Mission Hill Plans," *On Boston,* Citizens for Participation in Politics, December 1971; Levinson interview.

28. Carl M. Cobb, "Harvard to Build $22 Million, 800-Unit Housing Complex," *Boston Globe,* September 15, 1972.

29. "Harvard Plant to Service Institutions," *Boston Globe,* August 14, 1972.

30. Michael Lerner, interview by author, September 15, 2006, Roslindale.

31. Charlotte Ploss, quoted in Paul Restuccia, "Mission Hill vs. Harvard," *Boston Herald,* December 16, 1979; Bob Parks, quoted in Colin Nickerson, "Mission Hill–Harvard Fight Far From Over," *Boston Globe,* July 2, 1984.

32. Robb, "Saluting a Hero."

33. Nickerson, "Mission Hill–Harvard Fight."

34. Sharratt interview.

35. Dan Richardson, interview by author, September 1, 2009, Roxbury.

12. Public Housing on Trial

1. Lawrence J. Vale, *From the Puritans to the Projects: Public Housing and Public Neighbors* (Cambridge: Harvard University Press, 2000,) 167.

2. Vale, *From the Puritans to the Projects,* 200, citing letter from BHA chairman John Breen of May 20, 1939.

3. Laura Griffin, "Twenty-Five Thousand Families in Boston Lack Decent Housing," *Boston Globe,* April 22, 1968.

4. Vale, *From the Puritans to the Projects,* 303, 270.

5. Ibid., 308.

6. Ibid., 308.

7. Doris Bunte, interview by author, October 24, 2012, Dorchester; Bunte, quoted in Joanne Ball, "Bunte: From Public Housing Tenant to Public Housing Administrator," *Boston Globe,* October 27, 1984.

8. Barney Frank, interview by author, February 19, 2009, Newton, MA.

9. Vale, *From the Puritans to the Projects,* 309.

10. Bunte interview; Vale, *From the Puritans to the Projects,* 314; Inez Middleton, quoted in "Tenants Should Persist in Complaints, Ash Says," *Bay State Banner,* December 14, 1967.

11. Elliott Friedman, "White to Disclose Police 'Master Plan': Tours Housing Project," *Boston Globe,* February 15, 1968.

12. Laura Griffin, "Hope Dawns for a Brighter Day," *Boston Globe,* April 26, 1968; "Hub Asks Tenants for Views," *Boston Globe,* February 27, 1968; Griffin, "Hope Dawns."

13. Griffin, "Hope Dawns"; Ellis Ash, quoted in Ken O. Botwright, "Hub Tenant Plan Given $10 Million," *Boston Globe,* November 1, 1968.

14. Janet Riddell, "Tenants Vote for Voice," *Boston Globe,* March 4, 1969; Janet Riddell, "1st Tenants Up for BHA, Both Doers," *Boston Globe,* February 3, 1969.

15. Bunte interview.

16. Edward O'Neil, quoted in Riddell, "1st Tenants."

17. Vale, *From the Puritans to the Projects,* 327; Edie Goldenberg, "Dropout Won Diploma at Boston Night School," *Boston Globe,* July 13, 1971; Maria Karagianis, "Doris Bunte—The Pain and Triumph," *Boston Globe,* February 16, 1974; Bunte interview.

18. Janet Riddell, "Tenants Give BHA Roaches for Christmas," *Boston Globe,* December 18, 1969; Vale, *From the Puritans to the Projects,* 327–28.

19. Bunte interview; Andy Olins, interview by author, September 21, 2007, Brookline, MA.

20. "Mrs. Bunte: No Comment on White's Charges," *Boston Globe,* March 30, 1971; Robert A. Jordan, "Atkins Attacks White over Handling of Hearings on Mrs. Bunte," *Boston Globe,* May 14, 1971.

21. Fred Pillsbury, "Mayor Levels Charges against Another BHA Member," *Boston Globe*, March 30, 1971.

22. Fred Pillsbury, "The Bunte Hearing (Yawn!)" *Boston Globe*, May 6, 1971.

23. Herb Gleason, interview by author, April 26, 2007, Boston; Thomas Atkins, quoted in Christopher Wallace, "BHA Aide Defends Accused Member," *Boston Globe*, April 30, 1971.

24. Raymond A. Doherty, "Mrs. Bunte Assailed: White Demands Ouster," *Boston Globe*, May 18, 1971.

25. Christopher Wallace, "Public Housing Tenants' Group Supports Bunte," *Boston Globe*, May 5, 1971.

26. Robert A. Jordan, "Mrs. Bunte Backed by Black Leaders," *Boston Globe*, July 9, 1971.

27. "Mayor White's Hatchet Falls," editorial, *Boston Globe*, June 23, 1971.

28. F. B. Taylor, Jr., "BHA Adopts Unique Lease Spelling Out Guarantees for Tenants," *Boston Globe*, March 2, 1972.

29. Viola Osgood, "Hub Allows Tenants to Govern Housing Project," *Boston Globe*, December 21, 1972; Liz Roman Gardner, "Crime and Fear Decline as Tenants Take Over Housing Development," *Wall Street Journal*, April 18, 1973.

13. The Tenants' Movement and Rent Control

1. William H. Wells, "Boston Renewal So Far: High Rents Replace Low," *Boston Globe*, February 13, 1962.

2. "The Rich Get Richer . . . ," editorial, *Boston Globe*, January 27, 1969.

3. "Negro 'Rent-Strikers' Face Eviction from Roxbury Homes," *Boston Globe*, May 10, 1964; "Roxbury Rent Strike Starts," *Boston Globe*, May 5, 1964.

4. "Negro 'Rent-Strikers' Face Eviction."

5. Viola Osgood, telephone interview by author, January 25, 2007.

6. Ruth Gelmis, "The Bitter Blacks and the Five Rabbis," *Look*, April 1, 1969.

7. Anthony Lukas, *Common Ground: A Turbulent Decade in the Lives of Three American Families* (New York: Alfred A. Knopf, 1985), 429–30.

8. Arlene Grimes, "Tenants, Mindick Family Ink Pact," *Boston Herald-Traveler*, August 6, 1968.

9. "Students Back S. End Tenants in Rent Strike," *Boston Globe*, March 3, 1969; "200 Notices Sent to Landlord," *Boston Globe*, April 7, 1969.

10. Viola Osgood, "South End Tenants Given More Independence," *Boston Globe*, June 4, 1969; John H. Mollenkopf, *The Contested City* (Princeton: Princeton University Press, 1983), 193.

11. Joe Tibbets, quoted in Ken Hartnett, "He's Trying to Set His House in Order," *Boston Globe*, March 16, 1972.

12. Fred Pillsbury, "Budget, Staff and Space Needs Block Hub Housing Court Start," *Boston Globe*, May 1, 1972.

13. "First Housing Court Judge Cites Case Load, Asks Aid," *Boston Herald*, June 8, 1973.

14. Felix Vasquez, quoted in Marguerite Del Giudice, "Dorchester Residents Get Chance to Air Complaints at 'Backyard' Court Session," *Boston Globe*, May 21,

1976; Paul Garrity, quoted in Housing Court of the City of Boston, Case No. 11025, July 2, 1975; Alan Sheehan and Manli Ho, "Landlord Staying Nights in Jail," *Boston Globe*, July 4, 1974.

15. David R. Ellis, "West End Developers Veto Economy Units," *Boston Globe*, June 19, 1968.

16. Mary Honan, interview by author, October 12, 2010, Brighton.

17. Ray Flynn, interview by author, April 21, 1999, South Boston; Peter Perault, "Rent Control Debated," *Boston Globe*, October 2, 1969.

18. "Hub Tenants Ask Rent Control," *Boston Globe*, July 9, 1968; David R. Ellis, "Tax Bite for Rent Gougers," *Boston Globe*, July 13, 1968.

19. "Highest Rents in Brighton and Allston," *Boston Globe*, January 18, 1970; Joe Smith, quoted in Janet Riddell, "200 in Boston Fight Rent Hike," *Boston Globe*, February 8, 1969; Hale Champion, quoted in Jeremiah V. Murphy, "Hub Rents Too Costly—Champion," *Boston Globe*, February 18, 1969.

20. Peter Perault, "Boston Council Approves 'Modest' Rent Curb Plan," *Boston Globe*, November 2, 1969; "Rent Control Now as White Asks More," *Boston Globe*, November 21, 1969.

21. "Anger Descends on Landlord at Rent Board's First Hearing," *Boston Globe*, March 17, 1970.

22. Ibid; Anita Bromberg, quoted in Robert F. Hannan, "Tenants Ask Rent Rollback," *Boston Herald*, March 17, 1970; "Anger Descends on Landlord."

23. Joseph B. Levin, "Problem of Rent Appeals Begins in Trek to Offices," *Boston Globe*, November 27, 1970.

24. Robert A. Jordan, "Hub Council OK's Stronger Rent Control," *Boston Globe*, November 28, 1972; Kevin White, quoted in Robert A. Jordan, "White Signs Rent Act—'Now We'll See How It Works,'" *Boston Globe*, December 3, 1972.

14. People Before Highways

1. James S. Doyle, "Collins Threatens Inner Belt Roadblock," *Boston Globe*, October 5, 1962; Ed Logue, quoted in "Catlin Raps View That Inner Belt Is 15 Years Off," *Boston Globe*, March 14, 1962; A. S. Plotkin, "Cambridge Groups Map Opposition to Inner Belt Routes," *Boston Globe*, May 10, 1960.

2. A. S. Plotkin, "Jam Hyde Park High on Expressway Plan," *Boston Globe*, September 25, 1962.

3. Anthony DiNatale, quoted in George McKinnon, "2,200 Boo, Roar Protest at All Inner Belt Routes," *Boston Globe*, May 11, 1960; A. S. Plotkin, "Storm of Boohs and Hisses Greets Inner Belt Route at Boston Hearing," *Boston Globe*, May 13, 1960.

4. A. S. Plotkin, "Museum Feels Belt Road Would Injure Fragile Art," *Boston Globe*, May 4, 1960.

5. Plotkin, "Jam Hyde Park High."

6. Anthony Yudis, "Roxbury School Rocks with Shouts of Opposition to S.W. Expressway," *Boston Globe*, October 23, 1962; Val Hyman, interview by author, August 21, 2008, South End.

7. Robert B. Hanron, "Plans Unveiled for Southwest Corridor," *Boston Globe*, November 30, 1965.

8. Timothy Leland, "Go-Ahead Given for $100M Inner Belt Stretch," *Boston Globe*, February 3, 1966.

9. "Expressway Faction Fights Swamp Route," *Boston Globe*, July 6, 1969.

10. Alan Lupo, Frank Colcord, and Edmund P. Fowler, *Rites of Way: The Politics of Transportation in Boston and the U.S. City* (Boston: Little, Brown, 1971), 26.

11. "Belt Foes Rebuffed at Capitol," *Boston Herald*, October 16, 1966.

12. John Bassett, interview by author, May 12, 2012, Brookline, MA.

13. "The Churches Get Involved," *Boston Globe*, March 19, 1968; Alan Lupo, "Thorns in the Flesh," *Boston Globe*, March 2, 1969.

14. Tom Corrigan, interview by author, October 29, 2008, Farmington, CT.

15. Ron Hafer, interview by author, February 15, 2008, Jamaica Plain.

16. Fred Salvucci, interview by author, October 30, 2008, Cambridge, MA.

17. Hafer interview.

18. Lupo, *Rites of Way*, 51–53; Fred Salvucci, "Tomorrow's Transportation Needs Must Avoid Yesterday's Mistakes," *Boston Globe*, September 3, 1982.

19. Alan Lupo, "Road Protesters Mass," *Boston Globe*, January 26, 1969; Hafer interview.

20. Alan Lupo, "Road Protesters Mass."

21. Lupo, *Rites of Way*, 46–49.

22. Bassett interview.

23. Lupo, *Rites of Way*, 87.

24. Ann Hershfang, interview by author, November 7, 2008, South End.

25. Peter J. Howe, "1972 Turnabout in Master Transportation Plan Still Felt," *Boston Globe*, December 6, 1987; Hafer interview.

26. Chuck Turner, interview by author, November 14, 2008, Roxbury.

27. Hafer interview.

28. Alan Lupo, "A Whole Generation of Memories Will Go," *Boston Globe*, August 11, 1969; Fred Salvucci, talk delivered at Beacon Hill Seminar, November 1, 2007.

29. Ann Hershfang interview.

30. Lupo, *Rites of Way*, 96–97; A. S. Plotkin, "Sargent Urges More Public Transit: Halts X-Way Work," *Boston Globe*, February 12, 1970.

31. U.S. Department of Transportation Fact Sheet; Paul McMorrow, "A Ticking Clock for Cities," *Boston Globe*, August 26, 2011; Bassett interview.

32. Alan Lupo, "Fabled Eastie 'Fightah' Finds That New Folks Care," *Boston Globe*, February 24, 2002.

15. The Mothers of Maverick Street

1. Noah Bierman, "Massport Holds Its Cards Close," *Boston Globe*, January 4, 2009.

2. Dorothy Nelkin, *Jetport: The Boston Airport Controversy* (New Brunswick, NJ: Transaction Books, 1974), 49–52.

3. Nelkin, *Jetport*, 82, citing *East Boston Community News*, April 10, 1973.

4. Nelkin, *Jetport*, 82.

5. Caryl Rivers, "The Battle of Maverick Street," *Boston Globe Magazine*, April 13, 1980; Alan Lupo, "Remembering a 'Fightah,'" *Boston Globe*, December 6, 1998; Rivers, "The Battle of Maverick Street."

6. Alan Lupo, Frank Colcord, and Edmund P. Fowler, *Rites of Way: The Politics of Transportation in Boston and the U.S. City* (Boston: Little, Brown, 1971), 36.

7. Mary Ellen Welch, quoted in Christine MacDonald, "Their 2D Run at Runway: Maverick Mothers Still Questioning Authority," *Boston Globe*, November 30, 2003.

8. "King Branded as Don't Care Executive with No Feeling for Public," *East Boston Times*, October 24, 1968.

9. Anna DeFronzo, quoted in Lupo, *Rites of Way*, 36.

10. Thomas Russo, quoted in Janet Riddell, "'Tried to Do It Peacefully,'" *Boston Globe*, October 4, 1968.

11. Janet Riddell, "Mayor White Bars Maverick Street Truck Traffic," *Boston Globe*, October 3, 1968; Alan Lupo, "East Boston Truck Route Remains," *Boston Globe*, October 5, 1968. "Peace Comes to Eastie's Maverick Street," *Boston Globe*, October 5, 1968.

12. Alan Lupo, "Legislator's 'Drive' Fails to Save Neptune Road from Bulldozers," *Boston Globe*, April 24, 1969; Nelkin, *Jetport*, 76; Mimie Pitaro, quoted in Lupo, *Rites of Way*, 56–57.

13. Alan Lupo, "East Boston Motorcade Jams Traffic at Logan," *Boston Globe*, April 28, 1969.

14. Sallese, Welch, and Pitaro, all quoted in Lupo, "East Boston Motorcade Jams Traffic," *Boston Globe*.

15. Alan Lupo, "Airport Foes Tie Up Bridge," *Boston Globe*, May 5, 1969.

16. Lupo, *Rites of Way*, 57.

17. John Vitagliano, interview by author, January 16, 2009, Boston.

18. Ibid.

19. Alan Lupo, "Sargent Reassures E. Boston," *Boston Globe*, May 30, 1969.

20. David Langworthy, "Boston, Massport Unwind: Planes Still Fly, but Relations Improve," *Christian Science Monitor*, September 9, 1975; Nathan Cobb, "Loving and Hating Logan," *Boston Globe Magazine*, August 19, 1990; Renée Loth and Michael Rezendes, "The Battle for Massport," *Boston Phoenix*, October 26, 1982.

21. "Traffic Up, Noise Cut at Logan Airport," *Boston Globe*, March 20, 1982; Bryan Marquard, "Dave Davis, 80; Diversified Hiring at Massport," *Boston Globe*, November 9, 2012.

16. Shadow Boxing in the Public Garden

1. Bernie Borman, interview by author, February 13, 2009, Beacon Hill.

2. Mark Primack, "The Gorilla Who Tried to Steal the Sun from the Public Garden," *Friends of the Public Garden and Common Newsletter*, Summer, 1995.

3. Borman interview.

4. Henry Lee, interview by author, November 18, 2008, Beacon Hill.

5. Bob Kenney, talk delivered at Beacon Hill Seminar, October 30, 2008.

6. Lee interview.

7. Henry Lee, talk delivered at Beacon Hill Seminar, October 30, 2008.

8. Henry Lee, talk delivered at Beacon Hill Seminar, October 29, 2010.

9. Miles Mahoney, quoted in Joseph Rosenbloom, "White Plans Meeting to Rebut Rejection of Park Plaza Plans," *Boston Globe,* June 12, 1972.

10. Anthony J. Yudis, "White Takes Park Plaza Case to Sargent," *Boston Globe,* June 14, 1972.

11. Peter Lucas, "Hard Hats Push Hard Line on Jobs," *Boston Globe,* June 29, 1972; Governor Sargent, quoted in Primack, "The Gorilla Who Tried."

12. Robert A. Jordan, "White Vetoes City Council Vote on Park Plaza," *Boston Globe,* February 12, 1974.

13. Ibid.; Ian Menzies, "Park Plaza an Albatross for Mayor?," *Boston Globe,* July 4, 1974.

14. Primack, "The Gorilla Who Tried."

15. Ibid., Lee, Beacon Hill Seminar, October 30, 2008.

16. "The Road to Park Plaza Was Full of Detours," *Boston Globe,* November 24, 1976.

17. Primack, "The Gorilla Who Tried."

18. Lee, Beacon Hill Seminar, October 30, 2008.

17. BOSTON JOBS FOR BOSTON RESIDENTS

1. Martin Gopen, "Construction Hassle," *Bay State Banner,* November 16, 1967.

2. Levine and Harmon, *The Death of an American Jewish Community,* 122.

3. Alan Lupo, "Hub Blacks Demand Construction Jobs," *Boston Globe,* May 29, 1968.

4. Alan Lupo, "Hub May Bar Deals with All White Firms," *Boston Globe,* April 24, 1968.

5. Alan Lupo, "Five Construction Firms Told by U.S. to Employ More Negroes," *Boston Globe,* June 12, 1968.

6. Ian Forman, "The Economics of White Racism: The Labor Picture," *Boston Globe Magazine,* June 16, 1968.

7. Martin Gopen, quoted in "Employ More Blacks Hub Contractors Told," *Boston Globe,* August 20, 1968.

8. John A. Robinson, "Unions Ignore Black Dispute Meeting," *Boston Globe,* September 22, 1968.

9. Thomas Oliphant, "Blacks Meet to Map Specifics on Construction Jobs," *Boston Globe,* February 12, 1970.

10. Thomas Oliphant, "Two Black Groups Denounce Minority Plan," *Boston Globe,* June 28, 1970.

11. "Minority Work Plan Lags," *Boston Herald,* January 13, 1971; Kay Longcope, "Boston Plan Is Dead," *Boston Globe,* October 24, 1971.

12. Mel King, interview by author, September 20, 2012, South End.

13. Mel King, *Chain of Change: Struggles for Black Community Development* (Boston: South End Press, 1981), 189; Jerry Taylor, "Group Damages Equipment, Library Construction Halted," *Boston Globe,* April 13, 1976.

14. Gary MacMillan and Robert Anglin, "Two Thousand Workers Demonstrate at City Hall Plaza," *Boston Globe*, May 8, 1976; Joe Heaney, "Hostile 'Hard Hats' Demonstrate in City Hall," *Boston Herald*, May 8, 1976.

15. Kirk Scharfenberg, "Resident Jobs Plan Passes a Milestone; Mayor Expands Program," *Boston Globe*, July 21, 1985; Chuck Turner, quoted in Nick King, "Boston Jobs Policy Goes to Court," *Boston Globe*, November 28, 1982.

16. Chuck Turner, interview by author, November 14, 2008, Roxbury.

17. King interview, September 20, 2012.

18. Robert B. Carr, "White OK's Job Pact Favoring Residents," *Boston Globe*, September 7, 1979.

19. Scharfenberg, "Resident Jobs Plan Passes A Milestone."

20. Nick King, "Boston Jobs Policy Goes to Court," *Boston Globe*, November 28, 1982.

18. The Battle over Busing

1. Alan Lupo, interview by author, January 26, 2006, Jamaica Plain.

2. Renée Loth, interview by author, January 22, 2009, Dorchester.

3. Ronald P. Formisano, *Boston against Busing: Race, Class, and Ethnicity in the 1960s and 1970s* (Chapel Hill: University of North Carolina Press, 1991), 225; Hillel Levine and Lawrence Harmon, *The Death of an American Jewish Community: A Tragedy of Good Intentions* (Boston: Free Press, 1992), 218.

4. "State Gets Nation's 1st Imbalance Law," *Boston Globe*, August 18, 1965.

5. Ellen Jackson, quoted in Bertram G. Waters, "'Decentralization' New Rallying Cry," *Boston Globe*, January 21, 1968.

6. Thomas Aktins, quoted in Marguerite Del Giudice, "Recovery: The Boston Schools after the Siege," *Boston Globe*, May 13, 1979.

7. Jim Hennigan, interview by author, April 24, 2013, Jamaica Plain.

8. Antony Lukas, *Common Ground: A Turbulent Decade in the Lives of Three American Families* (New York: Alfred A. Knopf, 1985), 218.

9. Jim Hennigan, panel discussion held at the Old State House, May 18, 2004; Jim Hennigan, quoted in John Wolfson, "The Road to Perdition," *Boston Magazine*, August 2004.

10. James Worsham, "Sargent, Parents Have 'Useful Talk,'" *Boston Globe*, May 3, 1973; Muriel L. Cohen, "Balance Law Protesters March Today," *Boston Globe*, April 3, 1974.

11. Pamela Bullard, "300 Parents Form State Anti-Busing Group," *Boston Herald-American*, February 6, 1974; Fran Johnnene interview in *Sometimes They Sang with Us: Stories from Boston's Most Enduring Neighborhoods*. Volume III: Hyde Park, Jamaica Plain, Mission Hill, "Looking Back on Busing" (Boston: City of Boston and Grub Street Inc., 2010), 117.

12. Fran Johnnene, quoted in Maria Karagianis, "'My Rights Are Being Taken Away,'" *Boston Globe*, September 1, 1974.

13. "September: The Violence Intensifies," *Boston Globe*, May 25, 1975.

14. Stephen Curwood, "Atkins Denounces Sargent Balance Plan," *Boston Globe*, May 23, 1974; Michael Kenney, "The Imbalance Veto—How Sargent Decided," *Boston Globe*, May 12, 1974.

15. Ken Powers and Jack Cadigan, "Busing Rejected 30,798 to 2,282," *Boston Herald American*, May 22, 1974.

16. Mel King, *Chain of Change: Struggles for Black Community Development* (Boston: South End Press, 1981), 158; Mel King, interview by author, February 16, 2007, South End; King, *Chain of Change*, 158.

17. *Morgan v. Hennigan*, 379 F. Supp. 410 (D. Mass.) (1974).

18. Lukas, *Common Ground*, 240.

19. Herb Gleason, interview by author, March 1, 2007, Boston.

20. Ken O. Botwright, "Drenched Marches Plod On 'Like US Mail,'" *Boston Globe*, March 20, 1975.

21. Robert A. Dentler and Marvin B. Scott, *Schools on Trial: An Inside Account of the Boston Desegregation Case* (Cambridge, MA: Abt Books, 1981), 7–8.

22. Robert Guen, quoted in John Powers, "On June 21, 1974, Judge Garrity Ordered the Integration of the Boston Schools," *Boston Globe Magazine*, June 19, 1994.

23. Paul Johnson, quoted in Leonard Alkins, "Power and Protest"; Alkins, ibid.

24. Louis P. Masur, *The Soiling of Old Glory* (New York: Bloomsbury Press, 2008), 44.

25. R. S. Kindleberger, "Civil Rights Activists Torn over Busing Protests," *Boston Globe*, September 11, 1974.

26. Masur, *The Soiling of Old Glory*, 44.

27. J. Michael Ross and William M. Berg, *"I Respectfully Disagree with the Judge's Order": The Boston School Desegregation Controversy* (Washington, DC: University Press of America, 1981), 196–98.

28. Ruth Batson, quoted in "September: The Violence Intensifies," *Boston Globe*, May 25, 1975; Robert Hayden, interview by author, September 16, 2010, Oak Bluffs, MA.

29. Evelyn Morash, interview by author, November 6, 2008, East Boston.

30. Ibid.

31. Masur, *The Soiling of Old Glory*, 45.

32. Martin F. Nolan, "Ford Disagrees with Boston Busing," *Boston Globe*, October 10, 1974.

33. "September: The Violence Intensifies," *Boston Globe*, May 25, 1975.

34. Ross and Berg, *"I Respectfully Disagree with the Judge's Order,"* 368–71.

35. Lukas, *Common Ground*, 249.

36. "Black School Critique," *Christian Science Monitor*, January 27, 1975.

37. James Worsham, "A Way Out For Boston," *Boston Globe*, August 1, 1976.

38. "Atkins: Masters' Plan Surrender to Threats," *Boston Herald*, April 5, 1975.

39. Wendy Bauman, *Boston Globe* Busing Chronology, 1976.

40. Herb Hershfang, interview by author, November 7, 2008, South End.

41. Formisano, *Boston against Busing*, 99.

42. Kevin White, quoted in "His Decision . . . Sparked This Reaction," *Boston Globe*,

May 12, 1975; "September: The Violence Continues," *Boston Globe*, May 25, 1975; Johnnene interview in *Sometimes They Sang with Us*, 119.

43. Janet Palmariello, quoted in Robert L. Turner, "The Support Is Tentative, but the Criticism Is Strong," *Boston Globe*, May 11, 1975.

44. John Bassett, interview by author, May 12, 2012, Brookline, MA.

45. Formisano, *Boston against Busing*, 102–3; "Hicks-Bulger-Flaherty Statement on South Boston," *Boston Globe*, September 16, 1974.

46. Ray Flynn, interview by author, February 10, 2010, South Boston.

47. Hicks, quoted in David Rogers and Joe Pilati, "Antibusing Leaders Urge Nonviolence," *Boston Globe*, September 8, 1975.

48. Moe Gillen, interview by author, September 7, 2007, Charlestown.

49. Ibid.

50. Gillen interview in Moakley Archives, Suffolk University, February 14, 2006.

51. Formisano, *Boston against Busing*, 160–61.

52. Ted Landsmark, quoted in Carmen Fields, "'Someone Tried to Kill Me with American Flag,'" *Boston Globe*, April 7, 1976.

53. Mel King, quoted in Robert J. Anglin, "Victim of Beating by Roxbury Gang Lying Near Death," *Boston Globe*, April 22, 1976.

54. Lukas, *Common Ground*, 649.

55. Robert Creamer, "White Student Flight 31% since Busing, Says Expert," *Boston Herald*, March 31, 1976.

56. Dentler and Scott, *Schools on Trial*, 12.

57. "The Boston School Decision," text of Judge W. Arthur Garrity Jr.'s decision of June 21, 1974 (Boston: Community Action Committee of Paperback Booksmith, 1974); "Boston's Unfinished Journey," editorial, *Boston Globe*, June 19, 1994.

58. Ibid.

59. Johnnene interview in *Sometimes They Sang with Us*, 122.

19. Fighting for a Fair Share

1. Lee Staples, interviews by author, March 8 and April 13, 2007, Boston.

2. Staples interviews.

3. Robert S. Carr, "Foes of Auto Rate Hikes Give Bologna to Insurance Firms," *Boston Globe*, December 13, 1974; Howard Husock, "Getting Their Fair Share: It Was an Unusual Alliance," *Boston Globe Magazine*, June 14, 1981; Carolyn Lucas, "Fair Share Marks Ten Years of Help," *Boston Herald*, November 23, 1985.

4. Staples interviews.

5. Reverend Samuel J. Barrows, "Dorchester in the Colonial Period," in Justin Winsor, ed., *The Memorial History of Boson, Including Suffolk County, Massachusetts: 1630–1880* (Boston: James R. Osgood, 1880), 423.

6. Lew Finfer, interview by author, February 10, 2012, Dorchester.

7. Michael Ansara, interview by author, May 17, 2013, Cambridge, MA; Kit Clark, quoted in Kathleen Kilgore, "The Evolution of a Revolutionary," *Boston Globe Magazine*, May 18, 1975.

8. Ansara interview.

9. "Grant to Fair Share Launches Save Our City Program," *Boston Globe*, November 19, 1975.

10. Michal Ansara, "Fair Share Aims to Save Neighborhoods," *Boston Globe*, November 21, 1975.

11. Anna DeFronzo, quoted in Ansara, "Fair Share."

12. Ansara interview; Ansara, quoted in Kirk Scharfenberg, "Fair Share Looks Ahead," *Boston Globe*, March 29, 1980.

13. "Property Taxes: Homeowners Revolt," *The Fair Fighter*, November 1976; "Doulos to Pay $50,000 in Back Taxes," *Boston Herald*, August 28, 1976.

14. Joseph Driscoll, "500 Protest Tax Abatement Delays," *Boston Herald*, February 9, 1977; Tom Corrigan, quoted in Timothy Dwyer, "300 Protest before Mayor's House," *Boston Globe*, February 9, 1977; Dorchester Fair Share Flyer.

15. Diane Roberts, quoted in Debbie Simon, "A Majority Funds Strong Voices to Fight City Hall," *New York Times*, August 7, 1977; Mike Regan, quoted in Husock, "Getting Their Fair Share."

16. Caroline Lewis, quoted in Howard Husock, "Getting Their Fair Share"; Evelyn Hannigan, quoted in ibid.

17. Stephen Curwood, "'Lifeline' Groups Merge, Celebrate," *Boston Globe*, December 3, 1975.

18. Fair Share Campaign Brochure.

19. Renée Loth, interview by author, January 22, 2009, Dorchester.

20. Art Jahnke, "Populist Organizers Fight over Turf," *Real Paper*, October 23, 1980; Husock, "Getting Their Fair Share"; Staples interviews; Staples communication to Finfer, January 20, 1977.

21. Ansara interview; Tom Corrigan, interview by author, October 29, 2008, Farmington, CT.

22. Dudley Clendinen, "Boston Is Becoming the Hub of Arson," *New York Times*, June 16, 1982; Ansara, quoted in Ken Powers, "White to 'Look Into' Arson Grant Charge," *Boston Globe*, March 30, 1980.

23. Jahnke, "Populist Organizers."

20. A Downturn in Activism

1. Val Hyman, interview by author, September 11, 2008, South End.

2. Ibid.

3. Sarah-Ann Shaw, interview by author, January 26, 2007, Roxbury.

4. Gail Snowden, interview by author, November 20, 2008, Roxbury.

5. Renée Loth, interview by author, January 22, 2009, Dorchester; Shaw interview.

6. Alan Lupo, *Liberty's Chosen Home: The Politics of Violence in Boston* (Boston: Beacon Press, 1977), 118–19.

7. Gerard O'Neill, *Rogues and Redeemers: When Politics Was King in Irish Boston* (New York: Crown, 2012), 282.

8. Barney Frank, interview by author, February 19, 2009, Newton, MA; Ken Hart-

nett, "White Moves to Consolidate City Power in His Hands," *Boston Globe*, September 19, 1976.

9. Paul Grogan, interview by author, March 28, 2007, Boston.

10. Joe Heaney, "'Rent Control Stinks'—White," *Boston Herald*, February 12, 1976; William Edgerton, quoted in Michael Kenney, "Rent Decontrol Leaves Tenants, Owners Upset," *Boston Globe*, May 11, 1977; Jim Creamer, interview by author, August 19, 2010, Boston.

11. Douglass Shand-Tucci, *The Art of Scandal: The Life and Times of Isabella Stewart Gardner* (New York: HarperCollins, 1997), 196, citing Corina Putnam Smith, *Interesting People* (Norman: University of Oklahoma Press, 1962, 154).

12. Jack Canavan, "How One Neighborhood Foils Arsonists," *Boston Globe*, October 1, 1978.

13. Ibid.

14. Ken Hartnett, "Arson Case Laurels Earned by Bellotti as White Lost Out," *Boston Globe*, October 29, 1977.

15. Michael Kenney, "Undercover Units Proposed to Fight Symphony Rd. Fires," *Boston Globe*, March 31, 1977; "Dukakis Pledge Reported for Symphony Rd. Action," *Boston Globe*, April 25, 1977.

16. Canavan, "How One Neighborhood."

17. Michael Kenney, "The Business of Urban Arson," *Boston Globe*, October 23, 1977.

18. Paul Langner, "Residents Cheer as Arson Bill Is Signed," *Boston Globe*, July 16, 1978.

19. Gary McMillan, "Anti-Arson Group Gets Wider Role," *Boston Globe*, April 1, 1978; Governor Dukakis, quoted in Langner, "Residents Cheer."

20. Langner, "Residents Cheer."

21. Langley Keyes, interview by author, November 8, 2012, North End.

22. Bob Turner, interview by author, April 13, 2006, Dorchester.

23. "Taking The Neighborhood Pulse," *Boston Herald*, August 27, 1979.

24. Robert L. Turner, "White Faces Belt-Tightening Dilemma," *Boston Globe*, November 9, 1980.

25. Carol Surkin, "White Test: 'Have They Helped Me?'" *Boston Globe*, April 30, 1977.

26. Mary Thornton, *Washington Post*, September 18, 1982, quoted in Robert A. Jordan, "Boston Is Called a City in Decline," *Boston Globe*, August 23, 1982; Mitchell C. Lynch, "Boston's Renaissance Brightens Downtown but Masks Many Ills," *New York Times*, November 13, 1980; *Time*, August 20, 1982, quoted in, Jordan, "Boston Is Called a City in Decline."

27. Jordan, "Boston Is Called a City in Decline," citing a Brookings Institute Report.

21. BACK TO THE NEIGHBORHOODS

1. Jack Beatty, "Respect for South Boston," *New England Monthly*, September 30, 1984.

2. Kevin White, "Why I Finally Decided to Call It Quits," *Boston Herald*, May 27, 1983.

3. Thomas H. O'Connor, *Building a New Boston: Politics and Urban Renewal, 1950 to 1970* (Boston: Northeastern University Press, 1993), 280–81; Wayne Woodlief, "The Legacy of Kevin White: A Booming Inner City and Decaying Neighborhoods," *Boston Herald*, January 1, 1984.

4. "The Election for Mayor," editorial, *Boston Globe*, October 4, 1983.

5. David Nyhan, "The Race for City Hall: Track's Fine, the Field's a Decent One," *Boston Globe*, August 8, 1983.

6. James Green, interview by author, October 26, 2006, Boston.

7. Tunney Lee, interview by author, September 22, 2010, Cambridge, MA.

8. Ray Flynn, interview by author, February 10, 2010, South Boston.

9. Ibid.

10. Larry DiCara, panel discussion at Suffolk University, November 8, 2003.

11. Joe Sciacca, "Tenants Rights Top Issue," *Boston Herald*, September 11, 1983; Kirk Scharfenberg, "A New Force at the Boston Ballot Box," *Boston Globe*, September 26, 1981.

12. Alan Lupo, "Housing Policy and Déjà Vu," *Boston Phoenix*, April 27, 1982.

13. Adam Reilly, "Racial Healing: Former Mayor Opponents Ray Flynn and Mel King Discuss . . . ," *Boston Phoenix*, November 6, 2008.

14. *Time*, October 10, 1983, 30.

15. "Boston's Big Win," *Boston Herald* editorial, October 12, 1983; David Nyhan, "Boston New Players in the Old Game," *Boston Globe*, October 16, 1983; James Green, "King, Flynn and Populism," *Boston Globe*, October 28, 1983.

16. James Jennings, "Race and Political Change in Boston," in Clay, *The Emerging Black Community of Boston*, 314.

17. Ray Flynn, quoted in Walter V. Robinson, "Flynn, King Differ on Bias," *Boston Globe*, October 21, 1983.

18. Mel King, quoted in Robert A. Jordan, "'A Giant Step for the City' — King," *Boston Globe*, November 16, 1983; Ray Flynn, quoted in "The Vote Is Just the Start," *Boston Globe*, November 16, 1983.

19. Anthony Lewis, "The Politics of Civility," *New York Times*, June 14, 1984.

20. Reilly, "Racial Healing."

21. Langley Keyes, interview by author, September 27, 2011, Cambridge, MA.

22. Ibid.

23. Paul Grogan, interview by author, March 28, 2007, Boston.

24. JoAnne Ball, "Tent City: 18-Year Cause Culminates in Triumph," *Boston Globe*, March 7, 1986.

25. Peter Medoff and Holly Sklar, *Streets of Hope: The Fall and Rise of an Urban Neighborhood* (Boston: South End Press, 1994), 142.

26. "A New Direction," editorial, *Bay State Banner*, March 29, 1984.

27. Raymond Dooley, "Ray: Moving On," *Boston Globe*, July 11, 1993.

28. Doris Bunte, interview by author, October 24, 2012, Dorchester.

29. Governor Dukakis, quoted in John Powers, "A Brighter Future Promised for Parcel 18; Flynn, Dukakis Sign Pact on Roxbury Site," *Boston Globe*, August 1, 1985.

30. Scharfenberg, "Resident Jobs Plan."

31. Chris Black, "The Flynn Legacy: Even in Rome, Flynn an Influence," *Boston Globe*, September 19, 1993.

32. Pierre Clavel, *Activists in City Hall: The Progressive Response to the Reagan Era in Boston and Chicago* (Ithaca, NY: Cornell University Press, 2010), 3, 198.

33. Ray Flynn, interview by author, April 21, 1999, Boston.

34. Thomas H. O'Connor, *The Hub: Boston Past and Present* (Boston: Northeastern University Press, 2001), 255; George B. Merry, "The People's Mayor: Looking Back at the Flynn Years," *Christian Science Monitor*, June 28, 1993.

35. Rachelle G. Cohen, "One More for Marathon Man," *Boston Herald*, April 16, 1993.

22. Boston Today

1. *Boston Herald*, October 14, 2012.

2. John Avault, Boston Redevelopment Authority Research Division, November 2012.

3. Zach Patton, "The Boss of Boston: Mayor Thomas Menino," *Governing*, January 2012.

4. Jim Campano, talk delivered at West End Library, March 18, 2006.

5. Massachusetts Association of Community Development Corporations, personal communication, November 2012.

6. Ethan Bronner, "Community Leaves Its Stamp on Corridor," *Boston Globe*, November 2, 1986.

7. Robert Kenney, talk delivered at Beacon Hill Seminar, October 30, 2008.

8. Linda Tucci, "Making It Stand Out," *Boston Globe*, May 25, 2008.

9. Moe Gillen, interview by author, September 7, 2007, Charlestown.

10. Hillary Chabot, "Neighbors Aim to Silence Old Ironsides' Cannons," *Boston Herald*, November 7, 2009.

11. Peter J. Howe, "'Newcomers' Give Less of Themselves," *Boston Globe*, January 26, 1988.

12. Mel King, interview by author, January 15, 2007, South End.

13. Leonard Alkins, Panel Discussion, "Jim & Jane Crow Employment," "Power of Protest: The Civil Rights Movement in Boston, 1960–1968," John F. Kennedy Presidential Library & Museum, November 4, 2006.

14. www.bostonpublicschools.org, revised April 25, 2013.

15. Ibid.; John R. Connolly, "Real Reform in Student Assignment Lottery," *Boston Globe*, September 19, 2012.

16. Ted Landsmark, "It's Time to End Busing in Boston," *Boston Globe*, January 31, 2009.

17. Michael Graham, "Shameless Gov Enables Welfare Abuse," *Boston Herald*, July 13, 2012.

18. Paul McMorrow, "Hope for Homeowners in Mattapan," *Boston Globe*, July 30, 2013.

19. Val Hyman, interview by author, September 11, 2008, South End; Vanessa Calderon-Rosado, interview by author, December 13, 2007, South End.

20. Peter Gelzinis, "Thugs 'Stir the Pot' in Public Housing," *Boston Herald,* August 1, 2012.

21. Barry Bluestone, quoted in Thomas Grillo, "Boston-Area Rents Now 2d Highest in Country," *Boston Herald,* October 27, 2009; Dan Adams, "Tight Supply Means Rent Soaring in City," *Boston Globe,* August 14, 2012.

22. Rose Marie Ruggiero, quoted in Michael Rezendes, "East Boston Eyes Old Adversary, Etc.," *Boston Globe,* March 20, 1994.

23. Colleen Quinn, "Fight over Shadows, Development Returns," *Boston Globe,* May 10, 2013.

24. John Vitagliano, interview by author, January 16, 2009, Boston.

25. Donavan Slack, "Fewer Residents Get Building Jobs," *Boston Globe,* September 10, 2009; Chuck Turner, interview by author, November 14, 2008, Roxbury.

26. Jonathan Saltzman, "Turner Found Guilty of Accepting Cash Bribe," *Boston Globe,* October 30, 2010.

27. Paul Grogan, interview by author, March 28, 2007, Boston.

28. John C. Drake, "Feeney Forges Ahead with Community Summit Plan," *Boston Globe,* February 27, 2008.

29. Matt Viser, "Off the Sidelines," *Boston Globe,* May 4, 2008.

30. Grogan interview.

31. David Arnold, "Proud, but Still Defiant," *Boston Globe,* May 2, 1998.

32. Renée Loth, interview by author, January 22, 2009, Dorchester.

33. Michael Dukakis, interview by author, June 29, 2007, Fenway.

34. Ray Flynn, interview by author, February 10, 2010, South Boston.

35. Paul McMorrow, "The New Campaign," *CommonWealth,* Summer 2013, 36–37.

36. Michael Levinson, "His Parts Built a Stable Whole," *Boston Globe,* March 29, 2013.

37. Thomas H. O'Connor, "Menino Reaches a Mayoral Milestone," *Boston Globe,* July 13, 2009.

38. Lawrence Harmon, "Menino's Boneyard," *Boston Globe,* April 6, 2013.

39. Mel King, interview by author, February 16, 2007, south End.

40. Larry DiCara, quoted in Michael Jonas, "The Last Great Racers Look Back," *Boston Globe,* November 23, 2003.

41. John Vitagliano, interview by author, January 16, 2009, Boston.

42. John Avault, "Income Inequality in Boston," unpublished paper, November 2012.

43. Gail Snowden, interview by author, November 20, 2008, Roxbury.

44. Loth interview.

45. John Avault, Boston Redevelopment Authority Research Division, November 2012.

46. Neal Peirce and Curtis Johnson, "Boston Unbound: Tapping Greater Boston's Assets and Talents to Create a World-Leading Citistate," Boston Foundation, May 2004, 4, 12.

47. Avault, "Income Inequality in Boston."

48. Rev. Richard Conway, panel discussion at Boston Globe 68 Blocks event, January 30, 2013.

49. Renée Loth, *Boston Globe,* December 18, 2009.

50. Ron Hafer, interview by author, February 15, 2008, Jamaica Plain.
51. Peter S. Canellos, "The Legacy of Boston's 'Sandinistas,'" *Boston Globe,* November 2, 2010.
52. Alan Lupo, interview by author, January 26, 2006, Jamaica Plain.

Epilogue

1. Alan Lupo, interview by author, January 26, 2006, Jamaica Plain.
2. Mel King, *Chain of Change: Struggles for Black Community Development* (Boston: South End Press, 1981), 274.
3. Evelyn Morash, interview by author, November 6, 2008, East Boston.
4. Michael Lerner, interview by author, September 15, 2006, Roslindale.
5. David Parker, interview by author, February 20, 2008, South End.
6. Dan Richardson, interview by author, September 1, 2009, Roxbury.
7. Lew Finfer, interview by author, February 10, 2012, Dorchester.
8. Tom Lyons, interview by author, August 19, 2013, Boston.
9. Sheila Trafford, quoted in Michael J. Bailey, "City Loses Tireless Guardian of Its Most Treasured Open Spaces," *Boston Globe,* March 17, 2009.
10. Mel King, interview by author, March 3, 2007, South End.

Index

JIM VRABEL is a former newspaper reporter, longtime community activist, and historian. He was a founder of the Back of the Hill Community Development Corporation on Mission Hill and of the Academy of the Pacific Rim Charter School in Hyde Park, and served as assistant director of the Mayor's Office of Neighborhood Services, executive assistant to the Boston School Committee, and senior research associate and editor at the Boston Redevelopment Authority. Vrabel is the author of *When in Boston: A Timeline & Almanac* and of *Homage to Henry: A Dramatization of John Berryman's "The Dream Songs."*